PETER DORNAN has for more than 30 years been a physiotherapist in the field of sporting injuries and manipulative therapy. He has worked with many international sporting teams, including the Queensland Rugby team and the Wallabies, and has been an Olympic and Commonwealth Games adviser. He is a Fellow of Sports Medicine Australia and has written two books on sporting injuries, as well as designing and marketing a video exercise program.

He has been married to Dimity, a speech pathologist, for more than 30 years. They have two adult children, Melissa and Rod.

THE SILENT MEN

Syria to Kokoda and on to Gona

Peter Dornan

ALLEN & UNWIN

First published in 1999 by
Allen & Unwin
9 Atchison Street, St Leonards NSW 1590 Australia
Phone: (61 2) 8425 0100
Fax: (61 2) 9906 2218
E-mail: frontdesk@allen-unwin.com.au
Web: http://www.allen-unwin.com.au

National Library of Australia
Cataloguing-in-Publication entry:

Dornan, Peter 1943– .
  The silent men: Syria to Kokoda and on to Gona

Bibliography.
ISBN 1 86448 991 X.

1. Australia. Army. Battalion, 2/14th—History. 2. World War,
1939–1945—Campaigns—New Guinea. 3. World War, 1939–1945—
Campaigns—Middle East. 4. World War, 1939–1945—Regimental
histories—Australia. 5. Kokoda Trail (Papua New Guinea). I. Title.

940.541294

Set in 11/13 pt Plantin Light by DOCUPRO, Sydney
Printed by SRM Production Services Sdn Bhd, Malaysia

10 9 8 7 6 5 4 3 2

I dedicate this book to the legions of silent men and women who sacrificed so that succeeding generations might live in peace

I also dedicate it to my mother, Ronda, and my family—Dimity, Melissa and Roderick

In memory of QX13844

Foreword

I SERVED ALONGSIDE THE 2/14TH BATTALION IN SYRIA, and met a couple of their officers. Based on this slim association I feel that Peter Dornan has depicted in plain and clear soldiers' language what is usually neglected in books of World War II vintage—namely the background atmosphere of the time, and the way in which young, healthy and intelligent men gradually moulded themselves into a trained team of dedicated friends.

There is to my mind a slight tinge of scepticism in the public mind about mateship, but those of us who have experienced it under war conditions know how genuine it is. There is no finer, closer or less selfish relationship between men.

There is an old adage which describes war as 'months of training, days of fighting, and moments of extreme fear'; it develops a dependence and trust between men, and produces such fine and courageous individuals as Bruce Kingsbury, VC. He gave his life so that others could live, both on the field of battle at Isurava, and in peace at home.

I fully recommend the book.

Roden Cutler
December 1998

Contents

MAPS

Acknowledgements

A BOOK OF THIS NATURE IS ONE I could never have accomplished alone. I have relied heavily on the oral histories given to me by the men and women who lived through the events described. I am extremely grateful to the 50 or more individuals who have entrusted me with the precious memories of their experiences.

I owe much to the help and ready encouragement given by the two authors of the 2/14th Battalion histories, Bill Russell and Jim McAllester, and have made consistent use of Peter Brune's books on Kokoda and Gona. For assistance with my research I am indebted to many individuals in various public service departments (especially the Department of Veterans Affairs) and at the War Memorial in Canberra, and in the RSL.

I am obliged to Fred Fink, the Yandina district researcher, and to my patient typists, Elizabeth Niarchos, Carol Jackson and Prue McKeering, whose comments were always welcome. I am particularly grateful to my wife Dimity, who was my on-the-spot editor and a critical reviewer of the drafts as they emerged, as well as being my support system and cheer squad when I felt the problems were getting too large. I am also indebted to Michael McKernan and Devon Mills, my editorial mentors, for their wisdom and experience.

Peter Dornan
Brisbane

Explanatory Note

THIS BOOK FOLLOWS THE EXPERIENCES OF a handful of men who were part of the 2nd AIF (Australian Imperial Force). The 2nd AIF comprised four divisions (6, 7, 8, and 9) of about 14 000 men each, and fought in many theatres of conflict during World War II. The story revolves around the Seventh Division and one of its fighting battalions—the 2/14th.

In March 1940 the Australian Army adopted a system in which a division consisted of three brigades, each with three battalions, and various support units. The Seventh Division was made up as follows:

18th Brigade	21st Brigade	*25th Brigade*
2/9th Bn	2/14th Bn	2/25th Bn
2/10th Bn	2/16th Bn	2/31st Bn
2/12th Bn	2/27th Bn	2/33rd Bn

Unit structure and level of command:

Division	(14 000 men)		Major General
Brigade	(3300)	(3 to a division)	Brigadier
Battalion	(850)	(3 to a brigade)	Lieutenant Colonel
Company	(140)	(5 to a battalion)	Captain
	(1 HQ and 4 rifle)		
Platoon	(39)	(18 to a battalion)	Lieutenant
	(6 HQ and 12 rifle)		
Section	(11)	(3 to a platoon)	Corporal

ABBREVIATIONS

Military terms

Sec	Section
Pl	Platoon
Coy	Company
Bn	Battalion
'I'	Intelligence (Section)
'Q'	Quartermaster (Store)
RMO	Regimental Medical Officer
RAP	Regimental Aid Post
HQ	Headquarters
AIF	Australian Imperial Force
AWL	Absent without leave

Decorations

VC	Victoria Cross
DSO	Distinguished Service Order
DCM	Distinguished Conduct Medal
OBE	Officer of the Order of the British Empire
MBE	Member of the Order of the British Empire
MC	Military Cross
MM	Military Medal
BEM	British Empire Medal
MID	Mentioned in Dispatches

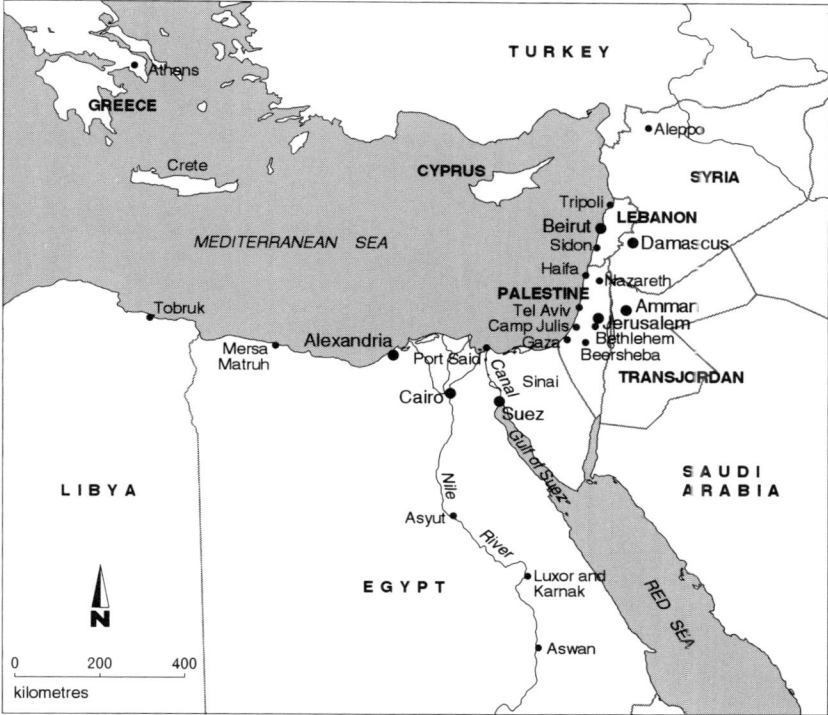

Map 1 The Middle East

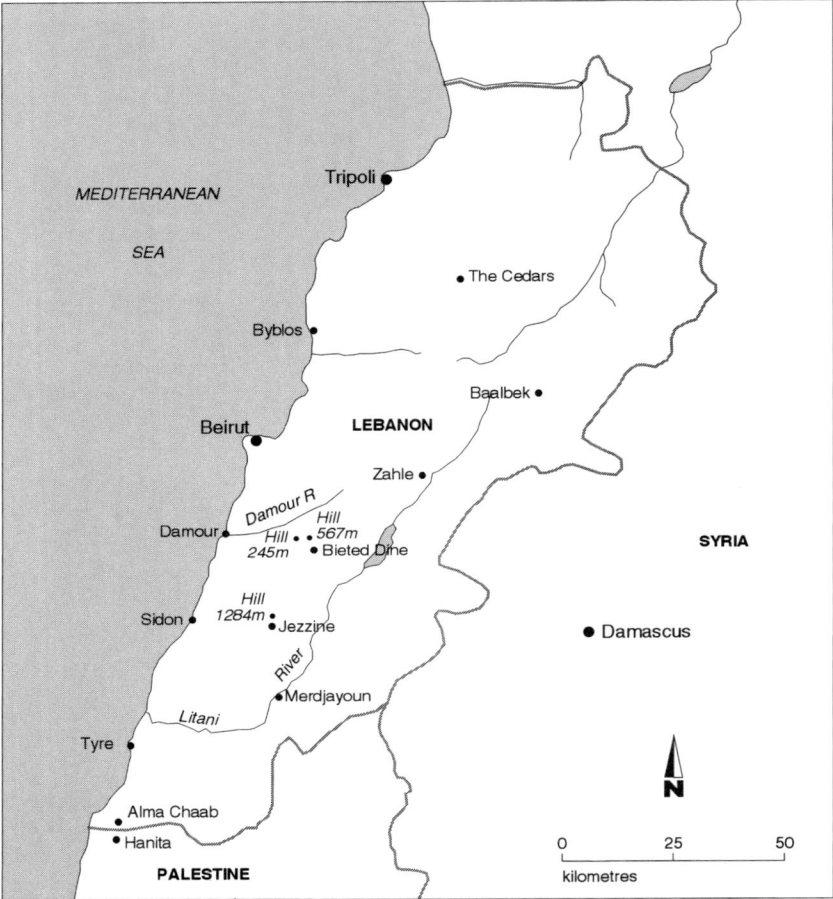

Map 2 Lebanon

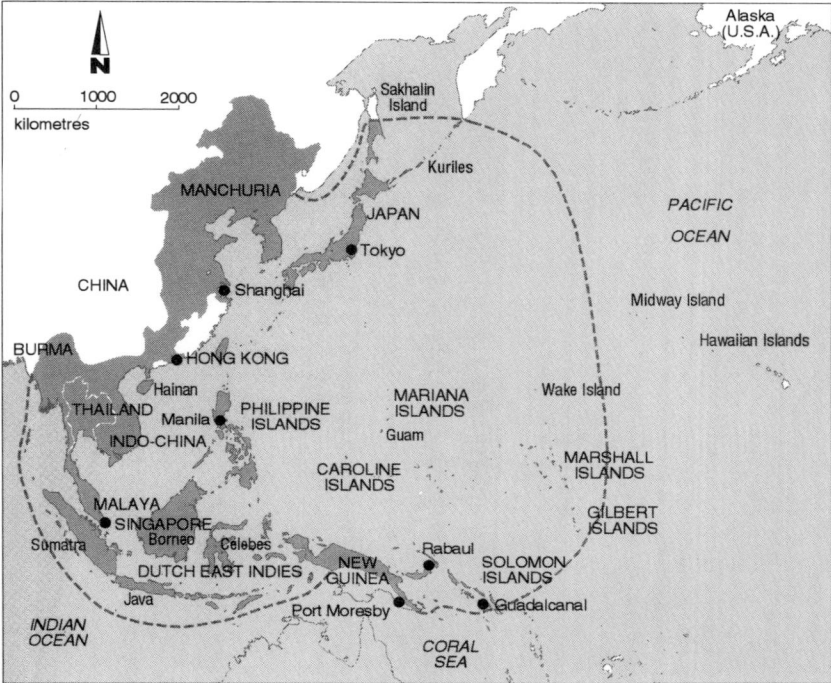

Map 3 Limit of Japanese expansion, July 1942

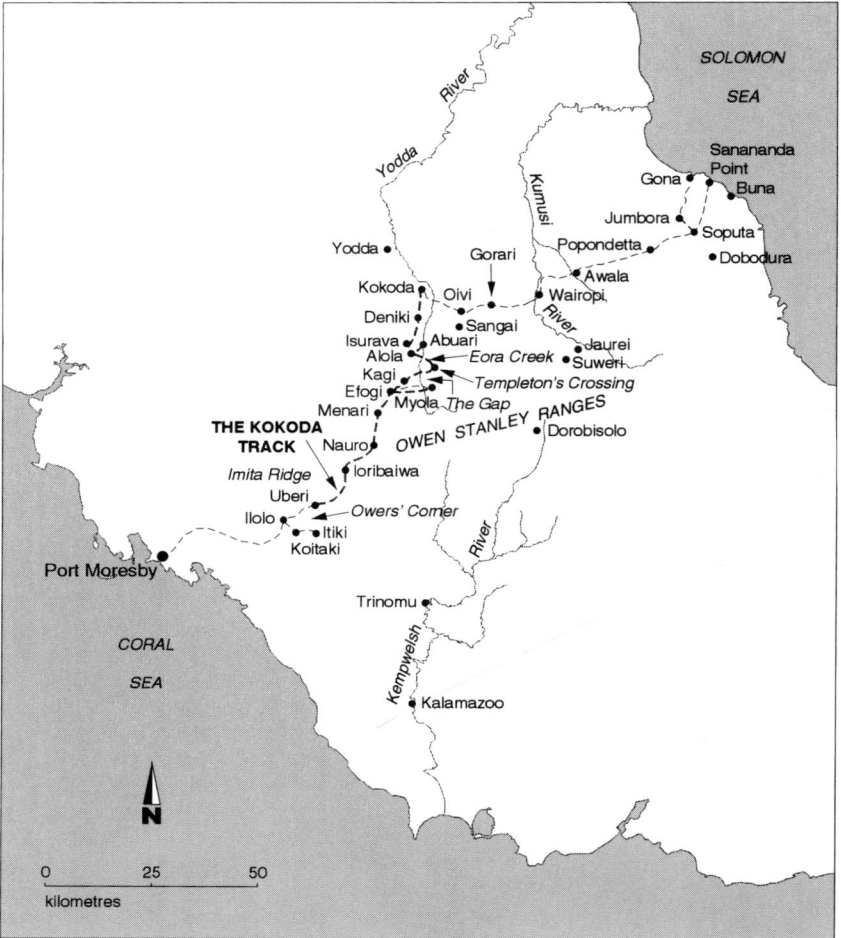

Map 4 The Kokoda Track and extension to Gona

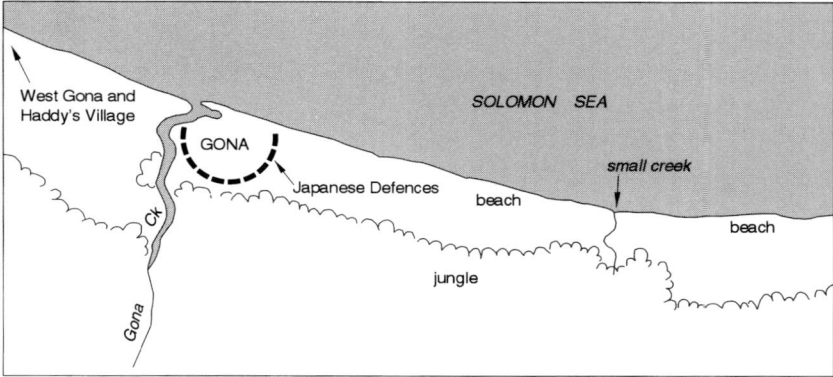

Map 5 Gona

Preface:
The Silent Seventh

A S A YOUNG BOY I ALWAYS knew my father had been a soldier. I would delve curiously into his metal army trunk, which he kept under the table in his study. On it were stencilled his name, rank, file code and battalion number, which all intrigued me immensely. Inside the trunk were small black and white photographs of unknown and exotic places. There was my father, in army uniform, posing beside the Sphinx, visiting Jesus' birthplace in Bethlehem in Palestine—wherever that was—and striding with his mates over ruins at a place called Baalbek in 'The Lebanon'. There were at least half a dozen medals with their ribbons and, amazingly, rolls of Japanese money, smelling of the camphor that had been sprinkled in the trunk.

When questioned, my father passed it off, saying the money was only a souvenir and was worthless. Why would it be there, then? And a souvenir from where? These were mysteries my father did not really explain to me.

In those early years I considered he was rather an aloof figure, not prone to extravagant displays of emotion or affection, yet I had no doubt that his life centred on our family. But he was definitely a little mysterious—particularly in the way he came to life in the company of his old army friends. On Anzac Day he would march with his brother-in-law; then later, with his friends at the RSL club, the mask would slip as the alcohol washed away some of his reserve. The men would often laugh uninhibitedly at some incident of long ago, then talk in hushed, respectful tones when remembering 'poor old Fred', who 'copped it' 'over there'. More mystery! It was a world I could not understand—a conspiracy of silence in their private club—their own unambiguous focus on a life I knew nothing about. And mateship: I did not understand the incredible bond between these men.

Later on, studying physiotherapy at university, I came to realise that the war may have had a considerable effect on my father's demeanour. To my surprise I found that he had a Repatriation Department entitlement for 'anxiety neurosis', and that he had been receiving regular treatment for the condition since the war.

I was interested, but didn't pursue it. Then I developed a special interest in sports medicine and, in 1972, I was given the opportunity to lecture in New Guinea on that topic. At the inevitable family slide night afterwards, I showed my father a photograph I had taken from Owers' Corner on the Kokoda Track. (Incidentally, both 'Track' and 'Trail' are valid. When the 21st Brigade were there in August 1942, it was 'Track'. In September an Australian journalist, Geoff Reading, needed a generic term to send to his editor in Sydney, and he called it 'Trail'.)

I said to my father: 'You should see it, Dad—apparently there was a bit of a fight there once.'

He answered: 'Yes, mate, I have seen it, and I have no great desire to see New Guinea again.' His curt reply surprised me, but I wasn't curious enough to follow it up. I was still unaware of the fact that the 'bit of a fight' had been a significant battle and that he had taken part in it.

A few years later, in 1975, when I was 32, my father died of bowel cancer at the age of 60. I remember my feelings of helplessness and shock in the final days as I carried his wasted frame to the car to transfer him to hospital. How could this happen? He was too young, otherwise healthy and, to me, almost invincible.

The Repatriation Commission attributed his death to attrition incurred on the Kokoda Track. What was this? My shock was complete. I must have missed something along the way. Too late—he had taken his secret with him.

My earliest knowledge of 'Kokoda' was that it was an effective mosquito repellent. We used it on the farm. My father had mentioned Kokoda in New Guinea intermittently over the years, but not in a way that involved him to any extent. It simply didn't mean a lot to me.

There was an awakening realisation now that this episode was not just a 'bit of a fight', yet how was I to know? My father and his friends never talked about it and it was never taught in schools. We remembered the Anzacs to the point of deification, but this whole business of Dad's war was grey to me. I *had* to find out. Why did he die so young and, just as puzzling, why did he not tell me about his experiences? I had always viewed my father through a clear Homeric lens of invincibility and great deeds, never knowing exactly what those deeds were. Now the lens was clouded a little. I needed to study World War II.

Over the next five years or so I searched and studied.

This self-directed commitment went a long way towards answering many of my questions. However, it wasn't until I had a chance to walk the Kokoda Track myself that I began to understand the personal stresses involved and the possible effects.

At the age of 40 I was invited by a Vietnam veteran friend, Doug Tanner, to accompany him along the track. I was to act as medico for fifteen of Queensland's top army and airforce cadets. Carrying a 25-kilogram pack, I suddenly knew, after two hours of climbing, a little of what my father had been through. Even though physically fit, I was devastated to realise that the struggle might be too much for me. Nothing in my life had prepared me for this extent of adversity; I was quite ready to turn around there and then.

However, hard against the rising tide of panic and impending failure, a quiet voice deep inside took command and ordered me to take stock—to be calm. I followed the order and responded by pushing myself, one step at a time, at my own pace, into the realm of mind over matter.

Many times, as the trek developed into an emotional rollercoaster, my new commitment and resolve forced me to confront myself. I was aware that my inhibitions were being peeled away, layer by layer, revealing a clearer image of myself, a core devoid of trappings. I unashamedly heard myself, at various times during the trek, calling to my father for help, seeking to draw on his achievements and those of others who had gone before me. On another level, I could readily see why a pilgrimage such as this could be compared to a religious experience. This, to me, was the Spirit of Kokoda.

It took us ten days to traverse the track, and the experience changed me profoundly.

Now, at least, I could understand a little of my father's patience and endurance. I realised his character was consistent with one who had been tested and could define his own limits. After the Kokoda Track, quite simply, nothing was too hard.

This revelation satisfied me for some years. But because during my own walk I'd never felt overtly threatened—I had not been fighting an enemy, only myself—I felt the full secret still eluded me. That secret would be revealed from another, completely different direction.

For the previous twenty years I had been studying classical sculpture and have my works displayed in prominent Queensland institutions. Prior to the 50th anniversary of the Kokoda Campaign, in 1992, I was asked by one of my patrons if I would create something to commemorate the occasion.

I decided to make a statue to honour the 607 men who did not return, and chose, as their representative, the only person in the campaign to receive the Victoria Cross—Bruce Kingsbury. My early research produced only thumbnail sketches of him, but eventually my trail led to his best friend, Alan Avery, who I found retired and living at Clontarf, a beachside suburb near Brisbane. Alan was most affable and pleased to offer me photographs and information on Kingsbury. He also told me in some detail about the action at Isurava. This was compelling to me, as I had never heard any soldier talk of his private experience of war. I was then referred to Stan Bisset, who was living at Noosa. He honoured me in a similar way.

When I unveiled the statue at the 2/14th Battalion's annual reunion, the event led some of the men to unsolicitedly confide in me about other private incidents in the Kokoda Campaign.

By the time I got home that evening I was very excited. It dawned on me that I had at last began to uncover the mystery that had teased and eluded me most of my life. I realised that here was a story of magnitude and richness that had not been recorded.

I decided there and then to write a book about the battle at Isurava. As my research continued, I found individual stories of young men, like my father, thrown first into the Middle East conflict and then sent to meet the Japanese in New Guinea. So the scope of the book widened. I even spent some time travelling through the Middle East.

As the results of my delving and oral history collection took on a workable shape, my interest became very personal. With a degree of fascination, I realised I had found a generation of forgotten, silent men. In the process, I also found a part of myself that had been unconsciously yearning for completeness ever since I first looked into that old trunk under my father's desk.

THE KOKODA TRACK IS FOREVER EMBLAZONED on the minds of those who fought along it—it will never be forgotten. And, like Gallipoli, it has become part of Australia's mythology. The date of Bruce Kingsbury's death, 29 August 1942, is celebrated by many as a tribute to the heroism and sacrifice of the Australian soldiers who took part in the Battle of Isurava. Military historians consider that, had the men not held on for the four days of the battle, the ordered strategic withdrawal that ensued might instead have been a rout, which would have meant a totally different outcome—particularly for Australia.

In a different way, and for different reasons, the Syrian Campaign of 1941—a good part of it fought in Lebanon— played a vital role in the war in the Middle East. And it was the first blooding for the Seventh Division's 2/14th Battalion; a rigorous preparation, as things turned out, for the trauma of the Kokoda Campaign.

But why weren't we told more about these major chapters of Australia's World War II record?

Now, several years later, these and other important questions still exist. At the Australian War Memorial in Canberra, in the Victoria Cross Room, most VC winners are accorded a large photograph and a detailed biography. Bruce Kingsbury rates only a small photograph and a copy of his citation. Why has he been overlooked? And the Isurava battle? Why was the Syrian Campaign overlooked?

Further reinforcing the mystery, I learnt that the Seventh Division had been dubbed the 'Silent Seventh'.

A good point at which to search for the reason for this silence might be the fact that the Seventh Division's Syrian and Kokoda Campaigns were both heavily censored at the time. The participants in the Syrian Campaign, for example, were ordered not to mention the battles, mainly because High Command were concerned that the public at home might not understand that the troops were fighting the Vichy French, the enemy—not the Free French, our allies.

It is difficult to compare battles, but Australian deaths in Greece totalled 320 and in Crete 274—both campaigns involving disastrous Allied losses. In Syria the number was 416—a very hard-won victory—but the troops were denied due credit because the press also was strongly censored.

The Kokoda Campaign was suppressed for other reasons. Firstly, the Supreme Allied Commander, South-West Pacific Area, General Douglas MacArthur, in his efforts to impress his superiors, badly needed an American victory. MacArthur censored all reporting, and even though United States troops did not enter the battle directly until after the Australians' final action at Gona, on the northeastern coast, he credited the Kokoda and Gona gains as an 'Allied victory'—not an Australian one. In this way he effectively prevented Australians at large from knowing of their army's achievements.

Secondly, MacArthur considered the 21st Brigade's strategic withdrawal from Isurava as being a defeat, and their efforts close to cowardice. He made this judgement thousands of kilometres from the battlefield, not realising the nature of the terrain, and in the belief that the Australians were fighting an inferior army, not the opposite—they were in fact outnumbered by at least five to one.

MacArthur's sentiments were echoed by the Australian commander-in-chief, General Thomas Blamey, in his now infamous Koitaki Address.

On 9 November 1942, after seven weeks of recuperating from their withdrawal, the proud men of the 21st Brigade, grieving for their lost brothers, were paraded at Koitaki in the south of the island—expecting perhaps some praise from their commander-in-chief for a job well done. Instead, the unknowing and seemingly uncaring Blamey insensitively blasted them for being beaten by an 'inferior enemy in inferior numbers'. To make matters worse, he virtually accused them of cowardice: 'It is not the man with the gun that gets shot, it's the rabbit that is running away.'

There is a lasting bitterness among 21st Brigade men towards Blamey and MacArthur, both for the sentiments expressed and for the very poor and incorrect Intelligence information used by the Brigade prior to and during the campaign.

Furthermore, the Syrian and Kokoda Campaigns and the battalions that fought in them have rarely been mentioned in the education of Australian youth. Even the expensive and otherwise successful 'Australia Remembers' history kits sent to schools in 1995 failed to mention the Isurava action or any of the battalions by name. In fact, there was a clear lack of reference to the Kokoda Track battles as a whole. The same applied to Syria. I suspect these omissions were due less to a 'conspiracy of silence' and more to the compilers' relative lack of knowledge of military history. But the point remains.

Another pertinent factor could well be the reluctance of the survivors, especially in the early years after the war, to talk loudly of their efforts and experiences. Psychologists have long reported that those who have suffered the atrocities of war find it difficult to communicate their experiences to anybody who has not encountered something similar. The fact is, most of them had to suppress their emotions, put the war behind them and get on with their life.

It may well be that among all these points lies the reason for Kingsbury's Victoria Cross being largely overlooked. Yet the award was the first VC won on 'Australian' soil and the only one given during the entire campaign. It was given for conspicuous bravery on the part of a young soldier defending his country against invasion; and it was won in the important Battle of Isurava. Isurava was arguably the highwater mark of the whole campaign, where the advantage slipped from the Japanese to the Australians. So it is strange that there is little official record of Kingsbury's life. Even W. B. Russell's history of the

2/14th Battalion does not make much mention of him, and *Men of the 2/14th Battalion*, by J. C. McAllester, admits that his story is virtually unknown.

THE DEPARTMENT OF VETERANS AFFAIRS COUNSELLING service reports that 75 per cent of World War II veterans suffered symptoms of what was called, after the war, anxiety neurosis, anxiety state or anxiety hysteria. This condition was the modern version of 'shell shock' or 'battle fatigue'. Over time, the matter was swept under the carpet as the world recovered from the conflict and 'got on with life'.

But during the early years after the war many of the men developed a long-term pattern: feelings of alienation ('I don't fit in'), sleep disturbances, nightmares, low tolerance levels, sudden mood swings, unsettled family and work life, and periods of substance abuse, in particular alcohol, as a coping mechanism.

By the time Australian troops returned from the tragedy in Vietnam, the condition was more clearly recognised and better diagnosed and was now known (as it is today) as post-traumatic stress disorder (PTSD).

While many veterans of World War II turned their energies towards their careers and families to keep themselves on track, the Department considers that about 20 per cent of the men who fought in that war developed *chronic* PTSD symptoms.

Another particularly sad outcome for some men was the gnawing, inescapable knowledge that they had survived the war when a number of their friends had not. One veteran of the 2/14th Battalion told me that he had pulled back a bush in the jungle one morning, to find a Japanese machine-gun aimed at him. He dived aside, but it killed three of his friends. For years, at army reunions, he would sit and drink and ask the question, of anybody: 'Why did *I* survive?' He admitted that he'd had 'a hell of a job with the guilt' and would often 'go on the grog or the pills' to try to understand why fate had allowed him to live but had destroyed others—an unanswerable question. But most are grateful that they survived, while still feeling strongly for the friends left behind.

A surprising number admit that rarely a day goes past when they don't think of some aspect of the war. Some are still very angry at the lost opportunities as well as for the legacies they endure.

It is not only the men who carried the burden, and perhaps carry it still. For the wives of many of the veterans there was another hidden cost of the war. To them the fears started the minute their husband walked out of the door to go off to fight. Often they wouldn't hear from him for weeks or even months. And when a letter did turn up, it was frequently riddled with holes from the censor's razorblade. One of the hardest times for the women was waiting for the arrival of the daily newspaper in order to look at the casualty lists, hoping they wouldn't see any names they knew.

After the war the wives played a more active and supportive role in what for many were difficult years. There were major readjustments to make and a good deal of love and patience was needed to get through those early years, as the women tried to come to terms with what was often a very different man from the one they had married.

This supportive role was complemented by the battalion's robust and vigorous Association, maintaining as it did the ethic of comradeship forged in wartime.

THE BOYS

1

Stan and Butch

IT WAS SATURDAY, 14 AUGUST 1993. He was at Ballymore in Brisbane and the Wallabies were about to play the Springboks—Australia versus South Africa. It was the second Test, and it had the makings of a Rugby classic.

Stan Bisset loved a good contest—just as Butch, his brother, had. And from the kickoff at Ballymore the two teams left no doubt as to their commitment. Stan followed every move, cherishing echoes of boyhood and past Rugby matches as he weighed the fortunes of either side. After a hustling start, a penalty from each team momentarily steadied the game and leveled the score at 3–3. Australia was soon on the push again, but then a brilliant intercept try and an ensuing conversion put the Springboks ahead 10–3. Dismayed, Stan sank back into his seat.

The Wallabies were spoiling for points and hit back with renewed urgency and intensity. The next few moments saw one of the great tries of Rugby. In a magical display the flying centre Jason Little wrongfooted four defenders one by one before darting under the posts to score Australia's first try.

Stan jumped to his feet, applauding the move, and caught something familiar in Little's posture as the footballer stood confidently eyeing his opposite centre, hands on his hips, completely absorbed in his own ability and worth to the team.

Perhaps it was Little's stance, perhaps it was the event itself, perhaps it was the thought of Butch. Whatever it was, the incident triggered something in Stan, who recalled himself in the same assertive position, wearing an Australian jersey and likewise playing against the Springboks. It had been the greatest crowd ever to watch a Rugby match in Brisbane—people had come from all over Queensland to see an Australian XV play the touring 1937 Springboks. Stan was deeply proud of his jersey and was playing in his first International. Tall, and weighing 88 kilograms, he was a fast, strong and aggressive second rower, and he too was aware of his own potential.

The fleeting memory of his brother comforted him. To the rest of the world he'd been known as Butch, but their closeness meant that Stan only ever called him by his given name, Hal—Harold, to be exact. Stan could see the two of them as young boys, running through the sandhills of Black Rock on Victoria's Port Phillip Bay. Stan was then six, Butch eight, and it was a life with few restrictions and plenty of interest. Besides the beach, there was a bit of scrub and ti-tree forest, where the boys played bushrangers and fought over who'd be Ned Kelly.

THEIR PARENTS, GEORGE AND OLIVE BISSET, owned and ran a large drapers shop in Prahran, a Melbourne suburb. The boys had two older brothers and a younger sister.

During these early years Butch was always the pale, fair-skinned golden boy, regarded by all as a lovely child, but very delicate and timid. Stan smiled to himself as he recalled, disbelievingly now, that as soon as evening shadows began to fall, Butch was always fearful of the ti-tree forest. He didn't dare to run errands at this time unless accompanied by Stan. As well, there were 'the gangs' that used to frequent the bush. Some older youths had built rough clubhouses there and would wear old World War I gas masks for effect. Several times Stan and Butch were terrorised by these bullies, and fought together for protection.

When the family moved to Warrandyte, an old gold mining town some 30 kilometres from Melbourne, and the older boys had left home, Stan and Butch grew even closer. Here they learned to fish in the river and to paddle a homemade raft of two kerosene tins joined by a board.

Stan winced as he remembered how, on one occasion during the floods, their raft had been whipped out of control by the roaring stream, to be caught fast by a low branch of a tree projecting over the water. He hadn't jumped clear in time, and his leg became jammed between the raft and the branch. The clutching, sucking current was threatening to drag him under. As cold panic started to grab him, he screamed to his brother for help. From the edge of the water, Butch immediately swung his feet around and pushed against the branch as hard as he could. There was just enough movement in the tree to allow Stan to whip his leg out. The raft spun off in a wild lurch and finally crashed against the bank. The boys crawled onto the grassy earth, gasping for breath, frightened, but elated at the close call.

During these years they mastered the use of weapons. First they learnt to shoot out the light of a candle at twenty metres with a 'pea rifle', a .22. They also practised firing a shotgun, and eventually both could shoot a rabbit on the run.

This open, country life seduced Butch to the extent that, in his late teens, he went jackarooing, first in the Riverina, then in Western Australia. It was the first time the boys had been separated and they were not happy about it. But the hard work made a tremendous difference to Butch's physique and general health. When he returned for Christmas several years later, at the age of 22, Stan saw a tall, powerful man with the country man's signature features of bronzed face, broad shoulders and strong arms.

But there was something else about Butch, too. He had grown up and found a great love of life. There was no mistaking that Butch was at a party—his laughter went before him and his obvious lust for life attracted people to him. He had also developed a forthright streak to his character which similarly was magnetic. His time on the land had stripped away any veneer or pretence in relationships. This toughness and straight-ness acquired in the outback had honed his innate personal integrity and allowed him to quickly judge character, to confi-dently call a spade a spade, and to stand by his convictions if need be. In all, Butch was a captivating figure, handsome, vital and inspiring. Girls liked him, rarely failing to be moved by his steely grey eyes, his courteous, attentive behaviour and his ready sense of humour. Not that he couldn't be riotous, if the occasion arose—which it often did—in male company.

When the time came for Butch to return to the outback, Stan resolved to improve his own fitness and to build up his weight. He attended the local gym and then, at the age of twenty, at the beginning of 1933, he even tried out for St Kilda Rugby Union Club.

THAT SAME YEAR SAW ANOTHER SIGNIFICANT event in Stan's life, as he was invited to join the Lord Somers Camp and Power House organisation, which was founded by the Governor of Victoria, Lord Somers, in 1929. The Camp system was modelled on a movement begun in 1921 by Prince Albert, the Duke of York, in England, in an attempt to bring together boys from the workforce with Public School boys in the hope that they would develop a common understanding and a sense of mutual appreciation and loyalty.

The Somers Camp, situated at Victoria's Western Port Bay, was only part of the process. Probably the more important function of the movement found expression in the institution known as Power House. It was here that a boy began fully to learn the spirit of service and duty and to understand that he had responsibilities, both to himself and to others.

Among the many characters with whom Stan enjoyed life at the Camp was Phil Rhoden, a law student who had been captain of Melbourne Grammar School the year before. Another was Nicky Barr, a gifted young sportsman who had previously attended several Camps. And, to Stan's delight, the Power House institution possessed many thriving sporting and social clubs, a number of which he joined, including the Rugby club. The challenges of this time shaped the pattern of his life for the immediate years ahead.

As 1937 got under way, Stan was re-elected captain of the Rugby club for the third year. He was also delighted at having persuaded Butch to return to city life and to join him at Power House. Butch quickly fitted into the scene and, as the season progressed, worked his way into the A grade team. He played front row and the brothers would pack down in the same scrum, as Stan alternated from lock to second row.

They both had jobs and life was good for the boys, yet they realised that many people in politics and in industry were becoming concerned at the world situation with its military and political unrest. Both Japan and Germany were blatantly chest-thumping and beginning to display their ugly, rampant nationalism by annexing the territory of other nations.

Australia was very much part of the British Empire, and most people considered such happenings to be Australia's direct business as well. With the worsening of the world situation and the possibility of war, wheels were set in motion to form an elite Power House army unit in line with Power House traditions.

But none of this stopped the local Great Game. The 1930s were proving to be a golden age for Victorian Rugby; indeed, 1937 was to be a special year as the Springboks were to tour Australia and New Zealand. As they were recognised as one of the best teams in the world, the forthcoming tour was viewed with great interest by all Australians. By the time the Springboks and their fearsome reputation reached Melbourne, the team had resoundingly beaten Western Australia and South Australia, and the normally Australian Rules–addicted Melbournites paid close attention to the game.

Stan by now had built his weight up to 88 kilograms and was pleased to be named in the Victorian team, along with his friend Nicky Barr. Even though the Victorians outscored the Springboks in the second half, they lost the game 45–11. However, Stan had played his heart out—enough to be selected in an Australian XV to play the Springboks in Brisbane.

'I'm in, Hal. You beauty!' he said excitedly to Butch.

'Good on you, mate!' Butch replied. 'We'll be there in spirit—to cheer you on.'

The game was played on a beautiful Queensland day, but it was soon obvious that the fine weather wasn't going to assist the Australian team.

As the game progressed, the Springboks dominated the scrums and rucks and quickly demoralised the Australians. Stan was everywhere and played the game hard, but as the contest continued he realised the older, more experienced players were not giving a wholehearted performance. There was no backup, no integrated play. The Springboks finished the game with a complete whitewash of Australia, and won 36–3.

Stan was disappointed with the result, but a Rugby identity, Syd King, urged him on.

'Stan, you've got what it takes,' King said. 'I reckon if you add a bit more weight you stand a pretty good chance of touring with the Wallabies in 1939.'

This extended tour was to be for ten months, playing a large number of matches, with Tests against England, Scotland, Wales and Ireland. The team was also to play games in several other countries, including France and New Zealand.

As it turned out, 1939 started off with a military slant, as word came through that Power House had been given authority to form its own training unit. The 14th Militia Battalion, based at Prahran, included four rifle companies, A, B, C and D. C Company was to be composed entirely of Power House members under the new arrangement.

Within weeks, 250 keen members had joined the company. Phil Rhoden, who was now a solicitor, was made second-in-command, with the rank of lieutenant. Stan and Butch joined up as privates, on the bottom rank. Once a week they would drill at the Power House, where they learnt military tactics and how to march and to use their army weapons. Butch very quickly established himself as the champion rifle shot of the company.

Stan had been steadily increasing his fitness and now tipped the scales at a strapping 91 kilograms—the goal being selection in the Wallaby team to tour the world later that year.

When the team was announced, Stan was delighted that his name was on the list. In fact, the selection of Stan, Nicky (Andy) Barr and Max Carpenter symbolised the pinnacle of achievement by Power House, as only a handful of Victorians had ever played Rugby for Australia.

In late July, with six weeks of sea voyage ahead of them, and amid cheers and sad farewells from friends, the young men boarded the P&O liner *Mooltan*.

WITH WAR CLOUDS SETTLING OVER EUROPE, there was a certain unease as the ship approached European waters. After the French Mediterranean seaport of Marseille, the ship was required to be blacked out. This was a new experience; really no more than a nuisance to the boys, but nonetheless a niggling, sinister shadow.

They crossed the Channel, disembarked in Devon and were driven to the beachside town of Torquay, where they stayed at the Grand Hotel facing the ocean.

They had been there only a few hours when Prime Minister Chamberlain informed the nation that Britain was officially at war with Germany. It was 11.45 am, Sunday, 3 September, and everything was about to change. The shadow became reality. Within minutes of Chamberlain's speech, Londoners experienced their first wartime air-raid alert; in Paris and Berlin, sirens sounded later the same day; and the citizens of all three cities took to their shelters.

To the boys the news was shattering, not least because the authorities decided to abandon the tour. Stan Bisset and Nicky Barr made enquiries about joining the Army and the Air Force respectively. However, the team manager decided that they should all return to Australia together.

They spent two weeks at Torquay filling sandbags to place around the hotel, and then travelled to London for the last week. Anti-aircraft balloons floated over the city and sandbags bolstered walls and stairways. The city was blacked out; everyone was carrying a gas mask.

The day before departure, the team was received at Buckingham Palace by the King and Queen. In 1921, King George VI (then Prince Albert, the Duke of York) had founded the movement on which Lord Somers modelled his Somers Camp organisation. The King knew that Stan was a member of Power House and spoke to him for a few moments about the Australian setup. Stan was then introduced to Her Majesty as the choir leader and singer of the team—in which capacity he'd proved himself in the weeks at sea—and she talked about music and the team songs they had composed during the voyage.

The next day the team left England, facing a hazardous trip back to Australia with the ship on full war-alert, zigzagging to avoid possible submarine attack.

On his return to work, disappointed with the failure of the proposed world tour, Stan had trouble settling down. He didn't return to the Power House C Company unit and even had

9

trouble becoming enthused with the football season as it got under way the next year.

Butch, meanwhile, had been promoted to sergeant in the company and, like everyone else, was keeping a firm eye on the situation in Europe and the Middle East. As soon as war was declared, Australia had raised a division of men to be dispatched to the Middle East to help the British forces in that area. This was the Sixth Division. (The first five served in World War I.)

By May 1940 Butch could resist no longer. He told his brother: 'I'm going to join up. The Sixth Division are making a fight of it over there in the Middle East. They've called for another division to go over—the Seventh. What with the Suez Canal and the oil from the area, it's pretty vital for the Brits.'

'Yeah, I saw that,' Stan said, not prepared to commit himself. 'I'm thinking about it. Who'll you join up with?'

'Well, I see the Seventh is going to have three brigades, the 18th, 21st and 25th. They're only raising one battalion in Victoria—the 2/14th—as part of the 21st Brigade.'

'The 14th . . . Jacka's mob from the Great War?'

'Yeah, I reckon so. It'll be great.'

The first 14th had fought at Gallipoli and in France with record battle honours. Its special hero was Albert Jacka, the first Australian to be awarded the Victoria Cross in World War I—at Gallipoli. After the war he became Mayor of St Kilda, completing a legendary career.

'Well, good luck, Hal. I'm not quite ready yet,' Stan said. At that the brothers shook hands. On 13 May 1940 Butch found himself on a train heading for Puckapunyal, the military's training establishment in Victoria.

For the next few weeks Stan explored his conscience, although even at this stage, watching the British Army being forced back through France by the unstoppable Germans, he had virtually accepted that his football career and the life it would bring would have to be put on hold.

By 4 June the British forces had been herded onto the beaches of Dunkirk, and the nightmare of World War II truly began. Stan went straight around to the town hall to join up. Like Butch, he duly found himself on a train to Puckapunyal. He was now a private in the 2/14th Battalion of the AIF.

2

Bruce and Alan

PRAHRAN, THE SAME MELBOURNE SUBURB IN which the Bissets operated their drapers store, had a reputation in 1928 as a knockabout sort of place. Two ten-year-old boys, Alan Avery, the smaller of the two, with an engaging smile and a larrikin grin, and his friend Bruce Kingsbury, almost gangly by comparison yet fluid and athletic in his movements, regularly raced their billycarts in the suburb's hillier streets—often dangerously. There were many near disasters but the boys calculated the risks and were exhilarated by the speed. Bruce's mother Florence, secure in her cosy house, would brace herself for screams or broken limbs, as she prepared to give the boys their tea. Bruce and Alan had been close friends since they were five years old, and the two of them often met at Bruce's house in the afternoon and at weekends.

When they left school, Bruce's results enabled him to pick up a scholarship to attend Melbourne Technical College, while Alan enrolled at Longerenong, an agricultural college in the Wimmera district of Western Victoria.

Alan's curriculum included stock, dairy and poultry farming. He lapped it up and, even though he missed Bruce, soon felt very much at home. Two years later, on graduation, his first job was on a sheep and wheat farm at Natya, a community in the Mallee country near the Murray River. It was hard work and the hours were long. For ploughing, it could take an hour

11

just to harness a team of eight Clydesdale horses. Guiding the stump-jump plough over the stubborn mallee roots would jar every bone in Alan's body, but the work seemed to fulfil a deep yearning. He loved the smell of horses and of the newly turned earth, and gained a feeling of security from the rhythmic jangle of the harness chains.

After two years of this life, Alan, at seventeen, had adapted to the hard, unremitting routine. He was growing tough, strong and resilient, both physically and mentally. The outdoor work was more than agreeing with him. He would write home regularly to his mother and two brothers, John and Jeff, and also to Bruce, who by now had finished his schooling at Melbourne Tech. Bruce was qualified to work in the printing industry but chose instead to work in his father's real estate office in Preston, another Melbourne suburb. His main duty at the office was collecting rents, and he admitted to Alan in a letter that he hated it. In fact, the life Alan was leading appealed very much to Bruce, to the extent that he finally obtained a position as caretaker for three months on a property about twenty kilometres from where Alan was working.

He hadn't told Alan of his plans, but as soon as he felt he could leave the property for a few hours he hitched the horse up to the sulky and started out on the rough country track to Alan's farm.

Alan was out in the fields burning mallee stumps when he saw the familiar figure. 'Bruce! Geez, where did you come from?' he exclaimed in amazement. Laughing with excitement, the boys caught up on each other's news.

Then Alan had an idea. 'After you've finished your job, what do you say we go for a bit of a stroll around Western Victoria and New South Wales—see what the country's like?' The idea appealed to Bruce, who wrote a few days later to his father and said: 'After my three months here, Alan and I thought we might walk to Sydney for a bit of an adventure.' The plan suited Alan ideally because, even though he enjoyed the work, his pay from the farmer was slow in coming. The times were hard and money was scarce.

IT WAS FEBRUARY 1936, THE BOYS were both eighteen, and it was a beautiful summer's day as they set off. They were a rather odd-looking pair. Bruce was tall lanky, well dressed and carrying a suitcase. He was always fastidious about his appearance, his neat, dark brown hair complementing his olive skin, and he wore a smart shirt complete with tie, and a suit. His face was rather angular with a high forehead, and his now handsome features were highlighted by a straight nose and engaging dimples in each cheek. Alan was still considerably shorter than Bruce, with pale blond hair flopping above the ruddy complexion of his round, open face. In contrast to Bruce he wore an open-necked shirt and a pair of tough, faded corduroy trousers.

The first town they came to was Piangil, after a hot twenty-kilometre walk. They tried picking grapes here but it was hard work and not very well paid, so they crossed the Murray River into New South Wales, ending up at place called Goodnight. Here they found an old hotel perched on the edge of the river. The Windsor Hotel was built in the colonial era, and it looked pretty good, with the bar commanding a majestic view of a wide bend in the river, revealing a small beach leading almost up to the hotel.

It was just on dusk, and a few of the local farmers had stopped in for a drink after work. They looked up as the boys made their entrance. The only man sitting down, a hardy-looking individual of uncertain age, broke the silence.

'G'day boys, where're you from?'

'We're from Melbourne, but we've been working at Boundary Bend. We're now travelling around—but we're keen to try any sort of work you might have.' Without pausing, Bruce added: 'Funny name for a place, Goodnight.'

'Yeah, well, it used to be the cry of the riverboat captain as he tied up at the end of the day's work. An' there's still plenty of work. But we only need strong young fellas. You fit?'

'Sure!' Bruce and Alan spoke together. 'What sort of work have you got?'

'It's pretty hard. Do you reckon you can throw a stone over the river from here into Victoria?'

The boys looked at each other but decided to go along with the question. The river was about 30 metres wide, not too far to throw.

'Yeah, we reckon we can.'

'Well, there's a catch. If you can throw a stone across, we'll find a job for you. If you can't, you'll have to shout us all a beer.'

Bruce didn't hesitate. 'Yep, we can do that. Just give us a rock.'

The boys hadn't noticed, but the man doing the negotiating had been sitting with one leg projecting straight out in front of him. As he stood up to lead them outside to the river, the leg emitted a familiar squeak and hiss.

'Wooden leg?' Alan asked. The question was out before he realised it.

'Yeah,' the man said, matter-of-factly. 'Johnny Turk got the original. It's probably still lying at the bottom of a trench at Lone Pine.'

The boys didn't know a lot about military history, but they'd heard about Lone Pine at Gallipoli. Alan considered asking more about the incident, but Bruce called to him to start looking for a stone to throw. The pair searched the river bank and the small beach, without success. They glanced into the bar, beginning to feel they were at the butt-end of a local joke.

Finally Bruce said to Alan: 'Y'know, those bastards are having us on—I just can't find a stone at all. What'll we do?'

'We'll have to go back in and buy them all a beer, I suppose. Damn!'

THEY WERE MET BY SMILING FACES. Bruce started: 'Um, we couldn't find any stones . . .' That brought the house down.

'Never mind,' the ex-soldier said, 'we'll shout you a beer and give you a job as well. Come on over to the bar. By the way, I'm Joe Smith.'

The boys introduced themselves and then settled into a school with several of the locals. The conversation eventually touched on the question of war and the changing political scene in Europe as Hitler had been making his presence felt.

'I hope you young fellas don't get involved in another war with Germany,' Joe said. 'I don't like the way things are shaping up over there.'

'Hell, no,' said Bruce. 'Anyway, it'll be a long way from us. I don't see that we need to get involved again.'

Alan agreed. By now, though, he was even more intrigued at how Joe had lost his leg, and the beer had given him the courage to ask. 'You know,' he said, 'I can't imagine what it's like to be shot at. Do you mind telling me what the Army was like? And the war? And Gallipoli?'

Joe wasn't at all fazed by Alan's curiosity. 'Well, quite simply, the Army was great. I met some tremendous fellas—blokes you'd trust your life with. After training and the experiences we had, we became thicker than thieves. I reckon we had some funny times and some great adventures, particularly in the Middle East. In fact, if you gave me a slip of paper and signed it, saying I wasn't going to get killed, I'd join up any day.

'However,' he added, 'on the other hand, war is simply hell. It's stupid! I'm still trying to work out why the blazes I was racing up a Turkish beach in the middle of the night. I remember it was fabulous coming into Anzac Cove late at night—it was lit up like Luna Park and I thought, there's going to be a bit of fun here, as well as a chance to help the Old Country. Then the bullets and the shells started coming, and they never stopped, day and night, for the next two months I was there. That's when I learnt the meaning of the word fear.'

'Is that when you lost your leg?' Alan ventured.

'Yep.' Joe's eyes had focused on some distant horizon. 'I remember the day and the time like yesterday. I'd spent some time up at Quinn's Post the week before that, and we got a message to say to be ready for a push. I was scared most of the time, but I didn't really learn the meaning of fear until I heard that bloody whistle blow. Whenever someone had to go over the top the captain would blow a whistle. I'd see them go up and over and most times get shot. Whenever that whistle blew, my stomach would turn over.

'Then it was my turn. It was exactly 5.30 pm, I remember, and it was the sixth of August—my Mum's birthday. We'd pounded the Turks with heavy artillery, then when they stopped, there was an eerie silence. Then the whistle blew, and the whole of the 1st Infantry Brigade jumped out to attack Lone Pine. That's when the fear reaction grabs you, after the artillery, and just on the whistle. Just before you leap out, your hands sweat, your mouth goes dry, your heart races like it's going to stop, and you feel like having a great dry retch. Some men even crap themselves. It's no shame—you realise this could be it. Your whole world focuses on the next few minutes and trying to survive. You feel like a rat caught in a cage slowly being lowered into a tank of water. But the fear makes you run and fight like a madman.

'We jumped out into no-man's land, and when we got to their front line we found the first trenches were covered with rafters and earth, with bloody loopholes so the bastards could shoot out at us. We raked the earth clear with our hands and bayonets, then jumped into the pits, in amongst them. It was pretty ghastly down there—it was too close to shoot, so mainly we used bayonets and fists, and fought like animals in the dark, grappling, stabbing, slashing . . . dying.

'By the second day of this, the bodies were piled four and five deep, and we just fought on top of them. By the third day, I was one of them. Someone had let a hand grenade go, and that put me out of the game. They fought on for two more days, and when they finally got me out I was more dead than alive. I can't remember anything else till I woke up on the hospital ship with no leg.

'As I said, war is hell and stupid. Looking back, I've had plenty of time to think about it. We should never have been there—it wasn't our war, particularly against Turkey. The politicians and British generals lost 2000 of us over those few days at Lone Pine. Sure, seven VCs were won, the most ever, but we were all wasted.

'So just you think carefully if Europe gets involved in another war, that's all I say.'

Joe moved his head slowly from side to side. He felt tired now. He wasn't bitter, or even angry. That was the way it was, and even though he admitted he was wiser with hindsight, he reckoned he'd done his duty.

'Y'know, I have to admit things don't look too good with Hitler. Still, just watch out for the politicians when they start rattling their sabres.' He looked around the room. 'It's getting late, boys. I think I'll turn in. Better practise with those throwing arms for next time you chuck a stone.' He laughed to himself, then limped down the corridor, his wooden leg squelching as it supported his now uncoordinated body.

The next morning the pair began two weeks orange picking, then, when the work was getting low, they moved on again.

Mostly they walked from town to town, but often they would hitch rides on wheat trucks, the occasional private car or, many times, horse-drawn wagons. They continued in this manner for some weeks, picking up whatever work was available in each district.

Outside Narrandera they took a chance and 'jumped a rattler' travelling through kilometres of glorious wheat fields. They decided to hop off at Wagga as the train slowed down through the centre of the town. As they did so, they were 'sprung' by the local police sergeant. That night they slept in the cell, although the door wasn't locked. 'I hope this is the first and last time we ever get to sleep in a slammer,' Alan said. Bruce agreed.

Finding work in the Leeton district, as it was harvest time, the boys were awed at the wild beauty of large flights of sulphur-crested cockatoos. Screeching interminably, drawn by the spilt grain, the birds almost blocked out the sun.

AFTER REACHING SYDNEY, BRUCE AND ALAN immediately caught the next train down to Melbourne, allowing them time to reflect on their journey. They were both feeling very satisfied with themselves—the trip had fulfilled most of their expectations, not least testing their self-reliance. However, they were aware that it hadn't exhausted their desire for adventure.

Content to await the opportunity, the boys settled back into Melbourne life, Bruce again employed in his father's real estate agency and Alan working as a nurseryman. Their world wasn't all work. There were dances, concerts, parties, and weekends away. And there were girls, two of whom, Leila and Ann, began to assume a certain importance. Life was sweet.

But the spreading cancer in Europe was becoming difficult to ignore in Australia. Alan and Bruce often found themselves discussing whether they should join the Army. By mid-1940, as the war escalated, each had made up his mind. Oddly, though, they didn't enlist together. Bruce faced opposition from his parents, which in the end he decided to ignore. He joined the Army at the Preston recruiting centre, while Alan, coincidentally, enlisted at another centre on the same day.

Each of them was then sent to the Army's staging station at Caulfield racecourse, unaware that the other had joined up. Hundreds of men were milling around the converted area, waiting in lines, sleeping on their suitcases, or playing card games or 'two-up' in groups.

Somewhere in the massed throng, Alan came across a nurseryman friend of his, Neil Gordon. The two of them proceeded to complete the formalities together, and next morning, first thing, they boarded the train for the ride to Puckapunyal, to join the 2/14th Battalion.

3

At Puckapunyal

PUCKAPUNYAL AT THIS TIME OF YEAR was dry, bleak and cold. The red clay ran across a bald, undulating plain, with an occasional hill and stunted gum tree breaking the monotony. The Training Centre itself wasn't any more inviting. The long rows of living quarters were simply rectangular wooden buildings with galvanised iron roofs, each hut designed to accommodate 22 men. This allowed two sections of eleven men to bunk there. Each section, led by its section commander, a corporal, would be allotted one side of the barracks.

The transport trucks dropped the new recruits at the nearby parade ground—the bullring—where they were soon brought to attention by a sharp, authoritative voice which froze them in their tracks. It belonged to the Adjutant, Lieutenant Ben Buckler, a Duntroon graduate.

'Gentleman,' he bellowed, 'my name is Buckler. From now on, you belong to the Army and the Australian Government. In a few moments, you will select your future company and platoon, then your uniforms and kit. Tomorrow, we are going to start teaching you to become soldiers. And not just soldiers! *Good* soldiers! A good soldier is someone to rely on, someone who'll do his job and trust you to do yours. Your life will depend on him, and his on you—you'll learn to work as a unit. You are going to learn discipline, to take orders and to give orders—you are all going to be good soldiers!'

The recruits were now introduced to the 'cattle sale', where they could select the company of their choice—A, B, C, D or HQ. Alan Avery and his friend Neil Gordon randomly selected A Company. They then had to choose from the three A Company platoons—7, 8 or 9. To help them along, a tall, ginger-haired officer barked at them: 'What about you two blokes joining my platoon?'

'Suits us, sir, which one?'

'9 Platoon. Hop to it!'

After collecting their uniforms and army gear, the men moved to the huts to be sorted into sections, three to each platoon. Alan and Neil were allotted sleeping space on one side of their hut, and were thus placed in Seven Section of 9 Platoon. Neil immediately started to examine his equipment.

Alan smiled at the recruit on his other side and introduced himself. The man was a young Aboriginal. He returned the smile, flashing a row of perfect white teeth, and said he was Harry Saunders. He appeared shy, so Alan offered him a cigarette. The two sat on their kitbags, smoking.

'Where're you from?' Alan asked.

'Lake Condah. From the Mission there near Portland. I was doing timber contracting work around there with my father and my brother Reg. Then all of a sudden Reg up and joined the Army in April. I was still a bit too young, so I went walkabout for a few weeks. Since I was getting close to Melbourne, I thought I'd try and join up too.'

Alan looked at him quizzically. 'Geez, you don't look old enough to join now.'

Harry smiled. 'Ha! I tried to get in two days ago under my real name, Henry James, but I think the doc thought I was too young also. So I had another crack at it the next day. Changed my name to Harry, saw a different doctor, and here I am. I'm old enough—I've just turned eighteen.'

Alan chortled. He liked Harry's spirit.

'I suppose we'll get used to the Army,' another man said. He walked past and threw his palliasse and kit down next to them. He was taller than Harry but, like him, strong and athletic and also very youthful looking.

'G'day, Lindsay Bear's my name. Most people call me

Teddy—God knows why!' The others laughed and introduced themselves.

'Well, I guess we're all in now, for better or worse,' Alan said.

'Yeah,' Teddy said, 'and I'm keen to get going. I'd like a crack at Hitler.'

'Are you from Melbourne?' Alan asked.

'Yeah, from Kensington. I used to make diecasting moulds for cars. Flamin' heavy work, but somebody said it would be easy compared to what the Army has to offer.'

'Well, I'm ready for anything,' Alan said, 'And so's my new mate here, eh Harry?'

Harry's face beamed.

Next morning they were awakened at six by the reverberating voice of the Adjutant. The cold morning air carried his message all over the compound, and Alan remarked: 'Strike, sounds like Little Sir Echo—what a voice!'

He didn't have time to comment any further, as another loud voice issued from the doorway. 'Good morning, men, I'm your platoon commander. You met me yesterday. Welcome to your first day in the Army. You've got half an hour to go down to the ablutions block, get washed and shaved, and be out on the parade ground. Snap to it!'

It was Lieutenant Gerry O'Day. Before the war he had been a member of Power House, and had gained his commission whilst serving in the Militia. Even though he was only twenty, a year or so younger than Alan, he was authoritative, tough and experienced in army life.

It was the first battalion parade, and the men were introduced to their overall program and what they might expect over the coming months—drill instruction, rifle drill, regimentation, field craft, bivouac experience and mock battle training. At the end of this period, they were told, they should be ready for war.

AS THE PARADE WAS BREAKING UP, Alan noticed a familiar figure in another unit across the ground. With a gasp of surprise, he realised the person was Bruce Kingsbury. At the same time, Bruce recognised him and came over.

21

'Geez, Bruce, what a surprise! What are you doing here? I didn't think you were joining up.'

Bruce grinned. 'I had a run-in with my folks. They wouldn't let me go, so I joined anyway. They'll be alright. There'll be a few tears, but I know what I want. We'll patch it up later.' He looked back across the parade ground. 'They've put me into an independent unit—the 2/2nd Pioneers.'

'Hell, what are we going to do now?' Alan asked. 'We always said we'd go away to war together.'

'Yeah, you're right. One of us will have to change . . . Let's toss a coin, choose either your unit or mine, then see if we can change.'

'OK. Heads we go my way—2/14th. Tails we go yours—2/2nd Pioneers.'

Bruce tossed the coin; it came down heads. 'Right, 2/14th it is. Let's go and see whether we can change straight away.'

At that stage the process wasn't too much trouble. A few days later, Bruce transferred to the 2/14th Battalion.

Alan introduced him to Neil and Harry, then took him to meet some of the other newcomers. They were a mixed bunch: Bluey Whitechurch, a grazier from a property not far from Puckapunyal; Ted Jobe, who used to work as a stonemason before the war, and had already acquired the nickname 'Tombstone Ted'; and Sailor Parsons, from Dover in England, who had done a hitch in the Merchant Navy.

'And here's another one,' said Teddy Bear, who'd come up to them. He pointed to a reclining figure on the palliasse in the corner of the hut. The man, idly thumbing through a book, looked up. 'Meet the Professor,' Teddy said to Bruce. 'He's a school teacher, our resident encyclopaedia. Want to know anything about anything—he's your man. And you know what? His specialty is Classics, all those old cultures and myths. He's just told us about this Greek chap Ulysses who fought against the Trojans and took ten years to get home . . . Wonder what his wife said!'

The Professor put the book away, stood up and took Bruce's outstretched hand. He was smiling. 'Hello, welcome to Seven Section. As a matter of fact,' he continued, 'Ulysses was away for *twenty* years—the Trojan War itself took ten years to fight.

His wife Penelope waited faithfully for him all that time. How about that?'

'Ah, that's the trouble with those Greek heroes,' Alan said. 'Larger than life! He probably had a lot more to keep her faithful than what us mere mortals have.'

There was laughter all round.

Yes, Bruce and Alan thought, they would enjoy it here. They fitted in. Seven Section was definitely a varied lot, a microcosm of the battalion as a whole. But they were all young. The average age in the section was nineteen years, about ten less than the battalion average.

As the weeks moved on, this eclectic assemblage of men bonded into a more disciplined unit as Lieutenant O'Day trained his charges.

The evenings were mostly free and Bruce, Alan, the Professor and Teddy would spend long hours playing four-handed solo-whist, the score being meticulously recorded in a notebook. Later they were joined by another committed card player from Eight Section. This was Ted Silver. He was a timber cutter before the war and, at around 190 centimetres, was the tallest man in the platoon. He was lean and tough with strong arms; his jutting jaw offset his broken nose, a legacy of many bush fights. Typical of the bushman breed, he possessed a laconic, rather happy-go-lucky nature, and readily accepted the obvious nickname he was given—'Hi-Ho'.

Sport added to the bonding process, football creating most interest. The Australian Rules team played most weekends, boasting some of Melbourne's better footballers. The Professor, who was a natural athlete, made the team, and played at halfback with a 7 Platoon sergeant, Mokka Treacy, a man known for his resolve and toughness.

THE TEAM ALSO BOUGHT STAN BISSET and his brother Butch to prominence. In it they forged a reputation not just as fair and tough men but as adaptable players able to switch from one football code to another. Alongside the rover, Maurie Valli, they were the ruckmen of the team and helped to engineer some great wins.

The brothers had both settled well into army life, with Butch quickly promoted to sergeant major of B Company. Stan was pleased to be posted to the same company, where he acquired rank as corporal in 12 Platoon. And his friend from Power House days, Phil Rhoden, now a captain, was second-in-command of the company.

Stan came under further notice from the officers when it was realised that he possessed a gift for singing. He led a small group of six B Company men who regularly entertained at the camp and at dances and concerts nearby.

Training in military skills continued, helping to forge a strong battalion spirit. At the rifle range, Bruce Kingsbury distinguished himself by becoming the top marksman of A Company. In B Company, Butch and Stan Bisset regularly topped the day's tally.

They were almost ready to head off to the war. However, as September stretched out, guessing games as to their date of embarkation and probable destination were put on hold. Instead, intense interest arose as the battalion played in the Grand Final. There were 20 000 troops from 25 units stationed at Puckapunyal at the time, and the ground was packed. The 2/14th team was playing against the favourites, the 2/2nd Medium Artillery Regiment. There was added pressure for the players, as the officers had backed their shirts on the outcome. It was a tough game, played at a fierce rate. The artillery regiment had appeared better on paper, but Stan, Butch and the Professor lifted the whole team's game and they finally won by five goals. Several of them helped the Professor to celebrate with smuggled beer supplied by the officers.

The news the battalion had been waiting for was posted on the main notice board the next day. The Seventh Division was to be sent overseas within a few weeks. Events moved fast after this. Eventually orders came that the battalion would be leaving for Sydney later that week to embark for overseas.

The news stimulated Bruce and Alan into starting an all day two-up session, followed by a dice game. By midnight they had each won £22. Then came the bombshell. Bruce said to Alan: 'Well, I've almost got enough to go down and see Leila and get engaged . . . married if I can.'

'What! Just like that?' Even as Alan put the question, he caught his friend's eye and suddenly realised Bruce was serious.

'Yeah, but I'll have to get some more money for an engagement present.'

In the morning Alan rounded up some of the men and started another game. The dice rolled well for him, but Bruce's luck had turned sour. He lost all the money he'd won. He looked at Alan in desperation. 'Listen, mate, I've done my dough. You'll have to lend me the £22.'

That night Bruce and Alan went AWL and hitched a ride to Melbourne. They met Leila Bradbury in the city next day, where Bruce promptly proposed to her. To his relief she accepted, and he offered her an antique family ring as an engagement ring. It was gold, with lovers' knots entwined in it. They had photographs taken at a studio and, with Alan's money, Bruce bought Leila a wristlet watch as an engagement present. Leila gave him a signet ring and had B.S.K. engraved on it. In the window of the jeweller's shop, was a display of military medals and decorations. Bruce looked them over, then said with a smile: 'I'm going to come home wearing one of those!'

His idea of marrying Leila before he went overseas wasn't possible, as it turned out. Leila didn't need too much convincing, but they found they couldn't marry without a licence, which would take a few days.

HARRY SAUNDERS HAD ALSO GONE AWL. He'd hitched a five-hour ride out to Lake Condah, where he and his brother Reg had been raised in a shack not far from the Mission community of 300 Aboriginal people.

Harry had mixed blood in his veins, as his paternal grandfather was a Caribbean Negro who had married a full-blood Aboriginal girl in South Australia.

They had settled at Lake Condah, where their son Chris, Harry's father, married a local Aboriginal girl. It was a part of Harry's heritage to be a warrior, as his people, the Gunditjmara, tribe, had fought many battles with white settlers to retain their land. Closer to home, he had another proud military tradition to live up to, as his father had fought in France during World War I. And his uncle, Reg Rawlings, for whom his brother Reg was named, had won a Military Medal and was killed in action in Flanders.

Harry had attended the Lake Condah school, where he found he was a gifted athlete. His father taught him to box, swim and play football and now, as he moved through the Mission gates, he was recognised and welcomed by everyone. He greeted them all, including his three younger sisters, Amy, Eliza and Christine.

That night he attended the local dance, where he was in demand as a partner, looking both conspicuous and handsome in his military uniform.

Saying goodbye, his father reminded him that Reg was already in Palestine and was now a sergeant. Harry said he hoped that he and his brother could get together over there.

On 18 October 1940 the battalion entrained for Sydney. They travelled through the night, arriving at Sydney Harbour late in the morning, ready to board HMT *Aquitania* at Woolloomooloo Pier. The grand old Atlantic liner of the Cunard White Star Line had been a troop carrier during World War I also, and even though she seemed heavier, taller and 'dated' compared with the *Queen Mary* berthed nearby, her striking presence excited the men about to board her.

As their ship headed slowly down the harbour, Bruce and Alan moved through the packed throng of men and managed to secure a spot on the top deck. In the bright afternoon sunshine, tugs, ferries and moored ships blew their sirens to salute the departing convoy. An armada of yachts and motor boats had flags waving from them, wishing the troops well. Finally the *Aquitania* and the *Queen Mary* moved out through the Heads and into the open ocean.

With the Australian coastline fading in the evening light, the men felt the loss of loved ones and familiar surroundings. But the moment of regret didn't last. Soon they were all talking, laughing, meeting new friends, and familiarising themselves with ship life. For many of them it was the first time they'd ventured far from home, let alone overseas.

Standing at the ship's rail, Stan and Butch felt a tremble of excitement—they were on their way!

THE MIDDLE
EAST

4

Tourists Abroad

THE SHIPS PASSED ADEN, HEADING FOR the Red Sea. Somaliland was on their left and Arabia to their right. They were now part of a larger convoy. As it negotiated the narrows, on its way to Egypt, the aircraft-alarm bells suddenly rang, warning everybody to get below. Anti-aircraft guns on the cruiser HMS *Carlisle* opened fire at a plane flying overhead—it was the first angry shot most of the troops had heard. After the 'all clear' signal had been given, they tentatively re-emerged from the holds. Off to starboard Stan noticed a large pall of smoke about twenty kilometres away. It appeared as if some vessel had exploded at sea. They were told over the loudspeakers that the plane fired at was a reconnaissance plane and that they should expect a visit at some stage by enemy bombers.

The men were also told that Italy had recently attacked Greece, which produced waves of protest and prompted speculation as to where the unit might be sent to fight—Greece, Egypt, or even Eritrea.

It took three days to traverse the Red Sea, the ships finally anchoring at El Kantara on the Suez Canal. After experiencing their first clash with Middle East hawkers, the men boarded a train and headed north over the Sinai Desert, towards Palestine.

Eventually, at dusk, they moved into Julis camp, situated on the coastal plain midway between Gaza and Tel Aviv and surrounded by Australian camps spread over a 35-kilometre region. Poor and generally dirty Arab villages dotted the terrain. Alan Avery was amazed at the primitive farming methods used to sustain life. The ancient olive presses, waterwheels and donkey-drawn wooden ploughs had not changed a great deal since biblical times.

Within a few days of settling in, Stan was paraded before Brigadier Stevens, commander of the 21st Brigade. The brigadier was a small man with rather sharp features, and inclined to be blunt.

'Well, Bisset,' he said, 'this is what it's all about. I'd like you to be our amenities officer. It'll mean organising a few social events, sports and that sort of thing. You can start tomorrow, if you like.' Something like a smile appeared on his face. 'Or we can nominate you to attend officer training at Cairo—a four-month course run by the British Army.'

'Sir, if I'm going to become an officer, I'd like that very much . . . but what about all the sergeants? I'm only a corporal.'

Stevens looked at him. 'Well, that's not your decision. That's my decision—*Sergeant!* You're off to Cairo.'

'Thank you, sir,' Stan replied, a bit overcome.

Later he sought out Butch and relayed the news to him.

'That's great,' said Butch. 'And with a bit of luck we might be there together. I've just heard I'm being recommended also. Maybe for the next month's intake.'

He punched Stan on the shoulder in mock anger. 'You'll be an officer before me, you bugger. Look, we've got a few days before you go—let's celebrate by going on leave and having a look at Jerusalem.'

As Stan and Butch sat in the bus and looked forward to their first glimpse of the glittering spires and domes of the Holy City, they could almost hear the echoes of heroic and tragic events enacted and re-enacted over the centuries by uncounted legions.

The brothers entered the Old City through the ancient Jaffa Gate, immediately impressed by the bustling life, the peddlers, and the many devout people of all races seeking to fulfil the human need to believe. In turn, they visited the important biblical sites—especially the Via Dolorosa and Golgotha, the Western Wall, and then, outside the city, Gethsemane. Finally, at Bethlehem, they saw the supposed site of Christ's birth.

Harry Saunders now received an unexpected visit from his brother Reg, who was in a camp only a few kilometres away. Harry welcomed him warmly and introduced him to a number of friends, including Bruce, Alan, and Teddy Bear.

The next weekend Harry and Reg wandered around Jerusalem together. Having moved a few months earlier from the simple existence of a peaceful Mission community in Victoria, and being suddenly placed in one of the oldest and most fascinating cities on earth, it was for Harry a strange and exhilarating experience.

Reg smiled at Harry's excitement, yet he was deep in thought. He'd felt he should claim Harry for his own battalion so that he could keep an eye on the lad, but their father had warned against that. Chris had thought it was probably better to keep his two boys apart—that way there was less chance of both of them being killed. Now Reg reassured himself. Harry appeared to be in with a group of friends who would look after him.

And so they did—in a way. They organised an excursion to the old and unsavoury Arab city of Jaffa, just south of Tel Aviv. The idea was to introduce Harry to the world of women in an infamous brothel known to exist in the harbour town.

While Harry was ushered along the corridor towards one of the bedrooms, several British soldiers, relaxing in the waiting room outside, loudly voiced their disapproval of the presence of 'blacks' in their brothel. Immediately some New Zealanders, sitting nearby, and affronted by the comments, reacted violently to this prejudice. Within seconds, Aussies, Kiwis and Brits became engaged in an all-in brawl in the waiting room.

Hearing the commotion, Harry came racing back along the corridor, but the madam, experienced with brawls such as this, frantically blew a whistle and instructed her girls to throw buckets of water on the fighting mob. The fracas was over as briskly as it began. The three British soldiers, battered and bruised, were trundled out and sent on their way, not too sure what had hit them.

The Australians and Kiwis then adjourned to a cafe in Tel Aviv and continued with an uproarious drinking session while they discussed the day's events.

Towards evening, Alan, Bruce and Harry were ambling along

a beautiful tree-lined boulevard when they noticed coming towards them two very disorderly Australian soldiers from another unit.

One of the soldiers caught sight of Harry's black face and lurched across the footpath towards him. He spat out: 'G'day, Snowball!' Harry's reaction was immediate. His right hand hardly seemed to move, but it was fast, powerful and accurate. The punch fairly exploded on the man's chin, jerking his head back. His body dropped straight to the ground like a bag of cement. Bruce and Alan shot amazed glances at each other.

The second soldier leapt forward, his eyes wide and glaring with rage. He drew his right fist back, telegraphing his intentions. 'Why, you dirty . . .' The hapless soldier was cut off in mid-sentence as Harry unleashed another furious straight right, also appearing to zip out of nowhere. It dropped the man, as a train might stop a raging bull. From the ground, he heard Harry say quietly but firmly: 'Get out of here, and take your mate with you.'

'Hell, mate, we're bloody glad you're on our side,' Alan quipped.

Harry was smiling. 'Geez,' he said, 'what do you know, twice in a day! First the brothel, then here.' He laughed out loud. 'Y'know, I didn't know I was black until today. Why didn't you blokes tell me?'

By next day Harry was the talk of the battalion.

That night, in the shower block, Teddy Bear was preparing for his evening ablutions when he caught sight of Harry, who was scrubbing his skin wildly, and laughing.

'What's so funny?' Teddy asked.

Harry replied, in tones of mock annoyance: 'Damn thing, Teddy, it won't come off. I've been scrubbing this black stuff on my skin for hours, and it's *still* there.'

They both snorted at the ridiculousness of it all.

CHRISTMAS CAME TO THE HOLY LAND, ushering in the new year, 1941. It was certainly a different Christmas for the men of the 2/14th Battalion. A desert setting, with turkey and plum pudding, traditionally served by the officers.

As the new year dawned, the men heard that the Australian

Sixth Division was engaging the Italians at Bardia in North Africa, and by the end of January they had overrun Tobruk. Harry wondered how Reg had fared as the shooting settled down. It appeared that the war in the desert might be over.

The Ninth Division had arrived at Julis camp, and in March they were sent to North Africa to reinforce the line there. In the meantime, the Sixth Division was sent to Greece, which had earlier beaten off Mussolini's invasion. Even though everything was quiet in the Mediterranean now, behind the scenes the war establishment realised it was not going to be long before Hitler, Mussolini's unholy partner, recommenced his pincer movement to take the Suez Canal, the Persian oilfields, and finally India. They expected one arm of the pincer to move along the top of North Africa and the other to come down through Greece and Turkey.

For now, though, the Seventh Division busied itself with exercises.

At this stage Thompson sub-machine-guns became available to the Australian Army, prompting Alan to apply for one. He wasn't a very good shot with the .303 rifle, and he reasoned that the larger weapon might improve his chances. The Tommy gun held fifty .45 bullets in a drum and fired 600 rounds a minute. After many hours on the practice range, he became quite deadly with it, managing close groupings from 60 to 100 metres. He found his accuracy improved by shooting in short bursts of five or six at a time. Any more and the recoil would lift the barrel high, sending his bullets to the birds.

Stan was now in Egypt, training to become an officer. The course was conducted by the British Army in Abyssia Barracks, about eight kilometres out of Cairo.

Within a few weeks he was joined by Butch and two others from the 2/14th, Merric Stevenson and Mokka Treacy. Mokka, who'd been the halfback in Stan's Puckapunyal team, had by now become great friends with Butch, and Stan was glad to show them the ropes. He introduced them to the big Mess-Naafi—where beer could be found, as well as a piano around which most of them would congregate at the end of the day. As well, there was a strong Rugby team which Stan captained. And there were other attractions around Cairo where the men could be entertained.

After they'd visited the Pyramids and the Sphinx, Stan had an opportunity to go upstream on a cruise of the Nile. Here, at sunset, among the pylons of ancient temples and ruins, he watched the feluccas as their lateen sails billowed and played against the last light. The war was a long way off.

By the end of February he had completed his training and graduated as a lieutenant. On his return to the battalion, he was informed that he would be the commander of 18 Platoon in D Company.

When Butch, Mokka and Merric finished their term a month later, they went directly to a special training battalion in Palestine as instructors, where they were to train reinforcements for the next three months.

In early April, the battalion received a warning order to prepare to move to an unstated destination. Over the previous few weeks, the Allies had suffered serious setbacks from their early victories. Hitler had sent Rommel and his Afrika Korps to recapture the positions lost by the Italians in Northern Africa. Displaying his mastery of mobile warfare, by 9 April Rommel had the Ninth Division and part of the Seventh Division bottled up in the Tobruk fortress in Libya, along with elements of the British Army. The defenders were preparing to withstand a lengthy siege in order to give the Allies time to prevent Rommel's run towards Cairo and the Suez Canal and then organise a counter-attack. The Sixth Division were also in trouble over in Greece and were battling through a heroic withdrawal in the face of a furious German onslaught.

To the men of the 2/14th, it appeared that at last their touring and training days were over. As almost the last elements of the Allied Army in the Middle East yet to meet the enemy, they placed bets on their probable destination.

They didn't have long to wait, as they shortly moved to the Mersa Matruh fortress on the North African coast, about 300 kilometres from Tobruk—the front line.

Mersa Matruh was previously a quiet Mediterranean resort town, and had been prepared and laid out as a fortress by the Italians in 1940, as they were advancing into Egypt—before the Sixth Division threw them out. Now the garrison was to be used by the Allies mainly as a provision depot and port for ships taking troops and supplies to Tobruk. As they'd been warned that the Germans could conceivably be there within 36 hours, the first priority was to reorganise the fortress's defences.

The 2/14th took over positions from a Scottish unit and occupied the most westerly corner of the land area. It was high summer and Stan was dismayed to find that a large part of this sector consisted mainly of sand. There was no vegetation to break the raw horizon, only hectares of low, flat sandhills and undulating wasteland, laid bare by the hot, desert-like conditions—a world stripped to its rocky soul.

At times, the temperature would soar to 49 degrees Celsius, creating almost indescribable working conditions. To the men of the Seventh Division the heat quickly became unbearable, seriously affecting their first task—to erect kilometres of barbed wire fences around the perimeter.

At the same time, they also had to dig anti-tank ditches in the rock-hard ground in anticipation of a German breakthrough. The task was made even more difficult as they were always on the alert for land mines, laid by the Egyptians and the British as well as the Italians.

Alan and Bruce realised they were now in the war zone as, during the first night of their occupation, high-flying German bombers scattered their payload over the fortress area, the bombs crashing like thunder in the darkness.

'Christ, what the hell's that!' Alan crawled out of his dugout and looked up at the heavens. He couldn't see any planes, but one of the stores and several huts in the next sector were on fire.

'Shit, I guess that's it,' Bruce said. 'We're in it now. We'd better dig those bloody dugouts deeper.'

They were both a little shaken, and Alan realised his mouth was dry. He gulped down some water from his water bottle, suddenly remembering the words of the old Digger at the Goodnight hotel. Yes, that was a fear reaction, he thought to himself.

The next day they were out digging trenches with the rest of the platoon, when all of a sudden nine German Stuka dive bombers screamed in low over the garrison, releasing their bombs onto specific targets.

'Come on, Al,' Bruce said, 'let's have a better look.'

The two men scrambled up a nearby dune and, almost

breathless, peered over the top. From here they had a grand-stand view of the scene as the Stukas shrieked out of the sky in a second terrifying dive, dropping bombs that had 'screamers' attached to them for effect.

'Crikey, what a bloody racket,' Alan yelled, his hands over his ears.

The men watched, transfixed, as the 'Shrieking Vultures' built up to another screaming climax as they delivered their 908-kilogram bombs before pulling out of a vertical plunge.

After the planes had wheeled off and disappeared into the horizon, Bruce grabbed Alan by the arm. 'Y'know . . .' He hesitated, then continued: 'Y'know, Al, it's more than possible one of us could get killed in this bloody war. We should make a pact. If one of us cops it, the other collects his private things—letters, photos and so on—and hangs on to them.'

Alan agreed immediately, and with that they made their way back.

Even though these air attacks occurred virtually daily for the entire time they were at Mersa Matruh, it was a mine that was responsible for the battalion's first war casualties. Unfortunately, they were from Stan's 18 Platoon. One of his men, Tiny Faber, stood on a concealed mine and was killed. Tiny's companion was wounded.

If Stan needed any further reminder that they weren't far from the heat of the battle, he could walk down to the port and watch the shell- and bomb-damaged warships limp in to the wharves, after being raked by the German Air Force as they ran the gauntlet from Mersa Matruh to Tobruk. Lying on stretchers, the Tobruk casualties were carried off the battered vessels into waiting ambulances.

As the weeks drew on, the hot, dusty weather and the occasional khamsin, or dust storm, which often lasted three or four days, created uncomfortable hothouse conditions. The scorching air, filled with swirling particles of sand, would hit the skin and eyes like razors and reach into clothing, bedding, food, and every personal orifice that wasn't kept closed.

But the climate wasn't without its compensations. Mersa Matruh had been a seaside resort as far back as Roman days, and was linked to the romance of Antony and Cleopatra. At every available opportunity, the men would bathe at one of the best beaches in the Mediterranean. In fact, except for the random moments of terror when bombers menaced the garrison, and apart from the sticky and blistering conditions, life was reasonably relaxed and not unenjoyable at Mersa Matruh.

Towards the end of May, rumours started circulating that there might be another move, and possibly action, in the near future.

'Y'know, I reckon we could be off to Syria, myself,' said the Professor.

'Syria?' Alan and Bruce asked in chorus.

'What about Crete?' chipped in Harry. 'Reg and his Sixth Divvy are being hammered by German paratroopers, I heard. What about Greece?'

'Well, look at it. Both the Germans and the British could use the Iraqi oilfields, and I've heard that Messerschmitts have been landing in North Syria. I reckon the Germans might try and invade the Levant, push on to Palestine, then on to Persia, perhaps.'

'The Levant? What's that?' Alan asked.

'It means, literally, the East—East Mediterranean. Yep, I reckon it'll be more urgent for us to go somewhere towards Syria, or even Turkey.'

Teddy Bear weighed in, 'Yes, I agree, but unfortunately I won't be with you fellows. My friend from school days, Lester Royale, wants me to join him in the carrier platoon. We joined up together, and thought we'd better fight together. Sorry, chaps. Besides, I like the idea of a Bren gun on top of an armoured vehicle.' He laughed.

The news was a bit of a blow to the section, as they had worked well as a team.

ON 23 MAY, THE 21ST AND 25TH Brigades of the Seventh Division moved from Egypt and back up to Palestine. The other brigade, the 18th, had been sent to reinforce Tobruk in April.

For the men of the 2/14th it was a long, hot train ride back along the Mediterranean. Every now and then, history would call to them as a Crusader castle became visible and then settled back into eternity, its chalk white towers and battlements hanging like a necklace on a dusty hilltop. Their journey finally finished near Nazareth, on the Plains of Esdraelon.

'I hope camping here isn't too prophetic for us,' the Professor confided to Alan and Bruce.

'What do you mean?'

'Haven't you heard of Megiddo? This is where St John writes in his Apocalypse about the last battle at Armageddon, the site of the ultimate clash between the Forces of Good and Evil. It's been almost fulfilled many times over the centuries, as everybody from the Egyptians to the Greeks has fought here—on the Plains of Esdraelon and the Valley of Jezreel, right next to it. King Saul died here, Gideon won his victory here, and in the Great War Allenby licked the Turks with the Australian and Indian Light Horse. If it *is* prophetic, hopefully it'll be the last battle for our enemies—not us.'

For the next few days, the battalion rejoiced in the greenness and coolness of the surrounding collective farms. The peaceful Jewish people showed their hospitality; a great many of the Australians felt quite at home, as they camped against a background of gum trees and an oasis of crops.

They didn't have long to wait for word of their next destination. Lieutenant O'Day called his platoon together and briefed them.

'This is it!' he said. 'We're off to Syria and Lebanon. We're fighting the Vichy French there. The brass think the Germans want to take over the region and use it as a base for a leap to the Persian oilfields, or to force a way through to Suez and maybe on to India. We haven't got too long to get fit again. As we'll probably be fighting over high mountains and passes, we'll be going for a few climbs in the hills around Nazareth here. The general says we're crossing the border on Sunday the eighth of June.'

'Hang on a minute, sir,' Hi-Ho Silver piped up. 'Did you say we're fighting the French? I thought they were our allies.' The men all looked at each other.

O'Day smiled. He was waiting for the question. 'We *are* fighting the French. The *Vichy* French. When Hitler overran France last year, he put in a puppet government to run the country. It was to collaborate with the Germans and was established at Vichy, a spa town south of Paris. Hence Vichy French.

'Now, General de Gaulle, over in London, has set up a resistance movement to liberate the French people. He calls it the 'Free French'.

'So this left a problem for all the French colonies scattered around the world—who to side with? The Free French or the Vichy French?'

O'Day warmed to his lecture. 'As you blokes might already know, after the last war, the Levant countries were divided up. As a result, TransJordan and Palestine were placed under a British Mandate, while Syria and Lebanon went to France. In fact, Beirut, the capital of Lebanon, is known as the Paris of the Orient—it's a beautiful city, apparently. It appears these two countries are sympathetic to the Vichy government, so the idea is for us to stop the Germans setting up control there.

'We'll be up against one of the toughest armies in the world—the French Foreign Legion. They have a "Fight and Die" creed, and probably won't give an inch.'

And indeed, the scene had been set. On the nights of 5 and 6 June, spearhead troops moved into position close to the border of the two countries. The full invading force comprised some 34 000 soldiers. There were 18 000 Australians, 9000 British, 5000 Free French fighters and 2000 Indians. The core of this force was the two Australian brigades—the 21st and 25th. The attack was to be a three-pronged thrust over the border: to Beirut via the coast road; to Zahle and Rayak airfield situated in the Bekaa valley between the Lebanon and Anti-Lebanon mountains; and to Damascus, capital of Syria, over the cruel Syrian desert.

Opposing them, the Vichy commander, General Dentz, had about 35 000 troops. These included his French Foreign Legion battalions, plus French-led Senegalese, Algerian and Moroccan troops.

The 21st Brigade was to lead the thrust up the narrow coastal road to Beirut, and the 25th Brigade would lead the central attack over the high, narrow winding road leading to Zahle. To the right, Australian, British, Indian and Free French forces were to push towards Damascus.

As the men of the 2/14th were waiting in their positions on

7 June, the night before the invasion, there was still murmuring, and some shock, at having to fight their supposed allies. There was a hopeful official thought that the Vichy French might not have their hearts in the confrontation. And even though the Australians were keyed for battle, there had been every indication that the invading force would meet with little opposition, and that they should cover the 100 kilometres to Beirut within 24 hours.

The troops were ordered to wear their slouch hats instead of their steel helmets, in an effort to 'show the flag' and in the hope that the Frenchmen wouldn't fire on their former allies. It was, after all, only a little over twenty years since some of the Australians' fathers, and indeed some of the present AIF members themselves, had fought against France's enemies during World War I. However, just in case, it was decided that they should also carry their helmets.

It was a hot night, being high summer. Stan moved around his men, who were generally having trouble resting. It was too hot for groundsheets, and most were too keyed up to try sleeping. He found some of them talking quietly among themselves and he joined their conversation, offering encouragement. He took the responsibility as platoon commander of 38 men very seriously. This was what he was trained for. For the first time, they were about to be tested under fire, and the adrenaline was starting to pump. Earlier there had been a general feeling of tenseness as he insisted that his team check and recheck their gear, weapons and ammunition, and ensured that everyone knew exactly what was expected of them.

Many had retired to their own thoughts: some no doubt thinking of home, some excited at the prospect of action, others fearful of what the morrow might bring. Some were reflecting, perhaps praying, calling for strength and hoping they would not be found wanting when called upon. Stan privately suspected that the battle would be no pushover, and had steeled his men for a no-holds-barred conflict. Pitted one for one against professional soldiers, the task would take some resolve.

He thought of Butch, whom he missed, but was quietly happy that his brother was out of the battle for the time being.

It was now 7.30 pm, a little cooler, but Stan's hands were

perspiring. They would be moving out in half an hour's time, so he closed his eyes and thought about his own fears.

He realised that during the next few hours most of his men would be challenged to put their life on the line. Some of them, himself included, might even be killed. At any instant, any of them could have to make a life-threatening decision—heroic or otherwise—driven by their training and their commitment to the cause and to each other. The risk of loss of life would be high.

Stan searched for the strength to lead by example. He had been tested in many ways in life up till now, but, he admitted to himself, never looking down the barrel of a gun! There was, of course, no question of backing out.

His earliest moral beliefs had been moulded by his staunch Presbyterian upbringing, and then finely tuned by his years at Power House. This institution had played no small part in forming his thoughts concerning love of country, King and Queen, and the Mother Country; and in ultimately influencing his—and Butch's—decision to enlist. He was strengthened by a strong, intuitive feeling that what he was doing was right.

He believed he was ready.

5

Southern Lebanon

'RIGHT, MEN, ON YOUR FEET!' The words galvanised the keyed-up troops. The waiting soldiers of B and D Companies briskly and efficiently formed a column. Moving around effortlessly in the dark, Stan's 18 Platoon fell into place, putting their private thoughts behind them. Just after 8.00 pm, they moved out of the holding area and prepared for the slog up to the border village of Hanita, the jump-off point about ten kilometres inland from the sea. By now the night was cooler and quite cloudy, with the diminished moonlight making the climb to Hanita hazardous as well as strenuous. It was a four-hour march over craggy mountain tracks and rocky pathways as the route swung through the hills. Stan could barely make out the austere landscape with the available light reflecting from a few native bushes.

Fully laden, with packs, ammunition, weapons and food supplies, it was a testing ascent for the soldiers and they were grateful to have a break when they reached the British post at the Hanita kibbutz. They arrived just after midnight, reviving themselves with drinks and cakes which they produced from their haversacks.

About an hour later, the B Company contingent moved out to secure their designated objective, leaving the three platoons of D Company to prepare for the attack on theirs—Alma Chaab.

The border was about a kilometre away, with the village of Alma Chaab situated two kilometres further north. It was known to be guarded by a garrison of French troops. The plan was for Stan's 18 Platoon to attack it from the south, catching the enemy in a pincer movement with 16 Platoon moving from the west. As there were impassable mountains to the east, 17 Platoon was detailed to move around to the north to prevent any retreat by the Frenchmen.

Just after 2.00 am, the three platoons moved out of Hanita and crossed the border. With the aid of their Jewish guide, they carefully made their way in the dark over the stony and hilly goat path. It was tough going, but adrenaline fuelled their bodies, allowing the men to move with a steady, purposeful, almost hypnotic rhythm.

In the antique light of a mountain dawn, Stan saw around him the windswept valleys and craggy peaks. As the earliest rays of morning sun filtered through the clear air, materialising out of the darkness ahead and slowly emerging from the forms of trees, rocks and shrubs, he could make out the silhouette of buildings.

The guide turned and pointed. He whispered to Stan: 'Alma Chaab.' The village was directly ahead, still largely protected from the first fingers of light by the hills to the east. Through his binoculars, Stan could make out a large stone building which he imagined was the main garrison blockhouse. It was a two-storey building, completed in a Mediterranean French style. To the left, facing west, was another, smaller blockhouse; behind that, on a third building, he could make out a sign, *Gendarmerie*.

By now, he reasoned, 16 Platoon should be approaching from the west, so he turned in that direction. On a strategic rise covering the platoon's line of entrance, Stan was disturbed to see a sentry post manned by four members of the French Foreign Legion. As he watched through the glasses, he could see the crouched shapes of five men appear out of the receding darkness from the northern direction and crawl to within a few metres of the post. He recognised the leader as Bluey Lee, a section leader from 17 Platoon.

Suddenly, the five Australians attacked the post. Stan could see men fighting hand to hand and others struggling on the ground. Morning sunlight flashed off a bayonet as an Australian swiftly raised his weapon and buried the blade deep into one of the sentries. The man dropped silently to the ground. Another Frenchman went limp and fell as he too was bayoneted. The other two sentries, realising they had been outfought, capitulated. This is it, Stan thought, it's on!

At that moment, 16 Platoon appeared in Stan's vision and continued past the now silent sentry post towards the smaller blockhouse. Unfortunately, the muffled sounds of the skirmish with the sentries had been enough to alert the garrison. The morning quiet was shattered as a French machine-gunner opened fire from a post situated on the flank of the small blockhouse. The noise echoed around the hilltops and invited spontaneous return fire from the Australians. Smoke and sound erupted around the village as a fierce firefight exploded.

The air immediately became thick with bullets, with 16 Platoon under fire not only from the machine-gun post but also from both blockhouses and the Gendarmerie at the rear.

Stan felt the pit of his stomach tighten. A sense of foreboding passed over him as he realised he was going to have to walk into the middle of the murderous scene. He took a few deep breaths and quieted himself, now in complete control.

'Right, men, this is the plan. I want to take the large blockhouse in front of us. Move up quickly to it, and give supporting fire to 16 Platoon whenever you can. Nine Section, come with me, up the middle. The other two sections, go either side. You know what you have to do. Let's go.'

Stan moved his group a few metres closer to the blockhouse, but seeing the situation seemingly deteriorate for 16 Platoon, he ordered his men to concentrate their fire at the machine-gun post. He sent off several rounds himself, then aimed a couple of shots at the windows of the Gendarmerie's post, where he had seen gun flashes earlier. He heard the glass shatter, followed by screams and curses in French.

By the time Stan's platoon had got near the large blockhouse, the situation had changed again. The crossfire from his platoon and 16 Platoon had forced the machine-gunners to retreat into the large blockhouse, and the shooting from the Gendarmerie had been completely silenced. The platoon quickly surrounded the small blockhouse and proceeded to enter it, while Stan's three sections continued to attack the larger building.

Over to his right, about 40 metres away, Stan noticed that one of his men had fallen and was lying behind a small brick wall. 'Who's hit?' he called to the section leader.

'It's the sarge, sir. Snow Lawley. Hit by some bastard from the blockhouse. I think he's dead. Pappy Ransom's also been hit—in the knee.'

'Take charge, Corporal,' Stan said. 'Nine Section, follow me.' Stan moved quickly. He and his men dodged from cover to cover while giving each other protection from the increasing fire coming their way. Within seconds they had surrounded the building. As the Frenchmen rushed out of the blockhouse to oppose them, they ran into a wall of deadly and concentrated fire from Nine Section, several of them falling dead outside the door. Stan saw that some were black—Senegalese men—although the unit was commanded by white French officers. He waited a few minutes. No more came.

'Hold your fire,' Stan called to his section, and he and a few of the men approached to within a few metres of the blockhouse. The door was suddenly flung open, the cordite-laden air ripe with French profanities. An agitated Vichy officer came racing through the doorway, brandishing a pistol. He was clumsily doing up his shirt with his other hand but froze in his tracks as he was confronted by Stan, who was pointing his .38 service revolver at the Frenchman.

The man was a major, Stan thought, as he quickly assessed the situation.

There followed a long, tense moment as the two men eyed each other, both realising a wrong move could end in death. Stan's eyes narrowed. 'Don't be a fool, we're all around you,' he said forcefully.

Stan didn't know whether his adversary understood him, but the tone was obvious enough. The Frenchman saw the other Australians emerging out of the morning shadows. He looked at the soldier next to Stan, Winks Wakefield, menacing him with the bayonet on his rifle. Seizing the opportunity, Stan moved quickly, ripping the pistol from the Frenchman's grasp.

A yell came from the side of the blockhouse. 'Quick, the bastards are escaping on horseback, behind the blockhouse!'

Stan reacted instantly. 'Look after this character,' he said to Wakefield. 'The rest of you follow me and try and stop them.' He moved to the side of the blockhouse, where he could make out some soldiers mounting their horses in the holding yard. The men were Senegalese, and definitely not keen to match the Australians anymore.

Stan and his men fired at them. Several of the riders fell, but a good number escaped as they galloped their horses expertly along a bushy track leading north out of Alma Chaab.

'That'll do,' Stan called. 'They'll be picked up by 17 Platoon.' He looked north at the naked hills and the purple-shadowed valley. 'They'll be waiting for them.'

By breakfast time the confrontation was over. D Company had taken the village, inflicted a great number of casualties on the enemy and taken numerous prisoners. Stan was upset at the loss of his sergeant, Snow Lawley, but was pleased at the performance of his platoon under fire. Their intense training had paid off and he was confident the bloodying would ensure that they finished the job as professionally and quickly as possible. For Stan's part, he was quietly satisfied that he had carried out his first challenge as a leader against a determined, entrenched enemy.

Later he received news that the officer he had captured had divulged important information, and he was congratulated on his efforts. Yes, he was satisfied.

IN THE DAYS THAT FOLLOWED, THE rest of the battalion crossed the border into Lebanon and steadily fought their way up the coast towards Tyre. They participated in several large engagements without significant casualties, forcing the enemy out of Tyre and pushing them further along the coast. The French withdrew to the fast-flowing Litani River, one of the first natural obstacles that allowed them to form a defence line, after they'd blown up the only bridge.

At the river the 2/16th Battalion, one of the two sister battalions of the 2/14th, was in the lead position, and Stan was intrigued to hear that a friend he'd met on the *Aquitania*, Alan Haddy, had volunteered to swim the 40 metres to the far side with a rope.

The powerful Haddy fought the rushing river as machine-guns and mortars were aimed at him from the heights. A mortar bomb staggered and wounded him, and a bullet went clean through his cheeks. However, he gained the other side, enabling the 2/16th to establish a bridgehead, which they consolidated during a prolonged and bitter fight. This victory allowed the other sister battalion, the 2/27th, to continue the push north towards Sidon and towards Merdjayoun in the east.

As the 2/14th continued along the coast road, D Company was moving among the villages, along the foothills about two kilometres inland, as flanking cover for the main battalion.

They had just left one village when they ran into a company of French Foreign Legionnaires. Stan's 18 Platoon was leading the way at point, when suddenly gunfire echoed around the stony hills as the two opposing companies traded shots with each other. Now conditioned to the heat of battle, Stan immediately ordered his platoon into an attacking position and, firing as they went, they helped to force the enemy out of the hills. They were supported by accurate artillery fire directed onto the enemy with great effect. Smoke, dust and noise filled the gullies as, after a time, the furious onslaught forced the Frenchmen to capitulate. Some began to emerge, showing a white flag. Others slowly came out of their positions with their hands in the air. From that encounter D Company captured 45 prisoners and killed nine of the enemy for no loss to themselves.

They weren't finished for the day, however, as at 4.00 pm they were ordered to cut the road between Merdjayoun and the coast.

This was 11 June. The brigade and supporting units were held up by concentrated enemy resistance at Merdjayoun on the Zahrani River, southeast of Sidon.

In the meantime, the 25th Brigade and its support units had pushed through the central highlands of Lebanon and taken all their objectives. They were now linking up with elements of the 21st Brigade at Merdjayoun, on the left flank, and were pursuing a spirited offensive a few kilometres ahead at Jezzine.

Further across to the right, the Australian, British, Indian and Free French troops were continuing their push towards Damascus, and were also meeting stiff resistance.

It was now very clear that this campaign was not going to be a pushover—the Vichy French were making the Allied forces fight bitterly for every inch of territory won.

As D Company was moved forward to the Merdjayoun road, it encountered several strafing attacks by enemy aircraft. The planes flew in low, selected their targets and then sprayed the advancing line of soldiers as they scrambled over the hilly terrain. Stan and his platoon dived for cover at the first sign of attack, but some of the others were caught in the open. Luckily, there were only a few minor casualties.

The battle continued over the next few days at the Merdjayoun road and Zahrani River, with all positions receiving regular bombing, strafing and artillery shelling.

Several days later, on 15 June, as the battle was turning in favour of the Australians, the 2/14th Battalion moved out with the object of executing a wide encircling movement to outflank the enemy and take Sidon. It was a gruelling march, in summer heat, in full battle gear with weapons and ammunition, up and down over little used mountain tracks, and always on the lookout for a stray enemy patrol. The 30-kilometre slog took almost the whole day and, as the exhausted troops perched on the hills, looking down on the beautiful little Crusader castle town of Sidon and the sparkling blue Mediterranean beyond, they received information that the town had already been taken by the 2/27th Battalion.

THE NEWS WAS WELL RECEIVED BY the members of 9 Platoon. 'Thank God for that,' said Alan Avery. 'I'm done!'

He was answered by Lieutenant O'Day. 'Well, don't rest on your laurels—I don't think we'll be here long. I hear one of the 25th Brigade battalions, the 2/31st, is under attack at Jezzine, due east of here. They're holding five Vichy battalions at bay. Also, the battle still isn't finished down at Merdjayoun. We could be called either way.'

The 2/14th spent the next two days digging in and manning defensive positions outside Sidon. Late on 17 June, they were ordered to move to Jezzine to assist the 2/31st Battalion.

Next day, just after midnight, 9 Platoon were awakened by Lieutenant O'Day. 'Righto, chaps. We might be in for some action. Some trucks will be here in half an hour. A and B Companies are moving up to Jezzine. Let's get going.'

At 1.00 am, the two companies commenced the drive to Jezzine. The rest of the force were to follow in a few hours time. After travelling ten kilometres, the men were debussed and continued the journey on foot. Then began a tortuous climb up to the mountainous heights of inland Lebanon, sliding and struggling in the dark over steep, stony tracks. At 9.30 am, under a hot sun, they came under enemy artillery fire as the Vichy had most of the route leading to the highlands and Jezzine covered.

'Tell you what, mate,' Bruce Kingsbury complained to Alan, 'this's not a lot of fun—some bastard shooting at us, nowhere to bloody hide, pushing uphill, hot as buggery, and all on an empty stomach.'

Alan grunted, barely glancing at the impressive panorama offered by the magnificent pine forest they were climbing through, set as it was against wild Lebanese mountainsides plunging down to the rocky foreshores below.

Finally, at 11.00 that night, after 22 hours of continuous effort, they rested in darkness on the slopes of a hill outside the town of Jezzine. Even though they'd had only one small sandwich that morning, exhaustion overcame hunger, allowing sleep to come easily.

They awoke to a view of the town and the ridges overlooking it. Jezzine nestled at the base of a high mountainous range, of which Mt Kharatt was the dominant peak. The town was in Allied hands, and in the preceding days the enemy had bombed the place and created tremendous damage. Vichy bombers had devastated several buildings including the Hotel Egypt, where the explosions had tragically killed seventeen men of the 2/31st Battalion. From their position, 9 Platoon also had a clear view of the 'Mad Mile', a tortuous stretch of road which wound its way up through the ranges beyond the town and where ongoing battles were being fought.

The road was the only supply link to the mountains beyond and it was a supreme challenge for the supply trucks to attempt it, as the Vichy French had every point on the twisting track covered with their artillery fire. Other targets were the

Don R's—the motorbike dispatch riders, daredevils who would drive fast under all circumstances to get the messages through.

'Hey, watch this,' Hi-Ho said to Alan. 'There goes a Don R. Five bob says the bastard'll make it. The Vichy folk'll try and knock him arse over. Anyone take me on?'

'OK,' said Bruce, 'you're on. Then I'll take five bob on the bugger in the truck behind him. I bet he won't make it either.'

As the company was resting that day, bets were placed on every military movement on the Mad Mile. It was a bizarre but satisfying entertainment. But the men soon realised it wasn't a good idea to bet against the Don R's. Their daring and skill under fire were remarkable and they rarely suffered a casualty. However, the brave truck drivers weren't always so lucky, as a number of them were hit.

The score was partly evened up the next day when a Vichy bomber flew overhead. Gerry O'Day said: 'It's a Maryland bomber. One of theirs—it must have been one supplied by the Americans before the war. And look, the Brits have that Bofors gun on to it.' The Bofors was a Swedish-designed anti-aircraft gun, requiring a crew of eight to run it efficiently.

Moments later, white smoke trailed from one of the plane's motors as the cannon rounds ripped into it. The smoke quickly turned black as the engine oil caught fire, then red flames streaked out behind the wing, fanned by the wind.

As the soldiers watched the drama unfold, they saw two objects suddenly shoot from the plane. Within seconds, silver parachute canopies unfolded from them, instantly checking their descent. The airmen were momentarily caught as they hung in space, then slowly and harmoniously swung and spiralled towards the earth.

When the airmen were a few hundred metres from the ground, the watching soldiers were startled to hear a Vickers machine-gun suddenly chatter into life from the direction of a British unit situated behind Jezzine. The Vichy airmen, allowed no escape, slumped limply in their harnesses as they came down.

Alan, Bruce and the others looked on incredulously as the dead men crumpled to the ground. 'Christ, sir, is that bloody well fair?' Alan asked O'Day.

'I guess anything's fair in love and war,' the lieutenant answered slowly. But he wasn't completely convinced himself.

'The Vichy, it seems, have been rather indiscriminately bombing anybody and everybody, including civilians. I guess this must be a payback by the Brits.'

Soon the men were ordered to march into a position behind Jezzine. The five-kilometre walk took them past scenes of wild mountain grandeur as they trekked along the edge of the Wadi Jezzine, a great canyon dropping off the edge of the Lebanese heights. The Cascade de Jezzine, a large, gushing waterfall, shot out over the rim of the canyon and plummeted to the floor of the wadi far below.

Jezzine was a small Arab village at the centre of a tobacco growing area. As the men moved north into the village, they passed residents who were moving out, away from the battle zone.

'God, I can see why they're leaving. Look at the flamin' bomb damage. No wonder the Brits got mad,' murmured Bruce.

There was a great deal of damage in the town, and the villagers were still in a state of shock. The troops waited there till darkness, helping the odd person where they could, then marched along the road eight kilometres towards the mountain behind Jezzine. They stumbled and climbed up the Mad Mile, free of shelling, then found a reasonable piece of flat ground behind this and bedded down for the night.

They were awoken to the sound of their artillery crashing heavy rounds at the large mountainous feature that loomed up behind them. They could just see a makeshift fort on the top of the hill. As they watched, wind turbulence would direct most shots over the hill, but every now and then one would erupt on the mountain, and a puff of smoke and dust would shoot from the spot, echoing the report back some seconds later.

'I reckon that fort's taken a pounding. What's going on, sir?' Bruce asked O'Day.

'When we went past the waterfall, back on the other side of Jezzine, I was briefed by Major Muir of the 2/31st,' O'Day said. 'I believe they're going to try and take the fort on that hill—1284 on the map. Brigadier Plant was with him. He fought at Gallipoli, and he reckons this terrain is worse than that— higher hills, more boulders and less cover. Well, good luck to them! We're in reserve, so we have to sit tight for a while.'

The men settled into their positions for the next two days.

Information trickled back concerning progress in other areas of the campaign.

On 22 June, they received news that Damascus had fallen the day before. The city had surrendered to an Australian, Colonel Blackburn VC, of the 2/3rd Machine-Gun Battalion. However, the middle push and the western push had come together and had got bogged down at Jezzine, so the Allied units were concentrating on taking the perilous heights of the 1800-metre Mt Kharatt behind it.

The enemy had dug in on two commanding spurs of the mountain, giving them full military control of all the roads and the surrounding area. The spurs, known as 1284 and 1332 (by their height in metres), were unapproachable from the right flank, as it dropped away into a sheer precipice. The frontal and left flanks had been attacked three times by the 2/31st Battalion; they had been repulsed each time, a clear indication of the advantage allowed to the defenders. It was reasoned that the only possible way to take 1284, the first feature in line to the 2/14th Battalion, was by an attack from the rear.

IN THE EARLY HOURS OF 24 JUNE, B and C Companies of the 2/14th linked up to make the attempt. Towards dawn, as the fog started to lift, the well-entrenched Vichy rained artillery and mortar fire on the six platoons and crisscrossed the mountain slopes with murderous machine-gun tracer, rifle fire and grenades. The attack began to falter as the companies started to take serious casualties. An urgent message was sent back to the battalion, finishing with A Company's commanding officer, Captain Phil Rhoden, who relayed the directive to O'Day: 'Off you go, Gerry. Up the southern slope of 1284. Try and take the pressure off B and C Companies, and link up with any of our other platoons already up there if you can.'

'Righto, men. On your feet, packs on. We're off,' O'Day snapped to his platoon.

'What's going on, sir?' Alan asked, shouldering his Tommy gun.

'We're going up that feature there—the one we've been looking at for a couple of days, Hill 1284. That fort the artillery have been trying to clobber, and can't—we have to take it.'

The men looked at each other. They had been watching the fort on top of Hill 1284 for some time and not been impressed with the possibility of taking it. And at this stage they didn't realise the 2/31st had tried over the last few days and had failed.

The only way up to the fort was along an old bridle path. The route was steep and winding, over loose stones and boulders, and moved over a series of rocky terraces. It was a 670-metre climb and part of the way appeared, from 9 Platoon's viewpoint, to be over exposed ground. The fort was in effect an area of enclosed ground, about 50 metres in diameter, protected by two-metre-high rock walls. The walls were fashioned from an old aqueduct that had been there since Roman times and had been used by the local shepherds. The Vichy had set up machine-gun emplacements around the walls, including a pillbox outside. From the bottom of the feature, the fort looked impregnable.

'We going up there, sir?' Hi-Ho pointed towards the mountain.

'Yep. Get going. We have to take pressure off the other companies who are caught there—the quicker the better. As well as your normal weapons we'll take 90 hand grenades—three to a man.'

A few minutes later, the men moved out. As they approached the lower slopes of the hill, they passed through a section of men from the 2/31st Battalion, then by 9.30 they began to climb the feature itself. It was building up to be a hot summer's day and Alan was grateful for his light khaki shorts and shirt, which were soon soaked with perspiration. He was particularly grateful for his metal helmet, which he kept tight on his head—unlike Bruce, who wore his at a rakish angle, pushed back, exposing a high expanse of forehead.

It was hard, frustrating work as the 32 men clawed their way up the craggy face of the mountain. There were no trees, only occasional tufts of short grass and the rocks and rubble to give them purchase. The support artillery had stopped firing to allow them to attain their position, and to their delight they found that the slope was so steep that the enemy couldn't see them.

After a couple of hours of struggle, the platoon finally

reached a position about 200 metres from the fort. Here the exhausted men caught their breath while O'Day set up platoon headquarters and sent out a couple of men on reconnaissance.

The defenders in the fort consisted of a company of the 2nd Battalion, Sixth Regiment, of the French Foreign Legion. The commander was a Captain Jacques Leport and his French-bred troops were known as a crack unit. His men started firing the instant the Australians appeared. They were not going to be taken easily.

'The only cover you have is some of the larger boulders,' O'Day said. 'Leave your packs here.' He looked at Dick Smith, known as WRD. 'WRD, you and Le Brun and Arlow—I want you to take your Bren gun around to the left flank. There's a narrow ledge leading up the western side of the hill—cover us. The rest, follow me along that narrow ledge to the right about 40 feet below the fort. We'll attack from there. Fire at will—shoot when you see a head.'

Alan and Bruce dropped their packs and looked at each other. Alan's pulse was racing; he could feel a pounding in his ears. He remembered the old Digger again: the rat cage being lowered into the water. This was icy fear. 'Good luck, mate,' he said, through thickened lips.

Bruce's mouth was also dry, but his helmet was still perched cockily on the back of his head. He shot a wry smile at his friend. 'Yep. You too, Al.'

As Alan followed the rest of the section around to the right flank, his legs were wobbly—tired from the climb, but responding to adrenaline. WRD had set up his Bren gun on its tripod, and fired bursts every time he saw a head appear. Alan could hear the gun chattering over to the left and realised he was now in the middle of his first real battle.

Ahead of him, Nine Section had engaged the enemy and were firing intently at the machine-gun in the pillbox and at the men behind the wall. As Alan watched, he saw Corporal Jock Lochhead and Jimmy Uren race up the hill, jumping behind boulders, and then lie flat against the pillbox. They threw some grenades into the gunner's slithole, and then cupped their heads in their hands as the explosion shook the small structure. The shock, instantly killing the two men inside, forced dust and flames back out through the opening.

Flushed by their success, Uren continued to run ahead. He stopped at a break in the wall which obviously led into the fort. As Alan watched, he heard a Vichy machine-gun burst into life, then saw Uren fall beside the wall, bullet holes blasted through his chest. The machine-gun had obviously been placed there to protect the opening. Uren, mortally wounded, had copped the full blast when only a metre or so from the gun.

Alan and Bruce looked at each other, shocked by the violence. By now they were spreadeagled on the ground, trying to protect themselves from the fire pouring down from the fort. Harry Saunders was over to Alan's right, peering up at the wall. Alan watched him take deliberate aim, then coolly shoot at whatever moved. On Bruce's left, the Professor, Ted Jobe and Bluey Whitechurch were lined up, with the rest of the section dotted along the ledge, all intent on their own personal battle.

In front of him, suddenly appearing above the parapet, Alan saw a long rifle with a lethal bayonet attached to it. The bayonet was three-sided, with fluted grooves racing along each of its sides and finishing at a sharp, glistening point. This design allowed air to be sucked into the body as the bayonet was thrust home, allowing a quicker withdrawal. It also produced maximum physical damage.

Alan shivered as his mind lingered on that repugnant image.

Two heads now appeared above the parapet, as the rifle was lowered at him. Alan took careful aim with his Tommy gun and pressed the trigger. He saw both men fall away, one throwing his head back, screaming, as he dropped behind the wall. 'Hell, I've hit him,' Alan yelled, his voice high with excitement.

He continued to let small, controlled bursts go as one Frenchman after another appeared above the wall. He was now settled and his fire was deadly. 'Another bastard!' he shouted to Bruce, as he watched his bullets trace along the wall and finish at a French uniform. Shooting ducks in a gallery, he thought.

By this time, the platoon had the range of the fort, and the inhabitants had learned not to put their heads up.

Then the grenades started. Two landed near Bruce and Alan, covering them both with dust, but luckily doing no harm.

'Shit, they're bloody real, mate,' Harry yelled to them. Alan turned in time to see Harry drop his rifle and his head jerk backwards.

'Christ, Harry, are you OK, mate?'

After a few moments Harry answered slowly: 'Yeah, I think I'm OK. I'm not much bloody help anymore, though. Can't hold the rifle.'

'For Pete's sake, Harry. Just lie there. Don't move. We'll get you out when this friggin' thing's over.'

Alan had hardly settled himself again when an order came from Lieutenant O'Day: 'Move up!'

Slowly, metre by metre, jumping behind available rocks and firing to cover each other, the main body of the platoon moved to within ten metres of the fort. The firefight continued at this rate for about twenty minutes or more, with machine-gun and rifle fire slicing the air and hand grenades exploding amongst the attackers. The men of 9 Platoon were getting low on ammunition, so O'Day sent an order for Ted Jobe to move back to restock their supplies.

Tombstone Ted had only gone a few metres when he was wounded, unable to continue in the battle.

A few of the invaders had now got to within three metres of the wall and were lobbing grenades over it. Suddenly they realised that some of the grenades coming back at them were coming from *outside* the fort. A party of bombardiers from the Legionnaires had moved out; O'Day spied them leaping like mountain goats from cover to cover, briskly throwing grenades at the Australians.

Without hesitation, Cappy Wilson—a corporal and one of three brothers in 9 Platoon—picked up a handful of grenades and, one by one, threw them at the bombardiers. His courageous and deadly attack blew up six of the Frenchmen. The rest quickly raced back into the fort.

BY EARLY AFTERNOON A LARGE PART of 9 Platoon had been wounded, but the attack was still being pushed with great ferocity. Realising that Ted Jobe was injured, O'Day sent another soldier back for more ammunition.

Further out to the right, Leo Deeley, of Nine Section, was

pouring concentrated Bren-gun fire at the Frenchmen. His deadly shooting cleared out a machine-gun post on the wall, allowing the platoon to approach still closer to it. As Alan watched, another Seven Section man dropped to the ground— Freddie Parsons. He crawled behind a boulder to treat his wounds. Bullets were coming from a hidden sniper somewhere, and he was making a difference. Two more men fell—one was Bluey Whitechurch. Seven Section was being whittled away.

Realising the situation, the platoon sergeant, Harry Morti-mer, crept further round to the right of the platoon. He had a good view of the fort and carefully aimed and fired. Three men dropped in a row, one whom he thought was the sniper. Mortimer edged out of his spot and was making his way back to the main body when someone lunged at him from his left. Before the war, Mortimer was a rabbit shooter and was trained to shoot quickly from either his left or right shoulder. The Frenchman was within a metre of him. Reacting instantly, he slammed the rifle to his left shoulder and fired. The Frenchman stopped in his tracks as the bullet hit him full in the chest. The impact spun him around and he dropped straight to the ground, dead—the bullet wound gaping out through his back.

The French, realising they weren't making a strong enough impression on the Australians, started firing heavy mortars at the persistent platoon. The rounds exploded with devastating force, sending rock, dust and shrapnel screaming through the air. Some of the men caught on exposed ground became casualties. Corporal McLennan and the other two Wilson brothers, Crawford and Kisher, were wounded as they and several others sought protection in the pillbox outside the fort.

Leo Deeley, still offering covering fire with his Bren gun, caught a mortar fragment in his leg. At the same time the explosion damaged his gun and put it out of action. He discarded the Bren and obtained a .303 rifle from one of his wounded colleagues, continuing to shoot it at the enemy even though his leg was paining and now useless.

O'Day noticed that, under cover of the deadly and well-aimed mortar fire, about twenty more bombardiers moved out of the fort. They were carrying haversacks of hand grenades and began moving among the boulders, throwing the grenades at will. The battlefield was alive with detonations as smoke, dust and explosions again blurred the scene. Through the haze and confusion, Alan caught a glimpse of O'Day as a grenade hit the lieutenant. The blast blew him off the ledge he was standing on, catapulting him three metres to the terrace below.

'Christ, Gerry's gone!' Alan yelled out to Bruce. But after a minute or two O'Day appeared over the ledge again, dazed, his shirt blown off and shrapnel wounds lacerating his arm and elbow. Showing his character, he quickly gained control. He applied a field dressing to his elbow, then deliberately and coolly organised his men to concentrate new fire solely on the bombardiers.

Alan joined in and began firing at the enemy, who were jumping from cover to cover and expertly throwing the grenades with great effect. On his right he could see his old nurseryman friend Neil Gordon move in beside him, and the two continued to fire in tandem.

It was hot—perspiration streamed down Alan's face, stinging his eyes and dripping from his nose. The glistening sweat highlighted the distended veins in his temple, giving the impression that they were about to explode. With his teeth clenched, Alan furiously shot at the darting Frenchmen, searching for signs that his bullets had found their mark.

A grenade landed not far behind him, the concussion momentarily dazing him. He looked back expecting some serious damage, and found only that the heel of one of his boots had been blown off.

He breathed a quick sigh of relief, and angrily fired his Tommy gun in the direction where the grenade had come from. He emptied his canister into a Frenchman about 30 metres away, watching with satisfaction as the bullets ripped holes in the man's jacket. He wrenched the empty canister out and was reaching into his haversack for a full one when another grenade suddenly exploded a few metres from him. The shock lifted him, then thrust him back to the earth. Immediately he registered a searing, uncontrollable pain surging through his spinal muscles.

A granulated grenade had ripped the shirt off his back and injected metal splinters into his spine and buttocks. The sudden shock sent his trunk muscles into a severe protective spasm, interfering with his immediate ability to breathe. Gasping for breath, he moved his hand behind his back and felt the lacerated flesh. There wasn't a great deal of blood, but his first impression was that he had been badly wounded.

'Christ, I'm hit,' he called, his cry almost lost in the heat and noise of the battle. To his side he could see Bruce—the top marksman—repeatedly and accurately shooting his rifle at the bombardiers. Ahead, several of the Frenchmen fell, and through slit eyes Alan gratefully observed the remainder retreat into the fort. He breathed to himself: 'Thank God!'

'You OK, Al?' Bruce asked. 'I think I got the bastard that threw the pineapple at you.'

'Yeah, mate,' Alan gasped, 'keep firing.'

In the few minutes of respite, his muscles relaxed a little and his breathing became easier. He could see that Leo Deeley had been wounded again, but was relieved to find that the Professor and Hi-Ho were still uninjured and firing incessantly into the fort. However, looking to his right, he suddenly noticed that Neil Gordon had been hit by the same grenade that had wounded him. Neil's back and leg were bleeding, and he appeared to be unconscious.

REALISING THAT THE POSITION WAS BECOMING untenable, and with no hope of getting reinforcements in time, O'Day knew that he would have to break off the attack and withdraw as best he could. One-third of his men were dead or wounded, Deeley's Bren gun was useless, there were no more grenades— and on top of this bad news, he could see 30 more Frenchmen emerging from the fort.

He ordered the platoon to withdraw by sections, Cappy Wilson's first. Wilson only had four unwounded men left, and they set to, carrying and manoeuvring the wounded out of the battlefield and down the precipitous slopes of the mountainside. Two men picked up Neil Gordon and half dragged, half carried him out of firing range.

Bruce, Hi-Ho, the Professor and several others covered their withdrawal, pouring deadly fire amongst the attacking Frenchmen, who were now moving forward again from rock to rock. Although he was in considerable distress, Alan crawled behind a boulder and helped deliver an effective crossfire. He saw at least two Frenchmen fall as a result of his own bullets, and three more drop in the face of a concentrated stand by the remaining Australians.

O'Day, although wounded himself, got Harry Saunders to his feet and assisted him to a position where he could be helped by Bruce and Hi-Ho, whom he now ordered off the mountain.

Alan had run out of machine-gun ammunition so, like Deeley, he grabbed a .303 rifle and fired compulsively and continually, managing to keep the advancing Frenchmen's heads down. Then, over the noise of the shooting, he heard a call from O'Day: 'OK, Avery and Deeley, we'll cover you. We're almost all out, come on down.'

Seeing he was one of the last to leave, Alan carefully stood up, checked his wounds, then braced himself, firing from the hip as he went. He groggily made his way back to O'Day, who, with Sergeant Mortimer and Corporal Lochhead, were covering him.

As they moved further around the ledge, about 70 metres from the pillbox, they came upon Corporal Cappy Wilson and three others lying wounded. Wilson had been hit in the chest and was lying unconscious. Quickly, O'Day gathered some of the able-bodied men and arranged for Wilson and the wounded to be carried or assisted off the mountain.

As they went past the ledge where Dick Smith was positioned, O'Day called out: 'WRD, can you and Le Brun keep the Froggies at bay with your Bren? It'll give these blokes a chance to get off this bloody mountain.'

It was a slow, painful trek down the corrugated feature as the remnants of the battered platoon crawled over the ledges and terraces, some stumbling, some being carried.

At 3.30 that afternoon, Alan staggered in to the forward post of the battalion and was sent straight to the Regimental Aid Post. He could barely breathe, and still wasn't too sure of the extent of his wounds.

'Jesus, mate,' Bruce said, 'you're a bloody hero. Look at ya back, it's a bloody mess!' Alan's back was a mass of blackened, coagulated flesh, and by now he felt as bad as he looked.

The Regimental Medical Officer, Captain Don Duffy, had been with the battalion since its creation at Puckapunyal. He was young, handsome and fit, and accepted the responsibility of looking after the men's health with great energy and dedication; indeed, he knew most of them intimately. At this stage he was under pressure, as the Main Dressing Station had been inundated with casualties from B and C Companies who had been wounded earlier that morning.

He was now also receiving the men from 9 Platoon, straining his team's resources. After he had examined Alan and cleaned most of the wounds, he said calmly: 'We'd better get you down to the field hospital on the flats, Private. You've got a lot of grenade splinters in your back—you'll need extensive surgery. I'll arrange for the ambulance to get you there straight away. In the meantime, I'll give you an injection for the pain.'

Within a half an hour Alan was breathing easier, and along with several other 9 Platoon members, including Harry Saunders, was helped on board the ambulance truck. By now Harry's wounds were beginning to inflame and swell and he was in pain, although a shot of morphine had helped. Bruce watched the ambulance head back towards Jezzine, then pass out of view as it moved down to the flats below.

THE BATTLE FOR JEZZINE CONTINUED OVER the next week or so. Stan Bisset was pleased to welcome back his brother Butch for the remaining few days of the fight in which the 2/14th were involved. In the aftermath of B Company being devastated on the morning of 24 June on the slopes of Mt Kharatt, the three platoon commanders who were killed or wounded that day had to be replaced. In fact, in the preceding fifteen days, during the bitter and prolonged fighting, the battalion had lost twelve killed and 47 wounded.

Butch and the other two new lieutenants from officer training in Cairo were recalled from the training battalion in Palestine. The three men were now firm friends. Butch took over 10 Platoon, Mokka Treacy 11 Platoon and Merric Stevenson 12 Platoon.

Butch was welcomed back to the company where he'd been the sergeant major, and it wasn't long before his goodnatured personality and strong authority earned him the title of 'The Boss'. He spent the next two weeks training and integrating with the platoon and preparing them for the next confrontation, which was coming up fast enough.

The battalion moved out of the Jezzine area on 2 July and moved up to a wadi about eight kilometres south of Damour. Here they went into reserve for the approaching Battle of Damour.

While this was being planned, Alan Avery was recuperating in the 2/9th Army General Hospital in Rehovoth, in Palestine. In the bed next to him was Harry Saunders, and spread around the station were other wounded platoon members.

Ten days after their fight on Hill 1284, Bruce, granted a day's leave, walked into the ward, beaming to see Alan and Harry looking very much alive and giving as much cheek as possible.

'Geez, it's good to see you, Bruce,' Alan said, 'How've you been?'

'I'm good mate. How're the wounds?'

'Ah, we'll be OK, won't we Harry? Mind you, I reckon I might have bought it there for a few seconds when I was first hit. Couldn't bloody well get my breath. They took seventeen shrapnel splinters out of my back, some of them in the rib cartilages—affected my breathing for a while. There's still a piece caught under my diaphragm, but they'll leave it there. Suits me—I'm going well now. Harry's OK, aren't ya, mate.'

'Yeah. Still got a bit of a headache, and a bit crook in my shoulder—otherwise good as gold,' Harry said cheerfully, waving his good hand around.

'That's good. Take a bit more than a Vichy grenade to kill you two bastards.' Bruce paused.

'Y'know, 9 Platoon really copped it. Gerry went up the hill with 32 men and came back with fifteen—the fight almost decimated friggin' Seven Section. Only two of the section are left—the Prof and myself. But the good thing is they've called Teddy Bear back as a corporal.'

'You beauty,' Alan chortled. 'We needed his bloody Bren carrier. How about the rest of the platoon?'

'Well, we all got back in dribs and drabs. WRD and Le Brun stayed up there with their Bren covering us. They shot about six more of the buggers and came down late in the afternoon. They got one bloke who obviously thought they'd gone and came out of the fort for a crap—they knocked him off into the latrine.' He suppressed a smile at the thought.

'Unfortunately, as you know, Jimmy Uren died up there. Cappy Wilson caught some shrapnel in his heart muscle and was unconscious for eight days. They reckon the metal went straight through a bloody sandalwood-covered diary he had in his chest pocket—it stopped a fraction short of killing him. What luck! The rest of the blokes are in various states of repair. But I reckon we caused such a lot of damage the Froggies didn't have enough men left to man their fort.

'The Prof and I and the others went down to the wheat fields on the lower edges of the spur the next day and brought up a few of the wounded from the earlier fights. And we brought in a dozen Froggy deserters as well—not much fight left in them! The day after that, the Froggies left the fort. When our blokes went in, they found 21 graves including Jimmy Uren's—Lord knows how many wounded they took with them. So even though we lost the battle that day, I reckon we won in the end.

'O'Day's pretty upset, though. They didn't tell him before the fight that the 2/31st had tried to take the fort with two platoons on the previous day. They were the chaps we passed through on the way up the hill. If they couldn't do it with two bloody platoons, how the hell were we to do it with one! Still, he's pretty pleased with us.'

He grinned at them.

'Incidentally, I brought you both some mail. One for Al—probably from Ann, by the writing—and the perfume.'

Ann was the sister of Leila Bradbury, to whom Bruce was engaged. The two couples had gone out together a great deal before the boys left for the war.

Bruce sniffed the envelope and passed the letter to Alan. 'Y'know, I reckon she's a bit keen on you, mate. You'll have to do the right thing by her, y'know.'

'D'you reckon?' said Alan. 'What makes you say that?'

'Inside information. She's keen.' Bruce laughed, winked and turned to Harry, deliberately leaving Alan bemused.

Bruce had a couple of letters for Harry. 'Who's this "Djambie" bloke they've addressed it to, Harry?'

Harry took the letter, smiling. He looked at it and said: 'It's from my cousin Dickie. He always uses our tribal name. We came from a group of warriors once—still do, I suppose. It's pronounced "Jarmbe", anyway—it's a tribal word from the Gunditjmara tribe.'

'Really?' said Bruce. 'What's it mean?'

'Well, basically, it means "mates", "best friends", or even "blood brothers". Just like Al and me here. We're *literally* blood brothers now.'

'D'you reckon?' said Alan. 'Does this battle make us blood brothers?'

'Yep,' Harry laughed, 'from now on, you're White Jarmbe, I'm Black Jarmbe—mates and brothers. You too, Bruce, all together.'

'Jarmbe, eh?' said Bruce. 'OK, from now on you're Jarmbe—nothing else. Whaddya reckon, Al?'

'Jarmbe it is.' Then he asked: 'How's the rest of the battle going?'

'Well, The Vichy have been a tough enemy, and I've heard casualties are high on both sides—almost as much as Tobruk, I believe. Right now, the whole of the Australian Army is merging around Damour, waiting to go. It'll be the biggest operation Australians have been in yet—bigger than the Sixth Division in Bardia and Tobruk. All our brigades in a combined attack around the city.

'The other bit of news, which you've probably heard, is that Hitler launched an attack on Russia and is trying to break through the Caucasus so that he can come down to the Middle East through Turkey. Fortunately, we're still holding them at Tobruk, although they reckon Rommel's being reinforced.

'In the meantime, I'll have to get back for the Damour show—one last punch before we get to Beirut.'

6

Pushing North

THE COUNTRYSIDE AROUND DAMOUR WAS SPECTACULAR, not unlike the wilderness of Jezzine, with high mountain features interspersed with deeply-ravined wadis. Over time, the enemy had taken creative advantage of the peaks, developing strong machine-gun and mine defences, which virtually precluded a frontal attack on the whole of the mountain range.

The Australian contingent were massing around the perimeter of the city. In view of the perceived invincibility of the mountain terrain, the overall plan engineered by Brigadier Stevens was for a massed right-flanking attack by battalions from the 21st Brigade and elements from the Sixth Division's 17th Brigade, along with other units. He considered this would work if, on the left, enemy forces on the coastal flats were kept occupied and if, on the far right, the road to the inland town of Biet ed Dine could be blocked. This would prevent Vichy reserves coming in from a back road from Beirut. The plan would be assisted by shelling from the Navy at sea, bombing and strafing from the air, and the utilisation of artillery and tanks cooperating in an all-forces attack.

A and B Companies of the 2/14th were ordered to carry out the flank protection role on the Biet ed Dine road. Bruce arrived back from visiting Alan and Jarmbe in hospital just in time to leave with the companies on 5 July.

Biet ed Dine was about eighteen kilometres east of Damour

and boasted a beautiful nineteenth century castle built by one of the early ruling Emirs. Captain Rhoden was in command of both companies for the operation, and their task was to capture two hilly features nine kilometres along the road—halfway between Damour and Beit ed Dine. A Company were to take Hill 245 and B Company the higher Hill 567.

To reach the road, the companies left the headquarters site at 8.00 pm, and manoeuvred in the dark along a precipitous goat path which zigzagged down into the sheer Damour River gorge, about 300 metres deep. After crossing, they then climbed the equally high and dangerous wall on the other side.

'Hell,' Bruce said to the Professor and Hi-Ho, 'I thought it was hard work getting up to Jezzine. This is bloody ridiculous—and it's dark.' The universal moan of the soldier! Traversing the narrow ledge, behind the column of men, surefooted mules carried ammunition for the mortars and other supplies.

At 12.55 am, the men became aware that the battle of Damour had begun as 60 Australian artillery guns opened fire on the French positions. Other battalions were also moving forward in the dark to begin their attack right along the Damour–Biet ed Dine line. The noise reverberated along the wadis and clifftops and signalled the start of return artillery fire, mainly from a French 75mm battery situated some kilometres south of Beirut.

'Crikey, listen to that barrage,' the Professor said. 'I hope the bastards don't send any our way.'

'Yeah, I wouldn't care to get knocked off this ledge—which I can't bloody well see anyway,' Bruce answered.

It was a physically demanding haul as the two companies marched and crawled up and over antiquated rocky paths, until finally, at 3.15 am, exhausted, they reached the Biet ed Dine road. Here the companies parted. B Company stayed on to make a rough wall of stone to block the road, then to plan an attack on nearby Hill 567, while A Company moved west to attack Hill 245. About an hour later, A Company were sheltering underneath a ridge below the hill.

Bruce waited, crouched beside the Professor, and watched the play of dawn light as it tinted the peak face of Hill 245 a gentle bluish pink, then watched with delight as it warmed to red. Dark shadows lay sharp and flat off the wind-honed edges and he steeled himself for the unavoidable charge up the terraced slopes.

'Here we are again,' he thought. 'Another hill, and no Alan this time.' He realised he was a little lonelier, but didn't dwell on the feeling.

As the sun gained height, 9 Platoon moved around to a ridge left of the feature and were forced to take cover as small arms fire suddenly opened up on them. The Professor yelled: 'Hell, where in blazes is that coming from?'

'I think it's coming from the top of the hill we are about to go up,' Bruce answered, matter-of-factly. Before he could add anything, artillery fire also suddenly shot over their heads.

The shelling was erratic, not causing much real damage, but continued most of the day, until just on evening Lieutenant O'Day, who was almost recovered from the action on Hill 1284, once again barked the order: 'Let's go, men.'

The small remaining contingent of 9 Platoon fixed their bayonets, and along with the other two platoons moved out of the cover of the ridge and charged up the mountainside. Miraculously, no one was shooting down at them. When they reached the top, they were relieved to find that the French unit had retreated. The hill was theirs. Bruce and the Professor smiled at each other, elated.

In the meantime, B Company, after completing the barricade of rocks over the road, also waited till dawn. As the sun's first rays silhouetted the desolate feature in front of them, Mokka Treacy led a patrol of twelve men up the slope of Hill 567. They had not climbed halfway when they were attacked by a Vichy post on the western knoll of the ridge. A vicious firefight ensued in the early morning light, and Treacy realised after some moments that they were outgunned and outnumbered. He signalled for his men to withdraw, but in the confusion and heat of the battle two of them were taken prisoner.

On his return, the commander, Bill Russell, organised a company attack on the feature. Mokka Treacy was to take his 11 Platoon up the western knoll, with Butch to attack the summit on Hill 567 leading the other two platoons, 10 and 12. At 7.15 am, they began their ascent, but as they approached closer to the summit the entrenched enemy rolled hand grenades down the steep slope. The sheer volume of grenades was causing casualties and not allowing the Australians a chance to retaliate, so the attack was called off after some minutes. For Butch, his baptism of fire was developing into an ignominious occasion.

No sooner had the heavily mauled platoons withdrawn to the barricade than they were approached by three Vichy armoured cars which appeared from the direction of Biet ed Dine. The vehicles stopped 150 metres from the wall, and before they could fire were met by a determined attack from the Australians. A 'sticky' bomb was launched at the tank and exploded next to it on the road. Bren gun, mortar and .303 fire then peppered the cars.

Butch noticed one of the 12 Platoon men handling a new Boyes anti-tank rifle. With a grin, he said to the man: 'Give that car a shot, Stan.'

'OK, boss. I'm not too sure how this bloody thing works, but I'll give it a go.'

Not realising that the rifle should be attached to a recoil stand, Stan Bruton lay on a rock, aimed at the armoured car, and fired. The recoil from the flash eliminator hit the rocks and acted like a double recoil, bouncing upwards and throwing Bruton some metres away on to his back. The shot hit the lead car and he quickly jumped up to shoot again, before the car could return the fire. He repeated this act several times, each time being catapulted upwards and finishing lying spreadeagled on his back, several metres from the impact point.

Butch, highly amused, amid guffaws of laughter, offered encouragement: 'Come on, Stan—give it to 'em!'

The concentrated barrage was enough to persuade the armoured car drivers to retreat a couple of kilometres back along the road.

At 9.15 am, the platoons attacked Hill 567 again. This time, with the support of mortar fire, they secured a hold just below the summit. Firing continued all through the morning as the Vichy tried desperately to blast the Australians off their shaky hold. Butch was everywhere, giving encouragement where it was needed and, as marksman, taking accurate potshots at the enemy, as he would at rabbits back home. The company managed to contain the frustrated Frenchmen until a final attack was ordered for 12.30 that afternoon.

At that hour, as the Australians raced up the hill towards the summit, they too realised there was no one shooting at them. As with Hill 245, the French had retreated, and the summit was theirs.

But it wasn't to be that easy. The hill was too important, commanding a magnificent strategic view of the whole area. It had been defended by a platoon of Senegalese French Foreign Legionnaires, and they had retreated only a small distance away. During the afternoon they made seven counter-attacks, but were driven off each time. Towards 5.30, the Frenchmen were joined by the remainder of the platoon who had been pushed off the top of Hill 245 by A Company.

Using smoke as a cover, and shouting as they went, they advanced to within 35 metres of Mokka Treacy's 11 Platoon, which was holding the peak at this stage. As the smoke cleared, a frantic firefight erupted as Treacy and his men desperately poured rifle and machine-gun fire into the determined enemy.

Finally, Butch, now in reserve with his platoon, and offering covering fire, yelled to his men: 'Fix bayonets, we're going up!'

By the time Butch and 10 Platoon had breached the crest, they were confronted with a stark scene. Twenty dead Frenchmen lay around the perimeter of Treacy's platoon, their shattered bodies and bloodstained clothes testimony to the closeness and desperation of the fighting. Some had their eyes still open, staring blankly into oblivion. The Australians, exhausted, were catching their breath and, even though they were in a state of shock, most marvelled at the damage they had inflicted and at their own luck. Miraculously, they had received no casualties. Butch, relieved to see Mokka unhurt, beamed and laughed. 'Good on ya, mate, you didn't need us, did you!'

'I dunno so much,' Mokka answered, sucking air deep into his lungs. 'We caught a prisoner who said the ones that retreated took away about 50 wounded. We didn't do that by ourselves.'

Later five enemy planes flew over and aimed bombs at the peak, but they dropped harmlessly into a gully behind the mountain. The following day, the company repulsed several minor attempts to storm their positions, but the enemy had been convincingly beaten by now.

On the morning of 7 July, the company linked up with the

A Company contingent from Hill 245 and were ordered to hold their positions while the rest of the battle for Damour continued. They dug in for the wait.

JUST PRIOR TO THE BATTLE OF Damour, Stan and his platoon were camped in an olive grove on the outskirts of the city, when Stan began to feel sick. Within a few hours he developed a roaring temperature of 106 degrees Fahrenheit and quickly lost interest in the proceedings. Several others also came down with the same symptoms. After consultation with Dr Duffy, they were diagnosed as having sandfly fever and were briskly repatriated to a hospital in Haifa. After three days in and out of delirium, Stan's temperature dropped and he began to recover.

He returned to his platoon, but by now, 11 July, the war in Lebanon and Syria was drawing to a close. In his absence Stan's 18 Platoon, with the rest of C and D Companies, had fought a fierce running battle for the city of Damour. His platoon was one of the first to enter the city and they brought in about 90 prisoners, a fair prize. The other battalions involved in the main struggle, in particular the two sister battalions, 2/16th and 2/27th, with their support units, virtually forced the enemy out of all its positions leading up to and in Damour itself. In the east, the Allied forces had successfully put on the pressure, right around the perimeter leading up to Beirut.

The Vichy forces surrendered. Early the next morning, on 12 July at 12.30 am, word was received that an armistice had been negotiated with the enemy, and that hostilities were supposed to have ceased by midnight of 11 July.

Lieutenant O'Day reported the news of the armistice to an excited 9 Platoon. 'Everything is going ahead. They are signing it tomorrow apparently, at the old seaport of Acre in Palestine. It's over!'

The agreement with the defeated Vichy French provided for the occupation of Syria and Lebanon by the Allies. The overriding intention of this treaty was to enable defences to be created along the northern border to prevent Hitler approaching the Middle East through Turkey.

Bruce and Alan were now given a grisly task, being selected

in a contingent to help find and bury the war dead. Along the coast road, particularly around Sidon, the enemy had dug trenches into the cliffs, usually close to caves. The Allied navy had pounded these structures relentlessly, killing many of the occupants—most of them dying by concussion.

As the contingent moved down the cliffs, the first thing they noticed was the putrid odour of death coming up from the trenches below them. Entering the first cave, they weren't prepared for the devastating sight that greeted them.

The dead sentries were black Senegalese soldiers; their twisting, rotting corpses were still sitting in position five days after the bombing. Their features were grossly distorted, as the bodies were swollen and bloated and now festering with maggots. It was a grotesque vision which Bruce and Alan knew they would remember forever.

Two of the detachment could stand the terrible odour and sickening scene no longer and escaped outside and vomited.

Alan attempted to lift and transfer one of the bodies and, to his horror, the soldier's decomposed limb came off in his hand.

'Christ,' said Bruce, 'we'll never do it this way!'

They searched around and appropriated some signal wire and tied it around the unfortunate man's trunk. In this way the bodies were towed to the waiting trench, where they were covered up and finally given a burial service.

The work continued for two days. The men agreed it was the worst job they'd ever had to do.

While waiting for Beirut leave, Alan put a proposition to Bruce. 'You know, I've almost had enough of this marching and infantry business, and I reckon I'm ready for a change. I'm 24, and I can't drive. What do you say we get a transfer to the transport platoon, take it easy with our feet, and I can learn to drive? Besides, I reckon the war's over here for a while—if something happens, we should be able to get back in a flash.'

'Yeah, why not?' said Bruce. 'I'm sure we could get back into 9 Platoon if Hitler comes through from the north.'

Bruce assured their mates in Seven Section that this was only a temporary adventure. 'We'll be back—we're just having a break while Alan learns to drive.'

Alan, of course, had driven tractors and was mechanically inclined, and it was no large challenge. Before long, he and Bruce were handling army trucks like veteran drivers, and were soon driving all over the Levant.

With experience came familiarity and a chance for a bit of larrikinism. The trucks had a hand accelerator as well as a foot accelerator, and for a lark, while driving, Alan would lie full length along the front seat and look at the road ahead with the side mirror tilted forwards, instead of to the rear—giving the impression that the vehicle was driverless. This trick brought much amusement to the troops. But after one such escapade, in which the truck bounced off the road, causing it to lose its tailgate, Alan became nervous that he might be in trouble.

The next day the battalion runner sought him out. 'Major Cusworth wants to see you in his office—immediately.'

Alan was aware that, if you lost an item of military equipment, the Army had the authority to take the money out of your paybook, and he was expecting the worst.

When he reached the major's tent, he was cordially invited in. This is a bit funny, he thought. He saluted smartly with his hat on, relieved to see that the major had a smile on his face. 'Sit down, Private Avery.' Alan sat down, still a bit suspicious. The major came straight to the point. 'I've got the good news that you've won the Military Medal.'

Alan, relieved, breathed a great sigh. He grinned in return, saying: 'Thank you, sir, very much! Very, *very* much!'

He immediately sought out Bruce, who had also been concerned about the loss of the tailgate.

'What'd he want, mate?' Bruce asked.

'I've just been given the MM,' Alan replied, a little incredulously.

'Really?' Bruce burst into excited laughter. 'Fair dinkum! That's bloody marvellous.' He laughed again, and continued: 'Anyone else get anything?'

'Yeah. The battalion picked up one Military Cross, four MMs and nine MIDs. 9 Platoon got two MMs—the other was for Leo Deeley. Butch Bisset's platoon got one also—Jim Jeffrey on Hill 567.'

THE BATTALION STAYED IN THE BEIRUT area for the next
month until the defeated Vichy soldiers had been repatriated to
France and the situation was deemed to be stable.

Beirut was indeed a beautiful city, and the men of the 2/14th
had some entertaining leave periods there. The city boasted
large promenades on the beach, with palm trees bordering the
streets. There were outdoor cafes, good restaurants, hotels,
bazaars, brothels and every convenience laid on for the occupation forces.

During this period it was part of Stan's job to liaise with
the local villages in order to get to know them and generally
to foster goodwill. He noticed that often they were hardly
touched by the war and the change of command—life still
following the seasons with an almost biblical simplicity.

It was also a time for the battalion to assess its recent
performance under conflict. The Syrian Campaign, as the Army
called it, had been unexpectedly difficult. The Australian casualties reflected the degree of commitment. During the five weeks
of hostilities, the Australians lost 416 men killed and over 1000
wounded, while the Vichy lost 521 killed and almost 2000
wounded. After the failures in Greece, Crete and Libya, the
victory was a boon for the Chiefs of Staff of the Allied forces.
Yet in Australia the news of the win was kept to a minimum
by a censored press which was forced to play down the fact
that Australians were fighting Frenchmen.

For their part, the soldiers received a general order that they
were not to mention fighting the French in their letters home.
Every letter was censored and any reference to the battle was
neatly excised with a razor blade.

In early September the battalion began a move north to
construct the planned defences. Alan and Bruce were in charge
of a truck carrying an inebriated Seven Section. Hi-Ho Silver
had just transferred to the section and they had all celebrated
by imbibing Arak, the local white wine. Teddy Bear, now the
section leader, and a non-drinker, amicably settled his charges
down for the long haul.

After some hours they were woken as they drove over the
Nahr Al Kalb, or Dog, River. The Professor blearily impressed
on them details of the conquerors who had engraved their names
on the rock face over the centuries, beginning with the great

Egyptian, Ramses II, in 1298 BC. Some of the inscriptions had been chiselled into the rock itself and were in various states of deterioration. Later ones were recorded on plaques cemented into the cliffs, including one for the 1st AIF.

The convoy moved on over deep valleys and gorges carved into the soaring cliffs, until they stopped for a break further north at Byblos—'The oldest city in the world,' said the Professor. He continued: 'We owe to Byblos the honour of creating the alphabet. As well, Byblos gave its name to the Bible.'

'Good on you, mate. Our own travelling guidebook,' Alan kidded.

Towards early afternoon they reached the ancient fishing village and seaport of Tripoli. Here the convoy turned right, then climbed quietly up into the hills, moving further back into antiquity and among unsurpassed beauty. They finally stopped their vehicles sixteen kilometres inland, in an isolated and desolate stretch of the landscape, where the battalion was to be thinly stretched over a wide frontier linking Tripoli and Damascus.

Stan's 18 Platoon, Butch's 10 Platoon and the two other platoons of D Company were given an outpost right on the front line. It was the most forward position and right on top of a very high feature, about 1500 metres, which dominated the main approaches where it was thought the Germans would probably come through.

The work of preparing the defensive positions was hard going. After laying kilometres of triple-apron barbed-wire fences right across the perimeter, they dug and constructed massive trenches and weapon pits.

Once a week, Stan would take his platoon down to a little mountain stream where they would do their 'dhobiing' (clothes washing) and freshen up a little. The water was cold but bracing. On one occasion after he'd finished cleaning himself Stan found to his horror, while washing his clothes, that he was actually scrubbing a long, writhing multicoloured snake. Considering his vulnerability, as he was perfectly naked, he made a dash for his revolver lying on the bank. In a heartbeat, he whipped the gun out of its holster and fired a bullet clean through the snake's neck, instantly killing it. Thank heavens for all that practice shooting rabbits and candle flames, he thought to himself.

Once a week, because of the ruggedness of the mountain, all their supplies would come up by mule train. On that day the men would search the foothills with their field glasses and then follow, with great anticipation, the mules' progress as the procession trudged up the mountainside. This was because the mule train was carrying rations of beer for the men and spirits for the officers. There was generally a celebration that night, and as Butch's tent was not far from Stan's there was plenty of opportunity for fraternising.

The brothers were relaxed now. The shooting was over, but Stan acknowledged an uneasy sensation that was difficult to identify—something niggling, unsettling, in the pit of his stomach. He thought it might be just a reaction to the loss of some of his friends in the recent campaign, but more realistically he considered it was probably because he and Butch had been in the firing line and had made it through. This time they were lucky—he had seen how fate can pick out who wins and who loses. He told himself that the reaction he was feeling was mainly one of relief, sprinkled with a few seeds of apprehension—next time, he realised, neither of them might be so lucky.

There seemed a need to make these moments more urgent—more precious.

High in the mountains, the October winds carried the scent of winter and the streams became edged with a filigree of ice crystals. The change in weather meant little to Alan and Bruce, who would regularly find their way over to 9 Platoon lines and continue their marathon card-playing sessions—generally with the Professor and WRD. At this stage, Jarmbe was very concerned about his brother Reg. He knew Reg had landed at Crete, but the battle for Crete had been virtually lost by the end of May. As he had not heard that Reg had been captured or killed, he had hopes that he was still safe somewhere. Bruce reassured him: 'Ah, he'll be OK, mate. He's resourceful. You've heard nothing bad yet—he'll make it!'

As with Stan's platoon, 9 Platoon would also have a regular weekly party as their supplies came in. On one such night, the Professor had invited the Catholic chaplain around for a few drinks. Fortunately Father Daly was no wowser. As the night progressed, and the beer flowed, they started a popular and deplorably rumbustious drinking game. This involved skolling a full 26-ounce bottle of beer while the rest of the party sang *'You're a bastard, so they say . . . drink it down, down, down,'*—along with other lines best forgotten. Then the drinker had to run up and over the side of the tent. Father Daly proved to be the best of the lot, as he could drink the whole bottle without pausing for a breath and remain standing after his tent climb.

STAN HAD BEEN SELECTED TO UNDERTAKE an intelligence officers course at Julis camp. He was eager to attend the six-week program beginning on 10 November, even though completion of it would mean leaving 18 Platoon.

First, though, he, Butch and a number of men from the company visited the northern Lebanese town of Tripoli. Walking around, the brothers were fascinated by its Byzantine and Ottoman history, its colourful bazaars, and the Crusader Citadel, which sits on a high rocky outcrop bordered by the sea on one side and surrounded by mountains on the other sides.

It was midday as they climbed to the tower of the citadel. Suddenly, from a mosque below the walls, a muezzin commenced his forceful chant, calling the faithful to prayer. Within seconds, voices from scores of other mosques joined in the chorus. It was an extraordinary moment for all of them as the energy of the combined prayers seemed to focus directly at them.

By the time Stan had finished the course and returned to the battalion, it was almost Christmas. The dark skies threatened snow, and two days before Christmas the first snowfall surprised and delighted the Australians. For most of them it was the first snow they'd seen, and within a few hours the Lebanese mountains and plains were covered, producing a magnificent white landscape. Before long, like children, the soldiers were engaging in aggressive snowball fights and building snowmen.

Bruce and Alan could easily find an official reason for commandeering a truck. In it they and their friends would regularly tour around Lebanon. One day they crossed into Syria and visited a classical Crusader castle there—Crac des Chevaliers, the Castle of the Knights. It stands near the road running between Aleppo and Damascus, and in medieval times anyone who controlled this area controlled inland Syria.

Another time they came across a grove of the last remaining cedars of Lebanon. 'You know,' the Professor said, 'there's only about 400 of them left—some are believed to be over 1500 years old. The whole of the ancient world used them. Even some of Australia's early stately homes were built from these cedars.'

The highlight, though, was a visit to Baalbek, down in the Bekaa Valley not far from the border with Syria. As they drove down the wide valley they saw, on a huge acropolis ahead of them, six massive columns looming out of the plain.

'Wow, look at that!' said Bruce.

'That'll be the Temple of Jupiter,' answered the Professor excitedly. 'Its columns are supposed to be the highest ever erected—over 70 feet tall. And just look at the size of the stones in the rest of the ruins. They're the largest ever used, I believe.'

Early in the new year the Seventh Division pulled out of the area. The 2/14th Battalion set up camp at Hill 69, outside Jerusalem, where they trained and were reinforced over the next two weeks.

News was filtering through that the Japanese had emerged as a desperate threat in the Pacific. They had invaded Malaya and were moving towards Singapore, where they were heavily engaged with the AIF Eighth Division. Elsewhere, the Americans were holding out in a vicious siege in the Philippines, at Corregidor and Bataan, against a fanatical and belligerent Japanese Imperial Army. Even though the situation was not good in the North African desert, as Rommel's counter-attack was driving the British Army back towards Cairo, this more urgent news caused the Australians to think they just might be sent to fight the Japanese somewhere—Java, or Singapore perhaps.

The prospect of meeting a different enemy, closer to home, led Alan and Bruce to rejoin the Infantry. Teddy Bear hosted the welcoming committee. 'Nothing's changed much, except we've got a new platoon commander. Lieutenant Cox replaced Gerry O'Day while we were in Palestine. We'll miss Gerry a lot alright. Come and join in.'

A few days later, Stan, who by now had been appointed as

the Intelligence Officer for the 2/14th, met the new commanding officer of the battalion, Lieutenant Colonel Key, for a briefing. Key had an impressive war record behind him, having commanded a Sixth Division battalion, the 2/8th, through Libya, Greece and Crete. Stan felt they could have every confidence in the new leader.

Later that morning he joined the troops as they entrained for a journey south over the Sinai. They moved through El Kantara staging camp on the Suez Canal, and when the train continued south towards Suez instead of heading west, betting money started to change hands, as now they obviously wouldn't be fighting in the Western Desert.

Finally the train stopped at Port Tewfik. There the battalion transferred to the Shell Oil wharf, ready to embark on the waiting troopships.

INTERLUDE

7

Home and Yandina

ON 30 JANUARY 1942, THE BEAUTIFUL 84 000-tonne trans-Atlantic liner *Ile de France* joined the convoy heading out of the Red Sea, bound for Bombay. The main body of the three battalions of the 21st Brigade were on board. The troops wrestled with mixed feelings as they left the immediate battle zone—relief, sadness for their lost friends, yet some excitement at the possibility they might be heading home. But the thought remained that they would probably have to fight the Japanese at some point.

As the voyage settled into routine, lectures on Military Intelligence continued. As the Intelligence Officer, Stan led discussions on issues concerning the Japanese, including aircraft and ship recognition. He also lectured to them on 'direction finding by the stars', as he considered this skill important for jungle fighting.

There was a concert on board the third night out. Among others, Stan entertained the men with a moving rendition of a popular Paul Robeson song, 'Going Home'. It was set to the largo movement of Dvorak's 'New World' symphony.

At Bombay, the battalion re-embarked on the *City of Paris*, and along with the rest of the convoy it moved out of Bombay harbour on the afternoon of Friday, 13 February. The date didn't bother the ardent gamblers of 9 Platoon, who continued with their legendary solo-whist card games, keeping score in their now well-used notebook.

As the journey progressed, wagers on their destination firmed on Singapore, as the latest information had it that the Japanese were closing in on the island city, Britain's jewel in Asia. The AIF Eighth Division were fighting there.

On the 20th, they received the disturbing news that Java was under Japanese attack. The spirited but under-resourced defence of the large island was led by two Australian battalions which had newly arrived there, ahead of the convoy, on the SS *Orcades*—the 2/3rd Machine-Gun Battalion and the 2/2nd Pioneer Battalion. The latter was the battalion which Bruce had originally joined but had left thanks to the toss of a coin.

The news of the Japanese advances caused the convoy to suddenly swing towards Rangoon in Burma, as Winston Churchill desperately wanted the Australians to offer relief to the besieged British troops garrisoned there.

However, the decision did not sit well with the Australian prime minister, John Curtin, who was influenced by several domino-type events closer to home. Singapore fell on the 15th, Darwin was bombed on the 19th, and Rabaul, in New Guinea, capitulated on the 23rd. Curtin, against the will of the war's chief strategists, called the Sixth and Seventh Divisions back home to protect Australia.

Thus, two weeks later, with the *City of Paris* about a day from the coast of Western Australia, a breath of fresh air wafted over the exhausted and irritable soldiers on board. They had barely tolerated the uncomfortable, cramped and oppressively hot conditions encountered during the Indian Ocean leg.

'Y'know,' Jarmbe said, 'I can almost smell the eucalyptus scent blowing off the mainland. I reckon we're not too far from Fremantle.'

'About bloody time,' agreed Hi-Ho. 'Another day staring at you ugly sallow bastards in this bloody heat and I'd've bloody well swum back home.'

The next day, amid scenes of excitement, the ships berthed in Fremantle harbour. The men noticed that there were American warships at anchor there.

The country's war footing was felt even more acutely when the battalion disembarked at Adelaide's Outer Harbour. The troops made their way by train to Springbank camp, about five kilometres outside Adelaide, and were impressed by the tremendous welcome and the obvious showing of people's relief at Curtin's decision to return the divisions in order to meet the Japanese threat.

'Geez, that was some reception,' enthused Bruce, 'but I wish we could get back to Melbourne. I'm busting to see Leila.'

'Yeah,' Alan replied. 'Still, I suppose we have to consider ourselves lucky. Fancy the whole of the Eighth Division being taken prisoner at Singapore! And all the Java battalions including your old lot being taken also. I guess that's one you owe me, mate—you could be in a Jap prison by now. Strike! Your life on the toss of a coin.'

After a few days of toughening up with long route marches and physical training programs, general leave was granted to the battalion. Members of 9 Platoon prepared for a night out in Adelaide.

'Hey, you coming, Jarmbe?' Alan called to his friend. 'Geez, you look a bit spivvy—all slick and oiled up. Where're y'going? You got a chick?'

Jarmbe broke into a pleased grin. 'Yep. A chap from one of the other units is setting me up for a blind date. We're off to dinner.'

'Yeah? You bastard! No such luck for us.' Alan in fact was missing Ann, and like Bruce was hoping there might be a chance for home leave later.

Jarmbe and his friend Alf, a tall, good-looking Aboriginal from Western Australia, met the two girls at a quiet restaurant. Alf introduced his girl, Ivy, who then presented Dot.

Jarmbe, quite simply, was overcome. Dorothy Banfield was petite, very pretty, with straight dark hair which fell about her olive-coloured face. The night moved in a dream.

After three weeks of his intensive courting of Dot, Jarmbe was told that the battalion was to be granted a week's home leave in Melbourne. This forced the issue for him and he promptly proposed to her. Even though she was delighted and flattered at the proposal, she hesitated, 'I'll write to you in the next few weeks after I get my thoughts straight.' Realising a 'maybe' was better than a 'no', Jarmbe simply said: 'I'll wait for you.'

Meanwhile, Bruce had sent a telegram to Leila: 'Expect home leave Tuesday or Wednesday. Bruce.'

The troop train arrived in Melbourne on 16 March to a rousing welcome home, as friends and relatives bustled to meet the returning battalion.

Leila and Ann had taken time off work, and with Bruce and Alan they enjoyed all the good things that wartime Melbourne had to offer. Bruce asked Alan whether he would 'pop the question', but was hardly surprised when Alan said he'd leave it for later. The war hung over everything and Alan hesitated to risk leaving a new bride a widow.

Also at the station to meet the returning troops was Jarmbe's father, Chris. He took Jarmbe straight to the nearest pub and shouted him a beer; the first he'd ever drunk with him. Chris confided his fears for Reg's safety, as he'd been missing now behind enemy lines for nine months, and he had heard no word since. Jarmbe shared his great concern. Then he proudly told Chris about Dot and his proposal to her. 'That's marvellous,' Chris said excitedly, and started to talk about the future.

The next day they travelled to Portland where Jarmbe had a great week back in his home town, being feted by his three younger sisters, his large extended family and his friends. He also went hunting with Chris several times, relishing the peace and security of the bush.

While the men of the 2/14th were well motivated to meet the Japanese, public concern for the protection of Australia was demonstrated in its crudest form to Bruce one day. Bruce didn't like wearing his army uniform around the city, because he felt it was ill-fitting. He was a snappy dresser and liked to look neat, so he changed into 'mufti'—civilian clothes—for his home leave. As he was walking through town to meet Alan, he was accosted by a young woman in the street who presented him with a white feather—the symbol of cowardice.

When he later told Alan, his friend asked, dumbfounded: 'What did you do?'

'What else could I do? I laughed, and kept on walking.'

During the same week, Stan and Butch also went home and spent time with their parents. The men were both officers now and a source of great pride to the family.

The week's leave finished too quickly. After a highly emotional farewell, the troop train dropped its passengers at Glen Innes, a town in northern New South Wales, where the battalion commenced hard training. Towards the end of the second week there, Captain Rhoden, who was now A Company commander, called for Bruce and Alan.

'Boys, I need two drivers to come north with me. The whole Seventh Division are to move to Queensland for further training before we meet the Japanese. Our new brigade commander, Brigadier Potts, wants me to take a couple of men to mark out a camp by tomorrow—or we'll be dismissed.' He smiled. 'Can you do it?'

After securing a truck, they drove all night. Bruce and Alan chatted idly, regularly taking a rise out of each other, and in doing so succeeded in entertaining Rhoden.

'Exactly where are we off to, sir?' Bruce asked at one point.

'A place called Yandina. It's a holiday resort about 70 miles north of Brisbane—on the north coast. There's a large mountain range behind—the Blackall Range—that's supposed to be fairly hard to climb, as well as being jungly, so it'll be ideal for training.'

Alan chipped in: 'What do you think of that big battle out in the Coral Sea a couple of days ago? Do you think it will slow the Japs down a bit?'

'Well, it will certainly mean a delay to them, and possibly more chance of them undertaking land invasion—maybe New Guinea, or even Queensland.'

Just on daybreak, when they were still some kilometres from Yandina, the first rays of the sun lighted an almost primeval scene as the nearby Glasshouse Mountains came into view, silhouetted against the sky. These were ancient volcanic plugs which rose from the surrounding plain like something from a forgotten Dreamtime.

'It's not too far past here, boys, I believe—a grassy paddock not far from the ocean,' said Rhoden, recognising the landmarks.

A little later, the three men set to to mark out the camp site in preparation for the rest of the battalion, which arrived next day by train.

Training continued now at a stepped-up rate. The Blackall Range offered challenging mountain climbs, and an opportunity to hack and crawl through jungle greenery. Amid all the activity, Jarmbe received two great pieces of news—a telegram from his father saying that Reg had safely found his way out of Crete and was now in Egypt, and a letter from Dot accepting his proposal of marriage. For a day or two Jarmbe found it hard to concentrate on the job in hand.

Taking a break from the hard slog, Stan took his Intelligence Section to Noosa Spit for a week to live off the land. Here they trained on the beach; to catch fish, Stan would throw a plug of gelignite into the ocean and always produce a full bounty.

Towards mid-July, Seven Section of 9 Platoon were required to live on the beach at Coolum, about sixteen kilometres from Yandina, for a period of reconnaissance and coast watching—specifically to report on suspected Japanese submarine activities.

'Wow. What a beach,' said Teddy.

'Just look at those rollers coming in.'

As the men watched the roaring surf, the morning sun shone through the cresting waves, rendering them a translucent green. The crashing foam raced up the wide, beautiful, deserted beach.

'Let's hit the water!'

Even though it was winter, the men stripped off and dived into the picture postcard scene.

Their job was to patrol the beach at night and to report any possible shore-to-sea signalling. They each carried a Tommy gun over their shoulder, then ran in twos to the outlet of the Maroochy River and back, four times a night, covering 40 kilometres in all. In the mornings they would listen to honeyeaters in the banksia trees and be woken by the screech of black cockatoos, which reminded Alan and Bruce of their trip in outback Victoria some years previously.

Yes, they agreed, this country was definitely worth defending.

THE CHANCE TO DO THIS CAME all too quickly. On 5 August the men were ordered to prepare for an immediate move north.

Once again there were hurried goodbyes—to the local people and to Yandina's idyllic surroundings. Bruce and Alan packed their playing cards, noticing that after all this time the notebook disclosed less than £1 outstanding between the various players. Then they were taken by truck to Brisbane to board the Liberty ship *James Fenimore Cooper*. Next day, at noon, they were under way to a destination unknown—somewhere to the north.

There were three ships in the convoy, as they were accompanied by another Liberty ship, the *James Wilson*, carrying the 2/16th Battalion, and a small Dutch ship, the *Both*, with troops of the 18th Brigade on board.

The Liberty ships were specially produced, being turned out in 38 days by the Americans to a brilliant new design. They were completely welded together, with not a rivet in sight. They were not particularly comfortable ships and as the convoy travelled further north the iron decks became red hot. When the seas grew larger out in the ocean, Alan would stand aft and look forward, amazed to see the whole ship twisting as it was thrown from wave to wave.

To the troops it was a safe bet that they were on their way to New Guinea. They knew that in March the Japanese had taken Lae and Salamaua on the northeast coast of the island, and that a large force of the Japanese Imperial Army was garrisoned at Rabaul on nearby New Britain. They also knew that in early June the news had come through that the large naval battle at Midway had helped to stem the Japanese thrust south. The Japanese had lost four aircraft carriers for one United States carrier, and this, coupled with the results of the earlier Coral Sea battle, effectively prevented an early invasion of Australia. However, Port Moresby, the capital of New Guinea, was looming as the next local prize for the Japanese.

The ships continued north, and on the fifth day the *Both* turned right, taking the 18th Brigade troops towards Milne Bay at the southeastern tip of New Guinea.

As the two remaining ships continued on to Port Moresby, a further day's journey, Stan Bisset congratulated his old friend Phil Rhoden on becoming second-in-command of the battalion, under Colonel Key. Earlier, Ben Buckler—'Little Sir Echo'—had been welcomed back to the battalion as the captain of A Company, which pleased 9 Platoon as they'd come to respect the man when he'd been the Adjutant during their time at Puckapunyal.

The next day would change everything again.

NEW GUINEA

8

The Kokoda Track

THE SUN BURST OVER THE CORAL Sea, heralding a simmering tropical day as the light danced and sparkled on the waves and then shimmered as the heat and humidity grew. Those on deck in the early hours in the clear air could make out the great peak of Mt Victoria, the highest mountain in the Owen Stanley Ranges. Incongruously, it was snowcapped. As the sun rose and the heat became sticky, clouds descended on the hills above Port Moresby, obscuring and darkening the jungle.

It became obvious that the war had exploded into New Guinea. Since 3 February, Port Moresby had been bombed by up to 80 Japanese bombers almost every second day, with many raids at night. In the harbour, the men could see the bombed wreck of MV *Macdhui*, a Burns-Philp motorship sunk some two months before. There were other wrecks as well, silent testimony to the effectiveness of the attacks.

An extra worry was the concern that some Japanese submarines were lurking in the area, as they had recently sunk three freighters. There was no small sigh of relief as the RAN corvette HMAS *Lithgow* pulled up alongside the Liberty ships and started ferrying the troops to land.

As they approached the wharf, the men could make out defence installations and were most unimpressed with the reality of the place. They'd had visions of a tropical paradise, green shrubbery and palm and coconut trees. 'Geez, we've been had!'

91

Alan said to Teddy. 'Look at that, not a bloody palm tree in sight or a dancing girl anywhere.' Teddy agreed; the place was like a desert and very bomb-scarred. The hills around the beach area were covered in brown kunai grass, except where it had been burnt off and was seared black, mixing depressingly with the ochre colour of the dirt.

Before 1942, there had been about 400 white civilians in Port Moresby. They had all been evacuated. Their flimsily built houses with corrugated iron roofs now formed a bomb-shattered village. Most of the official buildings of plaster and lathe had been damaged, leaving a virtual ghost town. The few shanties scattered around the waterfront offset the remnants of two pubs, the picture theatre, a Burns-Philp trading post, a couple of stores and some administration buildings.

Port Moresby had changed in character from a colonial outpost to an army garrison. The Australian militiamen who manned the small garrison were glad to see the fresh troops, as things had become pretty grim from their point of view.

Thanks to the surprise attack on Pearl Harbor by the Japanese on 7 December 1941, most of them had been posted there since the first few days of the new year. The intervening eight months had seen the deteriorating condition of the Allies' position bring about a belated 'backs to the wall' stance towards the defence of Australia. Some elements of the 49th Militia Battalion had been in Port Moresby since mid-1940, and were joined by the 39th and 53rd in January 1942 to form a scratch brigade—the 30th Infantry Brigade.

These Militia units were filled by volunteers, some of whom had been drafted with only 24 hours' notice—almost press-ganged into service—a point of some resentment. They were composed of raw, very young recruits with an average age of 18 or 19 years. They had been drafted for home defence service only, but this included territories. At the time, Papua and eastern New Guinea were among Australia's mandated territorial responsibilities. The AIF, on the other hand, could serve abroad. Its members derisively referred to the Militia as 'chocos'—short for 'chocolate soldiers'—as the AIF gallantly went off to fight anywhere in the world.

Through little fault of their own, the Militia battalions were inexperienced, poorly equipped and very unprepared to do battle as the Japanese approached. They were simply not trained, physically or mentally, to meet and match the invaders.

And approaching the Japanese were. In the nine months since Pearl Harbor, they had appeared to be unstoppable. As part of their so-called New Order, 'The Greater South-East Asia Co-Prosperity Sphere', they had ingested all the local forces and countries in their way. Their audacious grab for empire was reaching its climax.

Darwin had been bombed regularly since February, and when Japanese forces overwhelmed the small garrison at Rabaul in January and then landed at Lae and Salamaua in March, it was obvious that Port Moresby was next in line. This would effectively isolate Australia and make it ready for invasion.

The victorious Japanese Army now controlled an area within an arc that embraced the Western Pacific, passed through the Solomon Islands and New Guinea and ran south of the Dutch East Indies to Burma. Australia's nearest friendly neighbours on either side, the United States and India, were now disadvantaged strategically. Japanese triumph was at its height and it seemed that, at a time of their own choosing, they could take Papua. Port Moresby appeared ripe for the picking.

This tremendous tide had been checked by two naval battles—the Coral Sea battle, in May, and the Battle of Midway, in early June, where the Japanese fleet was crippled, thus delaying their immediate plans to take Port Moresby.

However, the Japanese still had intact their immensely powerful army and were in great strength at their now enormous base at Rabaul. Their naval reverses increased the urgency to capture Port Moresby and plans were put in place for deadly offensives over the Owen Stanley Ranges, through Kokoda, and also at Milne Bay. A third prong was planned to consolidate their gains at Guadalcanal in the Solomons, to the east of Milne Bay.

So now the Japanese had landed a task force in the Gona–Buna area on the northeast coast, on 21 July, and were preparing to march over the towering Owen Stanleys and strike Port Moresby from the rear.

When Stan reached the sleepy wharf, he was greeted by an officer who passed on the good news that the Allied counter-offensive was under way. The United States Marines had landed an invasion force in the Solomons—one at the large island of Guadalcanal and another at Tulagi, a smaller island. This was good news, as it suggested that the Japanese would be able to commit fewer reinforcements to the New Guinea campaign.

From the wharf, the rest of the troops were quickly transferred to army trucks. Alan and Bruce noted that they were driven by American Negroes—the first they had seen.

They slowly made their way out of the town, which had the appearance of being deserted. There were a few indigenous people around, the men carrying a long cane knife and wearing either shorts or nothing much; the women wearing either grass skirts or missionary-type dresses—'Mother Hubbard' or 'Mary' dresses, as they were called locally.

They passed the main airstrip in use, noting plane wrecks by the side of the runway, the legacy of regular Japanese bombing and strafing raids. This was called Seven Mile Airfield, and Bruce commented on the anti-aircraft guns around it— Bofors guns, the same as the British had used at Jezzine in Lebanon.

As the trucks left the coast and meandered up into the hills, the vegetation grew greener and thicker. For the next 30 kilometres, the scenery changed dramatically as they went through the Rouna Pass and around the spectacular Rouna Falls. Evidence of a more generous rainfall came in two ways here: several kilometres of prosperous rubber plantations, and their first evening tropical storm.

The drenching rain came suddenly at about 3.00 pm. It caused the trucks to skid and slide, and a few became bogged. In good spirits and eager to get going, the men quickly manoeuvred the transports back on to the road.

'I wonder where we're going,' Bruce said to Alan and Jarmbe as the truck skidded again.

'I don't know,' Alan said. 'I heard someone say the Kokoda Track.'

'Never heard of it,' Bruce replied.

They eventually pulled up at a clearing on the edge of the jungle, not far from what was known as McDonald's Corner and only a few kilometres from the beginning of the Kokoda Track.

P. J. MCDONALD HAD SERVED AS A Lighthorseman in World War I and had moved to Papua in 1924. After being involved in a number of ventures, he developed a rubber plantation in the area, and now he had been commissioned into ANGAU (Australian New Guinea Administrative Unit) as a lieutenant. His local knowledge was a great help to the brigade and they spent three days here in preparation for battle. The troops received lectures on how to survive in the jungle if lost or cut off, how to recognise native plants and foods such as taros and yams, and how to prepare them.

During these few days the men cleaned and checked their weapons, had their boots studded, checked their packs, pouches and haversacks for durability, and then packed a full scale of ammunition and rations for eight days. They had borrowed a foot-accelerated millstone from McDonald and spent some time honing their bayonets to razor-sharp condition. The minimum weight they could get their gear down to was 22 kilograms; but with a .303 Lee Enfield rifle or a Bren gun, and other battalion equipment passed around in rotation, each man rarely carried less than 36 kilograms—some as much as 45.

On the eve of the departure of the 2/14th, Brigadier Potts had a meeting with his brigade staff and at the same time received news that the Japanese had landed an extra 4000 men in the Gona–Buna area, including 1800 combat troops. This would boost the already confident 1500 strong who had landed on 21 July and were already forging inland towards the Australians.

Potts was a commanding presence—one his officers had great respect for. Physically, he was of average height with an immense, strong frame; emotionally, he was well equipped to lead his men into battle against an unknown and supposedly uncompromising enemy. He had already won a Military Cross and had been severely wounded in France in 1918 after serving in the Gallipoli campaign. In Syria he was awarded the DSO after the 2/16th's victories against Sidon and Damour, where he received a promotion in the field to command that battalion.

Stan appreciated Potts's decisive manner, and warmed to his subtle humour as the brigadier outlined his philosophy for the approaching conflict.

'Gentlemen,' Potts began, 'I'll tell you the way it is. Early in July, the Port Moresby commander sent elements of the 39th Militia Battalion and the Papuan Infantry Battalion—codenamed Maroubra Force—over the Kokoda Track to Kokoda. That's about 60 miles as the crow flies, but it takes seven or eight days to walk there. Further on, they had their first clash with the enemy at Awala, inland from Gona, on the 23rd—over a fortnight ago.

'After a brief fight, heavily outnumbered, they began a fighting withdrawal across the Kumusi River at Wairopi— here'—he pointed to the map on the wall—'then they withdrew back to Kokoda. The enemy forced them out of the village for a while, then the 39th mounted a counter-attack and briefly drove the Japs out of Kokoda and reoccupied the village. However, five days ago, the overwhelming pressure forced the garrison out of Kokoda.

'The 39th have withdrawn back over the Owen Stanleys. They are now at a village called Isurava on the Kokoda Track and are fighting a holding battle there. Our task is to get to Isurava, relieve the 39th, retake Kokoda, then throw the Japanese back to the Kumusi River. I don't believe we have a great deal of time, so speed is of the essence. To achieve this, we have to walk over the Kokoda Track. The only place for resupplying is at Myola, which is at least five days away—hence the rations.

'The 2/14th will leave tomorrow, the 2/16th the day after, and the remaining battalion, the 2/27th, will stay at Moresby in reserve. The 53rd Battalion, another militia crew, have moved up already and should be there soon. We've just heard the Japs have landed a few thousand more there against us, so we'll just have to kill for a bit longer. It shouldn't be a problem as long as we have our supplies and our reserves.'

His confidence was contagious but not necessary. The troops were eager for this confrontation.

As morning came on 16 August, the men of 2/14th Battalion broke camp and boarded the trucks once again.

The Kokoda Track runs from Owers' Corner to Kokoda over the defiant Owen Stanley Ranges. It was originally used by miners making their way to the Kokoda–Yodda goldfield as early as the 1890s, but since then very few Europeans had ever used it as it was considered too difficult.

The local people, however, probably used it for centuries

and it simply developed randomly as the villages and geographical features changed over generations. The track rarely followed the shortest distance between two points and it unreasonably climbed the highest peaks and dropped to the deepest ravines in the same few hours. The highest altitude reached was 2300 metres at Mt Bellamy, which brought bizarre extremes of temperature, as the thermometer could plummet close to freezing at night time and rise to 40 degrees Celsius or more in the morning.

Whereas the crumpled pathway would provide easy enough going for locals walking from village to village, the single track was not designed for hundreds of troops carrying heavy equipment. This deficiency would soon be obvious as the daily afternoon rainstorm churned the muddy route into a glutinous, sucking bog.

These possibilities were of little concern as the men of the 2/14th debussed and looked forward, with great spirits, to the challenge and the conflict ahead. They joked as they jumped from the truck, then helped each other to lift and balance their gear on their shoulders and waist.

They were fit—extremely fit. They all sported a deep Queensland tan, reminiscent of the mythical Australian bronzed surf lifesaver, and, wearing khaki shirts and shorts and a tin helmet, they were the best of Australian manhood.

As they walked off the road, down to Owers' Corner and on to the first few metres of the track, the extreme weight forced their boots into the thick mud and they had a sudden realisation as to what they might expect. The jungle quickly closed in on them. In a few minutes they were immersed in a world of green. Ahead, an enemy swollen with many years of victory was waiting. The Japanese soldiers were known to be vicious, cruel and fanatical, but the battlefield they and the Australians had chosen was to test them to the extreme. Its perversities, the physical and topographical obstacles presented by its special terrain, were to push physical and psychological endurance to the limit.

Within fifteen minutes, everybody was working hard and sweating freely. Their clothes became completely sodden. This was a new experience, as even the hardest marches at home or in Lebanon hadn't produced this uncomfortable result. The jungle humidity simply didn't allow for evaporation. Further, they realised that no amount of previous training could ever be specific enough and could *never* prepare them for the limits they were about to ask their bodies and minds to achieve.

The first section of the track was a reasonably easy hike downhill through bush for three or four kilometres, before slipping into the dark shadow of the jungle. Here Jarmbe detected some birds that may have been parrots. Every now and then the men would traverse a small glen that exploded with thousands of butterflies. There was an opportunity now to admire the wildflowers which were quite endemic.

These pleasures didn't last, for the pathway suddenly descended down a raw mountainside. This produced much slipping, sliding and minor bruising as the men weren't used to balancing their unearthly weight in this environment. The profanities and expletives reached new heights of colour as the picnic came to an end. First their thighs ached, then their calves began to scream, then burn, then quiver with fatigue.

By early afternoon the regular downpour commenced, which refreshed them but soon coated everything with a wet and greasy slime—adding to the treachery underfoot. Above them, the jungle closed over to form a canopy which the rain belted into, darkening their vision. Far below, they could hear a stream rushing. They finally descended to a brawling creek which was crossed by a single log, with a few stepping stones at one end. This was the first of about 250 rambling rivulets they would encounter. Most crossed without a dunking, then the track climbed a short steep slope to the village of Uberi, planted haphazardly on the banks of the Goldie River.

Mercifully, this was to be their first staging post. Even though they had only traversed seventeen kilometres, the terrain had forced them to battle all day to reach this point. It was obvious that sections of the route would now be better measured in time rather than distance. As they settled down for the night, for the first time, they were to complain about their screaming knees and thighs and feel utter exhaustion.

STAN (AS THE INTELLIGENCE OFFICER), COLONEL Key, and Albert Moore, a Salvation Army officer, had stayed behind at

Itiki at McDonald's Corner for a last minute update conference with Brigadier Potts. They started their walk some hours after the battalion, but caught up to them during the afternoon.

That evening, realising the amount of salt the troops were losing with their sweat, Stan arranged to have salt tablets ready for the men at the next staging post, as he had found out that the coming day's walk was one of the hardest on the track. He also advised the men to drink plenty of water in order to remain hydrated.

Stan left early the next morning with some of his 'I' Section and the Quartermaster staff to be first at the next site in order to arrange food, salt and bivouac sites for the troops as they came in.

Most of the battalion were stiff and painful on awakening. However, they soon loosened up as their bodies generated heat from the effort of walking after leaving Uberi. They were on the bottom rung of what was known as the Stairway to Hell—euphemistically called The Golden Staircase. Papuan labourers had specially built 2000 steps into a steep ridge which climbed straight up with no respite. Each step was formed by a log held in position by two stakes. They were uneven in height and width and were filled with putrid, cloggy mud, often 45 centimetres deep.

Roots of trees interlocked with the steps and the rain exposed slippery, dangerous wood ready to clutch at unwary exhausted feet. Men tripped, falling and sliding in every ungainly posture imaginable. Shins were bruised and heads were banged against trees or the next man's rifle. Often there was a domino effect as a whole section of men slid down the mountainside, producing another tirade of splendid obscenities. The troops soon found they could assist their legs by acquiring a body-length walking stick cut from a sapling by the side of the track.

Their stomachs ached as the diaphragm repeatedly and violently contracted to suck air into screaming lungs. This precipitated vomiting in some men and caused a headache in most. The heart thumped as respiration increased to cope with the increasing workload, and the sweating and salt loss began to produce calf and thigh cramps.

Very quickly the climb became more than a physical challenge. Each man searched for a private psychological or spiritual advantage as his physiological limits were pushed out further and further.

About mid-morning Alan became aware of a loud roar of engines overhead. Looking up through breaks in the canopy, he could make out a 'W' formation as a squadron of Japanese bombers flew low over the track, aimed for Port Moresby. Still gasping for breath, he spluttered to Bruce and Jarmbe: 'Hell, I don't like the sound of that.' The Professor, standing nearby, agreed. It was an impressive and frightening sight. There were 27 bombers in all, accompanied by a strong escort of Zero fighter planes darting like silver gnats around them.

Soon the men could hear a sickening *Karump! Karump!* as the bombs landed on Port Moresby airfield and echoed back up the Ranges. While they were grateful that the bombers weren't dropping their load on them, they didn't foresee the significance of the raid for their present campaign.

There'd been two rows of planes parked on Seven Mile Airfield, wingtip to wingtip. One line contained a row of C-47 Dakotas—the 'biscuit bombers', as they would be known. They were fully laden, bound for Myola with provisions and supplies for the advancing 21st Brigade. The other line were freshly fuelled and bomb-laden Flying Fortresses ready to go.

The Japanese bombs created an inferno on the airfield as the planes and bombs exploded. Virtually the whole fleet was either damaged or destroyed. It was, indeed, to have serious consequences later on.

On the track, after a 360-metre climb, the troops reached the top of The Golden Staircase. Most sank to the ground, gasping for air and for time to let their depleted muscles recover. Then they started down a 480-metre drop. This, surprisingly, wasn't any easier than going up. The thigh muscles were working in a reverse fashion here—decelerating violently as the knees checked the perilous descent. By now it was afternoon and the heavens opened up again, increasing the potential to slip as torrential running water and mud undermined the path.

Eventually, at the bottom, the mountains threw a final provocative challenge at them as they were confronted by a ghastly 600-metre climb up Imita Ridge. Darkness was now approaching and exhaustion was taking its toll.

Men were dropping out all along the track now, lying under

a dripping palm leaf trying to recuperate, or gasping on a log having a comforting cigarette, not believing that their unstable, jelly-like knees wouldn't respond to cerebral command.

Seven Section were doing it tough like the rest. Teddy Bear, as section leader, had grouped his men closer. He'd worked out that short-term goals at this stage seemed more attainable psychologically than long-term ones, and he advised his charges not to look up or down but simply to place one foot after the other—to focus on 'right now'.

The Bren gun was being rotated around his men, and although superbly fit, Teddy was exhausted and grateful to pass it on to Hi-Ho Silver. Hi-Ho was used to emergencies; before the war he was one of the leading figures fighting the disastrous 1939 bushfires in Victoria, helping to create firebreaks and organising relief for trapped homeowners. He was also strong and extremely fit, and his large hands held the Bren like a toy. The Bren-gunner was always placed forward of the section, so Hi-Ho yelled, 'See you later, Teddy!', and disappeared up the mountain into the fast fading light.

Some time later he returned smiling, after depositing the Bren at the top of Imita Ridge, and then proceeded to help his struggling friends attain the crest. But the torture was not over for the day yet, as they still had a four-hour walk down one of the steepest descents of the track as it wound through dense forests, finishing at Va-Ule stream. They followed the creekbed here for some kilometres, stumbling in the blackness over the eroded, uneven surface and the slippery, round, waterworn rocks, falling and twisting ankles in the process, still cursing. Eventually they laboured up a final steep ascent of about 100 metres, and staggered into Ioribaiwa.

Stan, his 'I' Section and the 'Q' Store men were already set up here and were gratefully met. After a meal the troops fell asleep in their wet clothing, as exhausted as they'd ever been in their lives.

In the early hours of the next morning, as light gathered to the accompaniment of a growing bird chorus, Alan and Bruce tried to focus on the unfamiliar scene. Whipbird calls signalled a full symphony of bird song. The jungle was cool and dulcet, and gradually, inevitably, the dawn concert was drowned by the humming and buzzing of insects.

They now contemplated crossing the Maguli Range where engineers had cut 3400 steps into the track. This climb proved to be a repeat of yesterday, with an extra psychological hurdle. There were many 'false crests' in this range—a series of ridges and spurs that goaded the walker into thinking he must finally be at the top, when in fact he wasn't. But the range had to be crossed for them to reach the village of Nauro.

Along the way, Jarmbe rejoiced in the cycle of nature evident in the jungle. The treetops played in sunlight, dappling the dead and rotting leaves on the clay jungle floor. From the rich compost mix, ferns and other plants forced upwards to fight for the scarce light.

Nauro was bounded on three sides by jungled mountains and by a swamp on the fourth. It was a catchment area for heat by day, and mosquitoes by night, and malaria was a concern. A wash in the cold waters of the swift-flowing Brown River soothed aches and pains, and once again they slept in their wet clothes, this time with their sleeves rolled down to ward off the mosquitoes.

A short day's walk to Menari, where they camped for the night, was followed next morning by a difficult negotiation through a huge log dam, presenting a testing obstacle over one of the streams. In the process, most of the troops finished with their boots full of water.

'Geez,' Alan complained, taking off his boots. 'Look at my feet—they're bloody swollen and the toes are starting to stick together.' He dried them as best he could, but they were soon as wet again with perspiration as they were from tramping through muddy bogs.

This was the fourth day that the men had suffered wet feet and some were starting to show problems, as the continual rubbing and squelching was producing blisters, fungal irritations and pulpiness of the flesh.

By now, nevertheless, the troops were gaining new confidence in themselves as they conquered each challenge that the Kokoda Track threw up. Their bodies were accommodating to the mountain topography and, even as they climbed higher and the air became colder, they found a fresh resolve to see the task through.

The path to the next summit was thick with jungle. The

rain, heard drumming on the canopy above, added to the torture. The ridgeline was called Mission Ridge, as there was an old Mission hut down below, but at this stage it created little reverence among the troops. It would later. Right now, they were intent only on forcing one foot in front of the other.

Finally they reached the ridgeline and broke out of the jungle. The rain eased as they gathered their breath, sitting in a patch of kunai grass overlooking a marvellous vista.

To the right could be seen Myola Ridge, with the crater lakes, their next day's destination, nestled behind it. The track could be clearly seen and it looked uninviting as the higher rainfall associated with the increased altitude had made a quagmire of it. Further to the left there was a clear view of the main crestline of the immediate Owen Stanley Ranges, with many jagged spurs and ridges culminating in Mt Bellamy at 2300 metres.

As they watched, tendrils of mist drifted off the southern flanks of Mt Bellamy and curled intricately through the river valley below. Far above, commanding the scene, stood Mt Victoria, its peak lost in swirling mist. This was the mountain they could see from the Liberty ship as it approached Port Moresby, and at this range its majesty was complete as its highest peaks soared to almost 4000 metres.

To the right of Mt Bellamy they could make out a gap where the track passed high in the ranges. Isurava was somewhere beyond that and it loomed as a daunting prospect—given what they'd already been through.

'I reckon that'd be Isurava through there,' said Bruce, pointing in the direction of the gap.

'Crikey,' said Alan, 'I wouldn't want to be those poor bastards making a stand up there—I hope they can hold on.'

BY THE TIME THEY REACHED THE village of Efogi they were all in good spirits, even though they were shivering in their wet clothes because of the 1500-metre altitude.

The battalion bivouacked in companies here, and in the evening each platoon built a roaring fire so that they could dry out and get warm. As usual, Stan had arrived earlier and arranged with the 'Q' men for the arrival of the troops. By the time Butch's 10 Platoon came through and began setting up camp, Stan had gone back to battalion headquarters and was starting to relax after the long day. Then Butch sought him out and invited him back for some food and a singsong.

The scene was one of unreality as the tired but buoyant soldiers celebrated the moment. Efogi was alight with campfires, men laughed and sang and, as the wind blew in from the northern valley, the village was lashed with gusts of bitterly cold rain.

Over coffee, Butch asked Stan if he'd sing a few songs. Stan began with one of his favourites, 'Sarie Marais', which he'd learnt from the Springboks in 1937. The men soon picked up the refrain . . .

O take me back to the old Transvaal,
That's where I want to be,
Way yonder 'mongst the mealies . . .

Stan continued with 'The Road to Gundagai', and then Butch asked him if he would sing a personal favourite, 'The Mountains of Mourne'.

Stan's rich bass voice suited the song well and the nostalgia was evident in his resonant notes. As the strains saturated the air, a strange sensation came over him—he was aware that his senses were suddenly more alert. He was acute to the feel of the darkness, the mouldy smell of the jungle, and the pungency of the wet, burning wood of the fires.

He looked at the men around the campfire. There were eight of them, hunched closely around the fierce blaze, either squatting or sitting on their haversacks or a convenient log. The others were standing just behind, either leaning on their mate's shoulder or propped against a tree. Occasionally, as raindrops hit the flames, gusts of smoke would puff up briefly and impair someone's breathing, causing a quick panicky cough from the unfortunate soldier.

Most had their half blanket and groundsheet wrapped around them for protection, but their knees were often exposed as their shorts, inadequate as they were for jungle fighting, were completely inappropriate for mountain heights.

As the fire danced, the men's faces were eerily illuminated. The haze of heat, smoke and mist created a 'Danse Macabre' effect. Who could know the men's thoughts—the oncoming battle, home, loved ones—the faces didn't give much away.

As he sang, Stan's eyes settled on Butch, who was characteristically joking with the man next to him. The hairs prickled on the back of Stan's neck as he had a sudden inexplicable sensation that he was about to lose his beloved brother. As the premonition grew, his strong voice faltered for a second and Butch looked up and caught his eye.

The moment passed.

That evening Brigadier Potts received a message that the fighting at Isurava up ahead was escalating, so at first light he left with a small reconnaissance party. He took with him some of his headquarters staff, including Stan, the intention being to forge ahead to Myola where he believed rations and ammunition for the coming action were waiting for him. He was hoping to resupply his forces quickly there and then continue on to Isurava to relieve the embattled 39th Battalion.

Myola was set between two old crater lakes formed eons ago. The empty lakes had just been 'discovered' by Lieutenant Bert Kienzle—the larger of the two, in fact, on the same day as Potts's arrival.

Kienzle was one of the few Europeans to have crossed the track before the war. He went in search of gold, found none, and instead developed a thriving plantation at Kokoda on the Yodda River. He built the airstrip there and knew the local area and people intimately. He was commissioned, like P. J. McDonald, into ANGAU as a lieutenant, and was responsible for organising and maintaining the carrying of supplies and wounded along the track. He eventually commandeered upwards of 1000 locals to achieve this onerous task and, because of his skills and the strength and caring nature of the native people, many a soldier's life was saved by the Fuzzy Wuzzy Angels, as they were fondly dubbed.

The dry lakes were the craters of ancient volcanoes and were covered with reeds. The ground underfoot was sodden but generally flat. Because of the 2000-metre altitude, the creeks flowing through the area were filled with icy water. The few huts set up next to the lakes contained three officers—a supply officer, an ordnance officer and Kienzle.

When Potts arrived, he was devastated to find that the

supply officer only had five days' supply—not enough for an offensive for his two battalions following behind. The Japanese bombing mission that the troops had heard on their first day's walk had effectively wiped out most of the supply aircraft on the tarmac at Port Moresby. In spite of this, the officers there had managed to send some supplies ahead by the remaining aircraft. But, in what was one of the great mysteries of the war in New Guinea, the rations and ammunition never turned up. They were lost somewhere between Port Moresby and Myola.

Potts frantically drafted a message to High Command at Port Moresby urgently requesting more supplies. He then continued his journey, aiming to reach Templeton's Crossing before dusk.

Stan remained behind at Myola and, later that afternoon, greeted the rest of the battalion as they marched in. The news that they would have to wait there for a few days for supplies to be delivered was upsetting to the impatient men. However, they duly made camp; then Stan, with Colonel Key and 'I' Section, moved ahead to Alola.

As a result of Potts's message, a single C-47 'biscuit bomber' appeared the next day and started dropping food and ammunition to the frustrated troops. As the plane swooped inside the crater the pilot, displaying great daring, lined up over a prearranged target area. At about 120 metres a 'bombardier', with similar dash, resolutely pushed the supplies out of the open cargo door.

This method of supply was repeated many times during the campaign, but there was only about a 50 per cent retrieval rate overall. The packages were often lost in the surrounding bush or jungle, or damaged if they landed on hard ground.

These derring-do exploits at least kept the troops entertained as their supplies slowly grew over the next few days. As well, Moresby dispatched 300 native carriers, hopefully to reach Myola as soon as possible. It was a gruelling eight-day journey for them, carrying ammunition, blankets, food rations and medical supplies, plus their own food, but this was the only other feasible way to remedy a potentially desperate situation.

Finally, at dawn on 25 August, fully supplied and ready to go, C Company left Myola and started off to Isurava, intending to bivouac overnight at Templeton's Crossing. Because of the supply position, it was only possible to send forward one company at a time—B, D and A followed later.

Once again the men's bodies were put into automatic drive as they climbed to 2250 metres—the highest point on the Kokoda Track. The swirling mists gave rise to intriguing moss forests—beautiful, green and subdued. Lichen and orchids proliferated, punctuating the emerald ambience. A complete canopy overhead created the impression of almost floating through a silent, dark green tunnel. Footsteps were soft and almost unheard. The vegetation had changed from jungle to rainforest with mosses, fungi and huge pandanus palms dominating.

With the forest came more rain and then mud, exposing slimy, jagged tree roots crossing the track. These malicious tentacles tripped up the men, stimulating the victims to surpass the standard and lustre of wit and language reached earlier.

Since they were marching at about 900 metres, they were alerted to look for a pass in the mountains which higher echelon officers had called The Gap. The officers expected it to be a narrow pass between unscaleable cliffs, where a small band of men could hold off an army—it was likened to the Pass at Thermopylae in Ancient Greece. High Command had formed the idea that a stand could be made here.

The Professor enlightened Seven Section: 'About 2500 years ago,' he said, 'Greece was being attacked by literally thousands of Persians. Just 300 Spartan soldiers held the Pass at Thermopylae, preventing the enemy from taking Greece.

'The Spartans all died,' he added laconically.

Bruce and Alan looked at each other, then at the thick jungle. 'I can't see much of a gap here—I've got a funny idea we'll be fighting in that stuff,' Alan said, pointing towards the thick, impenetrable jungle with his Tommy gun.

In fact The Gap turned out to be eleven kilometres wide and merely a depression on the summit, dropping to 2000 metres—a position by which pilots navigated their planes on the way over the Owen Stanleys. When the notion of holding The Gap with a small band of men and explosives arose, none of the brass had actually been along the Kokoda Track, thus giving rise to a myth.

The track was starting to slope down now, and as they descended, in the silence of the moss-covered track, they could faintly hear a creek rushing through the valley far below. As the ground plunged more steeply, they clutched at overhead vines and branches to slow their descent. The rush of the creek turned into a roar as they fought closer to it, battling deep mud holes now filled with putrid slush.

This was Eora Creek and the place was known as Templeton's Crossing.

TWO OTHER EVENTS WERE HAPPENING THAT day that were to have a great impact on the men and their mission.

At that very moment, a Japanese force was sailing off the coast of New Guinea, planning, at 2230 hours that night, to sail into Milne Bay and to come ashore and attack. This action was to deny Potts the immediate use of his reserve 2/27th, still at Port Moresby, as they were also in reserve for the expected Milne Bay invasion.

Secondly, by the end of this day, the Japanese were working out final plans to launch their offensive against Isurava. Major General Tomitaro Horii was the commander and he was flushed with the success of victory after victory, including Guam, Rabaul and Salamaua. He now had about 13 000 efficient, aggressive and confident soldiers under his command, some of whom had fought in Malaya and China as well. They were ready to overrun the weary 39th Battalion, present strength 300, who stood between them and Port Moresby. Horii was a colourful, dedicated strategist who led from the front, and was often seen riding a beautiful white horse, even high in the ranges. Physically he was short in stature and somewhat thickened—almost pudgy. He wore glasses, but his temperament marked him as a worthy opponent for Brigadier Potts.

This picture was about to change, however. This same day, Potts and his forward party, followed by Colonel Key and Stan, arrived at Alola, which was only about an hour's walk from Isurava.

The 39th had been holding their ground at Isurava now for ten days and had set up positions in a thin line around the perimeter of the village, which was situated on the side of a hill. The positions covered the high ground on the left, the track in the middle which ran along the side of the mountain, and the terrain down to the creek on the right.

The officers had set up a standing patrol three-quarters of an hour forward of Isurava and were aware of the gradual buildup of Japanese troops. Behind the lines was a three-man telephone post which relayed news to battalion headquarters further back and to another post just up the track from Isurava.

The situation was tense, if not desperate.

A young sergeant, Bill Guest, moved past the telephone post just outside Isurava while returning to his position. Guest had joined at seventeen and now, at 21, he was the old man of his platoon. His once fit body was emaciated from five weeks of hard fighting and from lack of food and sleep. Like the rest of his depleted battalion, he had been expecting to be overrun for some time.

The phone rang. The post was manned by his friend, Barry Harper, also a sergeant. Harper acknowledged Guest as he was passing, then answered the phone. His voice suddenly rose with excitement. He put the phone down and shakingly wrote out the message.

'Bill, I've got some great news,' Harper called. 'The 2/14th have been on the road for over a week and they should be here tomorrow.'

Guest stopped. 'Nah, it couldn't happen,' he said disbelievingly. 'We're gone, aren't we?'

'It's true, mate—they're at Templeton's now, and moving off first thing tomorrow.'

'You bloody beauty! The cavalry are coming!' Guest raced off to relay the message to the others.

Back at Templeton's Crossing the arriving 2/14th were finding it to be a thoroughly depressing place. It was permanently wet and everything was damp and covered with fungus. The roaring creek had large boulders the size of locomotives in it, where the water spumed and sprayed, drenching everything around it and throwing up a continual background bellow. The high mountains enclosing the valley starved it of light and added to the overall effect of cold and gloom. The men endured another wet and miserable night's sleep there.

They were now on the eastern side of the Owen Stanleys and getting near their target. From there, the Eora Creek valley opened into the larger Yodda valley and fell 1500 metres to where Kokoda nestled at the base of the ranges next to the Yodda River. All that stood between them and their goal of Kokoda now was Alola, Isurava, Deniki . . . and the enemy.

The men were glad to get going next morning, continuing their trudge for three hours. During this time they were treated to the slashing impact of a fierce tropical thunderstorm. As the moist air flowed in from the coast, it collided with the mountains and was forced upwards, condensing into massive thunderheads forming violent wind gusts.

The men instinctively ducked as lightning sliced through the wet skies, accompanied by crashes of deep-throated thunder. The wind blew in hurricane force, whipping over the treetops, shrieking through craggy ridges and forcing the rain before it. The driving rain bit into their faces and soaked them yet again as fire and water mixed in a violent concoction over the Kokoda Track.

As they climbed out of the valley, the storm waned and suddenly and unexpectedly gave way to morning sunlight—such was the versatility of the elements and the capriciousness of the terrain. To their astonishment, they found they had left the jungle and were now in primitively developed country and only half an hour's march from Alola.

Stan had again moved ahead with Colonel Key, to Alola. He was being based there with Brigadier Potts, who had taken over from the commander of Maroubra Force, Brigadier Porter, and had set up Maroubra Force Headquarters. Porter and the Intelligence Section had constructed a sand-terrain model of the area showing the topography, including valleys, peaks and tracks from Myola to the coast.

As the troops came through, Stan informed each platoon in turn of the lie of the land and the tactics that the Japanese might use. Soon Lieutenant Bill Cox and 9 Platoon gathered around the table. Referring to the model, Stan started his account.

'Behind Isurava and down the hill is Deniki, and then Kokoda, our goal. To the right is the long way to Kokoda, through Missima and Abuari. These two villages are being held by the 53rd Militia Battalion and they'll probably be relieved by the 2/16th Battalion coming up behind us. The Japanese are entrenched forward of Isurava and also in the valley between Isurava and Abuari on the right. Our forward scouts are out looking for them now.

'The Japs' normal tactics are direct confrontation followed quickly by wide flanking movements which can act as deadly pincers. In case you get overrun, take a good look at the model and remember your way home. At this stage we think they have the advantage of about two to one, but I'm sure we can hold. Anyway, good luck!'

With these sobering thoughts, the platoons moved out and enjoyed a heated meal supplied for them. They then moved off into the jungle again for the half-hour walk to Isurava. On the right of the track, the mountain dropped sharply to a river valley and then rose sharply again to the other track going to Missima and Abuari.

The river in the valley between the ridges flowed out to the Yodda valley and Kokoda, less than half a day's walk away.

As they moved closer to the battlefield, they could faintly hear gunfire echoing through the trees. Their immediate reaction was one of excitement mixed with a feeling of dread. They could make out the sharp crack of single rifle shots set against the occasional staccato of machine-gun fire. They could hear the heavier .303s duelling with the lighter-sounding Japanese .256s and knew they were close.

Suddenly a shell from a Japanese mountain gun exploded not far from them, sending reverberations along the ground and quivering the trees around them. Each man sucked in a quick, deep breath, his rifle at the ready. In a few moments the jungle was quiet again. Lieutenant Cox slowly stood upright and signalled to his platoon to move forward.

'Shit,' whispered Alan, 'what do you think that was—a mortar?'

'I don't know,' said Bruce, 'but I just about let it all go!' He recalled once more the old Digger at the Goodnight pub.

9

Isurava

BEHIND THE 39TH BATTALION'S MAIN DEFENCE perimeter, Bill Guest was resting with five of his mates. They were sheltering in a weapon pit covered by a groundsheet and were generally in a poor state. They had been elated at yesterday's news that reinforcements were on the way to Isurava, but it didn't take away from the seriousness of their immediate situation. Most of them were sick with malaria, dysentery or just plain exhaustion. Their eyes were sunken and hollow and their waxen skin hung around their faces under unkempt beards. Their clothes had degenerated to filthy, ragged pieces of cloth—neither they nor their garments had had a wash for as long as eight weeks. Their boots had rotted through, some held together by vines, the gaping holes exposing raw, often bleeding, flesh. They were low on food and what little they had was boring and not always nutritious. Fresh food and vegetables were simply not available and some of the men were developing bowel symptoms.

Remarkably, morale was still high.

Guest stretched and said to the others: 'I think I'll go down and fill the water bottles.' He collected the six containers and went down to the creek nearby. The banks were very steep, and in his weakened situation he half fell, half slid down to the running water. He managed to fill one bottle and then took a quick look around for any Japanese patrols that may have been trying to flank the main force.

Immediately, he froze. An unfamiliar figure was peering down at him. The man was tall, bronzed and wearing greens and a steel helmet. He had obviously sensed that Guest was no threat and had emerged from his cover, standing with a Tommy gun under his right arm and a grenade in his left hand.

Guest was transfixed. Finally he spluttered: 'Who the hell are you? Don't throw!'

The man, realising that this sad apparition was an Australian, called back: 'I'm the forward scout of the 2/14th.'

Guest yelled out: 'You bloody beaut! Come on over.' There were three other soldiers with the scout and they allowed Guest to lead them back to company headquarters.

Not far behind, the leading company of the 2/14th passed through Guest's area as they made their way to the front. A few of them stopped at his weapon pit, and one said: 'Y'know, Tom Blamey told us that if we capture Kokoda within fourteen days we can go back to Australia on leave.'

Guest laughed a little cynically. He thought to himself, this poor bastard doesn't know what he's up against. But the men from the 2/14th asked about the type of enemy they'd be fighting and wanted advice on jungle action. Guest and his mates told them as much as they could and gave them a quick rundown on how the 39th had got into such a desperate condition.

During that evening, Wednesday 26 August, and over the next day, the thin perimeter line was thickened as the 2/14th Battalion took over the positions of the weary 39th. The 39th largely went into reserve at the rear of battalion headquarters.

Butch's 10 Platoon went up to the vital high ground on the left and settled in. The rest of B Company, 11 and 12 Platoons, occupied an area to the left of the track known as the Cane Field and so were in the 'hot spot' for enemy activity. Bruce and Alan's 9 Platoon was also assigned to an area to the left of the track. By nightfall on the 27th, all companies were in position. Some twelve rifle platoons formed a solid circle around Isurava as they prepared their defences for what they knew would soon be a large-scale offensive by the enemy.

Even though they were aware that General Horii was

113

bringing up reinforcements, they didn't realise the magnitude of his resources. The men at Isurava were in fact outnumbered six to one, as Horii had brought up as many as 6000 infantry and engineer troops—soldiers who expected to easily add to their earlier string of victories, annihilate the Australians and quickly march into Port Moresby.

The 26th and 27th of August had seen sporadic fighting at Isurava when several clashes of patrols occurred. Horii's artillery bombardment increased on the 27th and harassment continued throughout the night. This was a new experience for the men of the 2/14th as they peered out through the inky gloom. With the rain playing tricks with sound and movement, they become acutely aware of their vulnerability as they had no trenching tools with which to prepare any shelter. Covered mainly by groundsheets, they spent an apprehensive, miserable night; they had been warned of the enemy's skill in jungle patrolling. In fact, one of the men in 15 Platoon was stabbed in the face while on duty and was lucky to escape with his life. Another was bayoneted in the arm without seeing his assailant.

All through the night the enemy used other unsettling tactics which further unnerved the men and kept them awake. The Japanese yabbered at top pitch, banged meal tins together and yelled out comments in broken English, adding to the confusion and unreality of the moment.

The 27th happened to be Stan's 30th birthday, but it almost passed before he realised it. He would have liked to move forward for a few moments to have a chat with Butch, but he knew it was just not possible.

FRIDAY, 28 AUGUST OPENED WITH A tremendous crash, shocking the apprehensive Australians into life as Horii released the full force of his offensive. As dawn filtered through the canopy, mountain guns and mortar shells shattered the morning stillness. The frightening effects of the explosions were amplified by the closeness of the jungle. Shrapnel erupted and whistled like a knife as it cut through trees and spun to the ground below. Heavy machine-guns opened up, cutting a withering path as their shells flattened the vegetation.

Then the hardened Japanese troops teemed out of the jungle,

supported by a wild, screaming cacophony from the rest of their forces behind the green screen. This was the first time the men of the 2/14th had seen the enemy and they'd expected to be confronted by the popular caricature of the Japanese—little yellow men with slanted eyes and wearing spectacles. To their astonishment, these were handpicked warriors, most of them over 1.8 metres tall, and trained for years in the art of jungle warfare. They attacked on three sides in waves of about a hundred, determined to give no quarter.

But it was no pushover for them this time. Everywhere, they were met and held by strong resolve and shattering fire, as the Australians matched them physically and emotionally. They raced into an inferno of Bren and Tommy gun fire, a fusillade of rifle shots and grenade blasts, and a wall of green and khaki uniforms.

Occasionally, by sheer force of numbers, some made it to the Australian lines, where they were greeted with frantic hand-to-hand combat. The dark, mouldy leaves of the jungle floor glistened with blood as men attacked with bayonets or grappled for an advantage, fists flailing and hammering. They rolled and faltered and died as the morning sun glinted and flashed on steel.

The 11 Platoon in the Cane Field took a great deal of this attack, and very soon their commander and many of his men lay killed or wounded. Butch's friend, Lieutenant Mokka Treacy, took over command of the platoon early that afternoon and helped them to repulse several more attacks.

As the day grew longer, Butch's 10 Platoon relieved Mokka's platoon at this key position. The sugar cane patch was about the size of a normal street block, so Butch placed his men in sectional positions around it. The cane was about 1.5 metres high and the field was hot, humid and claustrophobic. George Woodward, a Tommy-gunner, and a stretcher-bearer, Lindsay Elphinstone, went to the right of the platoon, behind a log, as cover. Their position afforded a reasonably clear view 30 or 40 metres up the track through the surrounding jungle, where they could see the Japanese flitting about. From here, the platoon kept up constant fire.

The Japanese probed several points around the perimeter, trying to outflank the besieged men, but the Australians' resistance held. Time and again, successive attacks threatened to overrun the defenders as the battle continued. The enemy would melt out of the jungle, then, forming lines and yelling 'banzai', make a fanatical burst as they threw their lives away against controlled gunfire, most of them not making the Australians' territory. At one stage they tried to camouflage their attack by hiding behind billowing smoke pouring out from pyrotechnic candles. The ghostly effect was disturbing for a while, but as their forms appeared through the haze they were quickly cut down.

As night fell and the firing ebbed, the two commanders took stock of their situation. Their armies had each received a mauling but General Horii clearly was frustrated, as he had not expected this sort of resistance. He had watched the battle impatiently from a vantage point about a kilometre north of Isurava, and now realised that the weakened 39th Battalion had been reinforced by fresh and determined troops who could match his in tenacity. Not willing to lose the momentum of his offensive, he brought up his two reserve units to complement his five in-line battalions. This would allow him to make an intensive, all out attack, hopefully to overthrow the Australians in a decisive confrontation.

Brigadier Potts had no reason to be overjoyed either. He now realised he was facing an enemy far greater in numbers and resources than Military Intelligence had previously reckoned. His request for his reserve 2/27th Battalion at Port Moresby still hadn't been authorised, and the battle was being dictated by the enemy on a ground not of Potts's own choosing. However, there was some consolation in appreciating the spirit of the troops under his command. They had met the 'invincible' Japanese in head-on confrontation and remained in some control of the situation. They estimated they had killed up to 350 of the enemy and wounded perhaps as many as 1000 of them, while they themselves had sustained less than a handful killed and about 30 wounded.

The men settled down for the night, buoyed with confidence, but keeping watch in the darkness.

At first light it began again. Their fitful sleep was shattered by the bombardment as mortars, mountain guns and hand grenades once more thundered in the air.

As the firing grew thicker, a message came through for Lieutenant Cox to take 9 Platoon further forward to reinforce 13 Platoon, which was under heavy attack. Moving forward to reconnoitre the area, Cox received a fatal wound. The platoon sergeant with him, Jock Lochhead, then went back to organise the move. At this stage the Professor, who had had to stay a day late at Myola, was reporting back to the platoon and met Lochhead beside the track. As they exchanged greetings, a mortar shell exploded near them and threw them both violently to the ground. As the Professor slowly regained his senses and crawled to his feet, he realised that the sergeant was seriously wounded, with a gaping hole in his head from a mortar fragment.

He got Lochhead to his feet and supported him back to the RAP a few hundred metres behind the lines, where he lay him on a stretcher. The orderly examined Lochhead, then bound his head wound and gave a discreet sign to the Professor that it didn't look good. Fighting to stay conscious, the sergeant whispered to the Professor: 'Tell Teddy he's now in charge. I'm not going to be much help.' He then lapsed into a coma. As the Professor made his way back to the platoon, he passed Lieutenant Cox's body lying beside the track.

Across the battalion area, as leaders were hit, the position had become confusing. It was difficult to determine responsibilities for sections, platoons and even companies. The jungle closeness and the battle noise added to the uncertainty, as men were unable to hear orders, see signals or even have contact with their section leaders. The green screen had levelled the battle into a close-fighting, personal war.

WHEN THE PROFESSOR RELAYED THE MESSAGE to him, Teddy Bear had no hesitation in forming a plan as to what was needed. In fact, this type of situation was to be repeated many times over the whole battalion as the day wore on. As key officers and leaders were wounded or killed, men of lower rank quickly and ably filled their shoes. Men of certain character, with their years of training, confidently assumed a leadership role and easily led from the front.

Teddy had already realised that, unless someone took charge, his platoon would slowly be picked off one by one and any advantage they may have held would be lost. He ordered all the remaining able men of the platoon to meet him at a central point. At this stage there were only about fifteen men left, including some from other platoons who had wandered into the area.

He told them: 'You all know the situation. Coxie and Jock Lochhead have been taken out. The sarge left me in charge. My plan is simple and direct. First, go and collect as much ammo as possible and stockpile it here, so that we have a ready supply of hand grenades and bullets. Then I want you all to assemble back at this spot on the track in fifteen minutes. We're going to spread out along the track, then advance and create as much damage as we can.'

From the dead and wounded, the men salvaged Bren gun and Tommy gun magazines, .303 clips and as many grenades as they could carry. They loaded their weapons and stuffed grenades into their pouches, then stockpiled the rest.

As they moved into an attacking position on the track, Alan clicked a full magazine into place on his Tommy gun, while Bruce directed a bullet into the breech of his .303. They briefly caught each other's eye and gave a dry smile. There was nothing to say—they were professionals and this was what they were trained for. Alan was on Bruce's right, and Teddy moved up to Bruce's left. Jarmbe fell in on Teddy's left, with Ted Jobe next to him. Hi-Ho Silver and the Professor joined in, as did the Wilson brothers. With several others holding a spot, the line extended some 50 metres across.

Alan glanced at Jarmbe who was waiting, sitting on a fallen log, running his thumb and forefinger up and down the sharpened blade of his bayonet. He flashed a toothy grin back, accompanied by a wink.

'Hey, Jarmbe,' Alan called. 'I want you to keep smiling. It's dark in the jungle, and I don't want to lose you.' The chiacking lightened the moment as Jarmbe bared his ivory teeth in a smiling chocolate face.

Just as they were lining up in their final positions, the Bren-gunner approached Teddy. His voice was quivering, his lips and hands trembling. 'Teddy, my gun won't work.' His hands were fumbling with the reload bolt. 'I don't think I can go.' The fear was palpable. Teddy took the Bren, examined it, released the safety catch and pulled the trigger. The man paled as the gun exploded into life. Realising the extent of the man's panic, Teddy said: 'Never mind, mate, I'll use this. You fall in behind and follow us up.'

Teddy told them that no man was to fire until he gave the order, and then called: 'Now, move!'

At that same instant, the Japanese decided on a break-through. Teddy could hear them crashing through the undergrowth towards Seven Section's line. There appeared to be about 50 in this wave. He gave the order to fire when they were 30 metres away.

'Now! Make every shot count!' The jungle erupted as never before—all hell broke loose. Every weapon in the confined area loosed its payload as machine-guns and rifles from both sides filled the air with screaming bullets. Everywhere men cursed, shouted or screamed as the spinning lead found its mark. My God, thought Teddy, no one is going to live through this. Bullets whistled past him, crashing into trees, ripping under-growth apart and slashing everything to pieces in the immediate vicinity. As bullets ricocheted off trees and rocks, they emitted a terrible whining sound as they spun and funnelled dangerously out of control, adding to the terror of the firepower. Teddy gripped the handle of his Bren and, firing from the hip, slowly moved to the apex of the Australians' line.

The enemy swarmed towards the thin line, cursing, yelling and firing, only to fall to the ground, their threats choking on the blood that gurgled through great gashes in their lungs as Teddy's bullets rammed home. They continued to drop under the Bren gun's assault—four, five, six of them, clutching at their stomachs or chest as they fell.

Meanwhile, to his right, Bruce was firing and reloading his .303 as fast as he could. He was an excellent shot and didn't waste any bullets. The clinking shells ripped out from the ejection chamber as he dropped one after the other of the enemy.

A few metres further to the right Alan was firing his Tommy gun from the hip at anything that moved. Two Japanese suddenly materialised from behind a clump of palms, and charged towards him. He fired a burst from his gun through

119

one man's chest and saw the blood spurt on his clothes and run from his mouth as the man fell in a limp heap.

The other man continued over towards the Professor who, for an instant, had thought of the battle of Krythia at Gallipoli and how, as the Australians moved forward over open ground, the air had been so thick with bullets that after the battle some were found welded together, having collided in midair. Now his eye caught the movement of the charging Japanese.

Physically exhausted from his morning's exertions and a little stupefied by the pounding crescendo of the gunfire, he reacted almost too late. As the enemy lunged, the tip of the bayonet sliced through the air centimetres from the Professor's face and tore off his shoulder webbing. Shocked into action, he automatically brought his rifle butt up to protect himself. The next bayonet thrust struck the wooden stock of the butt and the blade slid along it, jamming momentarily under the depressed bolt of the Professor's .303. In the same instant, the Professor kicked the man hard in the shins, quickly gaining the advantage. As the Japanese screamed in agony, the two men were close enough for the Professor to smell the man's stale breath and his sweat-stained clothing.

The Professor wrenched his rifle free, spinning the enemy's rifle completely out of reach. This had the effect of exposing the man's throat and chest and in that eternity of a second the Japanese realised his vulnerability and the inevitability of the outcome. He was helpless. The Professor, seizing the advantage, was preparing to thrust his bayonet home when he caught sight of his assailant's coppery face. The helpless eyes stared back at him and the Professor knew that he would see those eyes forever.

He finished the stroke off, sickening as he felt the metal crunch through the man's sternum and ribs. As the bayonet sliced into the lungs, air gurgled and blood spurted freely from the wound. The man dropped instantly to the ground without a sound, taking the Professor's rifle with him. The Professor put his foot on the man's chest to release the weapon and was beginning to shake from exhaustion and relief when he noticed another Japanese soldier racing towards him. A blast from Alan's Tommy gun dropped the charging man several metres from the Professor.

Meanwhile, Teddy was moving ahead with his Bren gun, still firing incessantly. He would empty the magazine, throw it into the bush, then replace it with a full one. Now he suddenly caught sight of blood on his shirt. Hell, he thought, I've been hit. But where? His chest seemed alright; he could breathe. He panicked a little, but eventually found he'd suffered a shrapnel wound to his nose. Amazed that he hadn't felt any pain, he continued his crusade, his machine-gun spurting at the nonstop wave of Japanese. Seven, eight, nine, ten men fell as the murderous bullets found their targets.

After half an hour of this concentrated fighting, the barrel of his Bren started to retain so much heat that he could barely hold it, so Teddy placed its two legs in the 'carry' position, parallel to the barrel. As they were still relatively cool, he held these to steady the barrel and went on fighting. The killing field by now was almost completely denuded of vegetation and cover. Tree stumps were cut off and vines were lying on the jungle floor. The bark was splintered off larger trees and palm fronds, and the canopy no longer cut out the sun.

Suddenly Teddy realised he could no longer hold the gun, as his left hand would not work. He found that a bullet had ripped through the back of his hand, which was bleeding freely. He couldn't make a fist or move the fingers. Damn!, he thought—it was useless! He put his arm inside his shirt front to support it and went on firing the gun one-handed.

Tiring now, he could still fire accurately enough, although with a lot more effort—twelve, thirteen of the enemy fell. At this stage he and the others were getting low on ammunition, so he quickly detailed two men to race back to their supply dump and bring up some magazines for him and for Alan's Tommy gun. He shoved the new magazines into his haversack, loaded one into his Bren and had gone only a few steps when he realised his right leg wasn't working properly. He noticed blood pouring from his left calf muscle and seeping through the gaiter. Two bullets had penetrated it. As he could still bear weight on the leg he continued to advance, dragging the leg behind, using it as a support.

Slowly but steadily the men saw that their drive forward was telling on the enemy and making considerable ground. Teddy kept firing, producing more casualties. Finally he was staggering and realised he could go no further, but it was enough. The enemy had been badly mauled and now retreated back into the green, as quickly as they had appeared.

With the lull in the fighting, Bruce and Alan gathered around Teddy and examined his wounds. Alan took out one of his field dressings and bound the damaged hand. 'I reckon you've had enough of this blue, Teddy. You'd better go back to the RAP and see the Doc.' The other wounded men were being tended to and were also making their way back, taking advantage of the break in hostilities.

Grimacing in pain and supporting himself on Bruce's shoulder, Teddy said: 'Yeah, I think you're right. I'll go back for a spell.' He turned and said to Bruce: 'I reckon they're only having a breather—they'll be back for sure. Take my Bren. It's pretty hot, but keep firing and keep moving.'

Bruce took the Bren gun, checked it over briefly, put in a new magazine and grabbed several from the stockpile.

Teddy slowly limped back from the battlefield, utterly exhausted and beginning to feel pain, as his injuries were now starting to become inflamed and to swell. He slowly made his way back a few hundred metres to the Regimental Aid Post and Dr Duffy.

AS TEDDY MOVED BACK, HE WAS passed by Sergeant Bob Thompson from Signals Platoon. Company headquarters had informed Thompson of the furious fighting on the right flank where 9 Platoon was. He was told there was a danger of a breakthrough and that battalion headquarters was under threat itself, so he and a party from his platoon were dispatched to help reinforce this vital area.

After assessing the situation, Thompson and his men acknowledged Bruce and Alan, then joined the recovering line. As the senior ranking soldier, Thompson decided he should go forward to reconnoitre the area where the Japanese had retreated, and he parted a bush in order to move ahead. But a Japanese soldier had started to do the same thing from the other side of the bush. Thompson found himself staring eye to eye at the man less than a metre away. It was the first Japanese he had actually seen, and he recoiled in fright. The soldier also registered alarm, then retreated like a gazelle back to his own lines.

The fleeing man was followed by a grenade from one of the Australians, the action being rewarded with screams from the point of the explosion. This seemed to have the effect of heralding the next wave of Japanese attacks. That instant, they surged out of the jungle into the Australians' positions.

Bruce didn't hesitate. He swung his Bren gun around towards the oncoming warriors, aimed it from the hip and raced towards the enemy. Without a second thought, he yelled: 'Follow me! We can turn them back!'

Once again gunfire filled the surrounding jungle as the line immediately moved forward in support. The thump of grenades smashed against Bruce's eardrums, mixing with the short snap of rifles, the deep-throated chatter of the Tommy gun and the sharp bursts of his own Bren gun.

Out of the corner of his eye, Bruce noticed one of his own men fall out of the line and drop to his knees as a line of bullets crashed through his thighs. Bruce's eyes narrowed, as if he was shielding himself from a glaring light. His senses were sharpened and focused, and his lean forearm muscles stood out like cords as he fired his gun.

He was now about two metres in front of the line, leading the way. His helmet was characteristically tilted on the back of his head, displaying his full forehead, and he felt in complete control of the immediate situation. He was aware of the fact that he was calm, and it felt sweet. It was as if everybody else was moving in slow motion except for him. He realised he had ample time to assess the position, to aim and then direct his fire. He chose his targets and watched the effect of his murderous columns of fire as one by one the bullets found their mark.

Behind Bruce the men were inspired by his actions and increased their efforts. Alan was vicious as he expended one magazine after another—firing the 50 bullets into the midst of the charging Japanese, flinging the spent magazine into the bushes, then clipping on another. Nobody was counting now as wave after wave come surging out of the jungle towards them, only to be met and stopped by a solid wall of fire.

Bullets flew past Alan as a Japanese soldier suddenly stood

only ten metres from him, firing an automatic weapon in an arc. There was a thud as one landed on the butt of his Tommy gun, jarring it momentarily in his hand. He felt another bullet zip through the cover of his money belt on his left side and expected to see blood come. Recovering from the shock quickly, he levelled and fired his own gun directly at the soldier, grouping the fire at the man's chest, completely shattering him and his weapon.

As the fractured rifle fell next to the man's body, Alan could see the sixteen-petalled chrysanthemum engraved on its butt. It was proof that the weapon was a personal gift from the Emperor to the soldier.

Jarmbe, Hi-Ho, the Professor and the rest of the line, standing a few metres from the green wall of enemy troops, were firing incessantly and slowly forcing the Japanese back into their jungle lines, over the bodies of their dead comrades.

A strong smell of cordite rested in the air, the fumes mingling in Bruce's nostrils with the odour of sweat, jungle mould and the oily heat from his Bren gun. He could see that their fighting advance was making a clear difference. 'We've got 'em on the run! Keep at 'em!' he shouted. Still leading by example, and oblivious to the spinning bullets flying around him, he emptied another magazine into the receding enemy.

One last disciplined effort of determined fire from this unique battle line finally forced the remaining enemy to give up their attempted breakthrough. The Japanese retreated further and then melted into the jungle, leaving behind many casualties.

As they did so, one soldier, unnoticed by the exhausted Australians and intent on a last punch at them, climbed a four-metre-high rock bordering the edge of the battleground. The experienced Japanese troops were not used to defeat and were now stinging from the humiliating experience they'd just been put through by Bruce and the others.

Alan was a few paces behind Bruce, who was standing and looking at the destruction. Alan heard a single shot. He looked up, noticing the Japanese soldier lying in position on top of the rock, as the echoes of the sound he would hear for ever reverberated like cannon fire.

Bruce gave a muffled gasp and dropped straight to the ground. Alan watched him fall with disbelieving eyes. He yelled

'No!' through gritted teeth, then turned towards the rock. 'You rotten bastard!' he screamed. Instantly he raised his Tommy gun and swept a burst towards the sniper. He saw the bullets raced up the rock, chipping pockmarks into it and creating clouds of dust. He saw the man fall and dearly hoped the bullets had found their mark. There was no more movement and no more noise, but he knew he would never be sure that he had nailed the assassin. His immediate priority now was with Bruce, whose body was completely limp. A small, red-tinged hole showed in Bruce's shirt where the bullet had entered his chest over the heart.

Alan intuitively knew the worst, but had never felt so strong as he carried his mate from the battleground back to the RAP. It was a gruelling few hundred metres walk through the boggy jungle track, yet he didn't falter. He kept searching Bruce's face and body for some sign of life, muttering to himself as much as to Bruce: 'She'll be OK, mate—we'll get you to the Doc. Hang on!'

The Regimental Aid Post was sited behind battalion head-quarters just beside the track. It was bordered by a large rock and some clumps of trees stretching back into the jungle. A large space about the size of a house block had been cleared, and groundsheets and anti-gas capes acted as both ground cover and top cover. Much of it was open to the skies; a quagmire of mud lay among the stretchers and other equipment. As far as possible, the field dressings, wrappings, drugs and medicines were kept under groundsheets, but this was not always feasible, particularly when the battle casualties started to pour in during darkness and rain.

Dr Duffy had a staff of seven medical orderlies who worked tirelessly and devotedly. At this stage they were under pressure, as the incoming casualties from the morning battle around the perimeter were starting to mount up.

Duffy had just left the RAP for a quick visit to the battle area when he encountered Alan not far from battalion head-quarters. Alan lay Bruce down beside the track as the doctor checked the inert body for vital signs. He searched for a pulse and found none. Then he drew back Bruce's eyelids and noted that the eyes didn't react to light. Duffy looked up. 'I'm sorry,

Alan, your mate's dead.' Alan dimly heard him add: 'He'll be alright here.'

Duffy took the bottom half of Bruce Kingsbury's dogtags and placed them in his haversack with the others.

As if in a dream, Alan remembered the pact he had made with Bruce back in the Middle East. He mechanically pocketed several of Bruce's personal belongings for his family, then slowly worked the signet ring off his limp finger. Bruce had asked him to return it to Leila if anything should happen to him. He then moved off in a daze.

He was in a deep state of shock as he slowly moved back to the platoon's position. His brain was still addled from the bombardment and violence of the morning and his ears were still ringing. Suddenly he felt very exhausted, physically and emotionally.

A terrible loneliness gripped him. He stopped at the side of the track and crouched on a nearby log. Supporting his head in his hands, he could not keep the emotions suppressed any longer and began to sob uncontrollably and unashamedly.

SLOWLY ALAN BECAME AWARE OF HIS surroundings again, and conscious of the sound of gunfire building up on both sides. He realised the Japanese were, characteristically, trying to out-flank them after the failed frontal assault this morning on his platoon. The aggravated hostilities were coming from the area of 10, 11 and 12 Platoons on the right. At the same time he could hear concentrated gunfire further over to the left.

Butch's 10 Platoon were still holding the vital Cane Field with the men guarding a section of jungle seemingly alive with enemy. All that day, like the rest of the battalion, they had weathered frontal attack after frontal attack, often repulsing as many as a full company of attacking Japanese.

George Woodward, still in his position where Butch had placed him the day before, was making the most of his clear view of the enemy flitting across the track in front of him from left to right. They were, in fact, making their way over to the area in front of 12 Platoon, preparing for an assault later that day. Woodward, a Tommy-gunner, with Lenny Meade, the Bren-gunner in the section, set up a strong crossfire along the track and its sides. They poured magazine after magazine into the area, accounting for a great number of enemy casualties. In all, that day, the platoon repulsed eleven frontal attacks on their section—causing a great demand for ammunition.

Butch came around every hour or so, either bringing ammunition or checking on the positions and rearranging his men if necessary. He carried a Tommy gun; often he would be caught by the enemy while moving around the perimeter and have to fight his way clear. He would check on the wounded, giving them an encouraging or humorous word as he saw them transported or assisted back to the RAP.

As the long day wore on, the Japanese, in one final great thrust, came swarming out of the bushes and infiltrated the platoon positions. Furious hand-to-hand fighting took place as the area filled with bodies of the dead and dying. Lenny Meade noticed a Japanese officer, complete with binoculars and samurai sword, charging at him. The murderous fire of the Bren gun almost cut the man in half as he fell a metre or so from the log that acted as cover for Meade and Woodward. On a whim, Woodward jumped over the log, grabbed the sword, and was back in a flash, breathlessly showing his prize to his mate.

'Isn't it a beauty, Lenny?'

'You bloody fool!' Meade yelled at him. 'Jesus, you took a risk!'

Woodward agreed, but the trophy seemed worth the risk. He smiled foolishly, then continued firing.

The fighting was so intense in the confined area that it was impossible to stand and move without becoming a target. As the enemy penetrated further into 10 Platoon's territory, communication between sections and even individual members became more difficult and confused.

Butch, trying valiantly to resupply his men with ammunition, stealthily moving from section to section, walked into the middle of this blazing inferno. No one saw the secluded machine-gun spurt flame as its bullets ripped through his shirt and abdomen. He dropped and rolled off the side of the track looking for protection. Grasping his mid-section, he realised very quickly that his wounds were extremely serious, and probably fatal unless he could get help—a possibility that seemed remote at this stage as he was on his own.

He had a cache of hand grenades and his Tommy gun with him, so he prepared for a last stand. He would not go quietly, he thought.

In the fading light of the jungle dusk, he propped himself against a fallen log. Placing one hand over his mid-section to support his wound, he positioned the grenades with the other hand ready for throwing. He then rested the Tommy gun on his leg, placed his finger on the trigger, and waited.

A little further forward and up to the right, on a scrubby ridge, Lieutenant Lindsay Mason, the commander of 12 Platoon, was leading a desperate battle against overwhelming odds. All that day, they could see the Japanese down below infiltrating the ridge on their left and the continuing battle with 10 Platoon in the Cane Field. They could also see 11 Platoon under Mokka Treacey a little further over, and realised that he too was under pressure.

Mason's platoon had been taking potshots all day at the enemy, but at 4.00 pm the Japanese positioned some machine-guns on the next ridge and started firing into the platoon's position. For two unrelenting hours the bombardment saturated the area, and as the bullets swept over the scrub and vegetation the scything movement had the effect of cutting everything in its path. By 6.00 pm, they had completely denuded the area and caused many casualties in Mason's platoon.

While the Australians were recuperating from this devastation, the Japanese launched a blistering attack, charging out of the jungle in company strength. Mason's platoon recovered quickly and met the now familiar onslaught with a resolved front. As had been happening all day around the perimeter, the Australians stood their ground as a solid line, and once again the air was thick with lead as the proponents met in a toe-to-toe confrontation. By sheer audaciousness and firepower, the enemy were slowly pushed back into the jungle.

Another wave quickly followed and the killing field was steadily being littered with dead and wounded as the crossfire cut through the flesh of anyone in its path. Twice more the enemy came at them, and twice more they held their position. At this stage Mason had lost fourteen of his men on that knoll and now he realised that the sheer weight of numbers was going to wipe out his remaining men piecemeal if he did not call a withdrawal. They were exhausted after holding on tenuously for over an hour, so, above the noise of the gunfire and with the sounds of the dying and wounded men screaming in his ears, Mason ordered his men off the knoll.

As they effected a fighting withdrawal, one man came forward to provide covering fire. He had been wounded three times himself already, twice in the shoulder, but accepted a position in front of the still charging enemy. Acting Corporal Charlie McCallum was the original strong, silent type. He was a farmer and a champion woodchopper from Gippsland in Victoria and at 83 kilograms he was fit and strong. Quietly spoken, he had the nickname 'Silent'.

With great calmness, he picked up a wounded mate's Tommy gun and placed it against his left shoulder, while still manning his own Bren gun and firing that from his right hip, stalling the enemy in their tracks.

When he ran out of ammunition for his Bren, the enemy rushed him, but he kept them back with a burst from the Tommy gun in his left hand. Deftly, with his right hand, while still firing the Tommy gun in his left, he replaced the magazine of his Bren gun and continued to fire with that.

Somewhere in the sturdiness of the figure, in the hard, quiet eyes, in the cheeks tanned by a lifetime in the sun, you gained the impression of ploughed fields, of the dust from a tractor in the warm light of evening. He appeared out of place here but he wasn't reaping grain now, as the rows of Japanese kept charging at him. As they made their rush, one got close enough to grapple with him and actually managed to tear away one of his utility pouches. McCallum wrenched himself away, putting a blast through the man's chest as he lay clawing at the pouch—a hoped-for souvenir.

The moment was close and desperate as dead and wounded men piled up at McCallum's feet. There were possibly as many as 25 lying there, those still alive writhing in their agony or cursing the absurd bravery of the Australian.

Finally Mason and some of the other members of his platoon yelled to him that they were all clear. Taking a last burst, McCallum left the area and calmly returned to the remnants of his platoon, bringing both weapons with him.

His utter disregard for his own safety and his magnificent

courage in the face of tremendous odds was an inspiration to his comrades as the withdrawal proceeded without loss.

AS THE PLATOON REGROUPED AND PREPARED to defend their new area of jungle, a message came from Colonel Key that the position must be retaken and held at all costs. This was a lot to ask the eighteen remaining men of the devastated platoon—all of them carrying a wound of some degree. However, after McCallum's display of contempt for the enemy, the weary men lined up, ready to charge into that hell again.

The Japanese had brought up a supply of hand grenades and were now holding the higher ground. They instantly started hurling the grenades at the Australians, who had no choice but to lie flat and try to protect themselves from the splinters of hot metal as the shrapnel whistled past their ears. By the time the Japanese had thrown more than 100 grenades at them, Mason realised they would never retake the ground. His platoon was being decimated at a great rate and he soon only had a handful of active men beside him.

Suddenly, Mason's world was thrown upside down as a grenade exploded not far from his head. His face and body were peppered with hot metal and the concussion shocked him into a stupor that left him dazed and disoriented. Supporting his head in his hands, he staggered off into the jungle, his immediate vision a heaving sea of green and black.

He lost all track of time and now, in the pouring rain, as dusk was giving way to nightfall, he was startled to fall over some bodies lying limply on the muddy ground.

'Shit!' he yelled, as he scrambled unsteadily to his feet. The expletive probably saved his life. In the murkiness of the jungle twilight, he caught sight of a recumbent figure propped against a log. The soldier was more dead than alive, with one arm posed ready to throw a hand grenade at him.

'Who's that? Answer quickly or I'll throw,' the reclining man called out.

'Hell! Hang on—it's Lindsay Mason from 12 Platoon. Who the heck's that?'

'You almost bought it Ickle! It's Butch Bisset. I've been gunned, and I'm pretty well stuck here. I'm out of ammo and down to my last grenade, but I've accounted for a few of the bastards.'

'Butch! What's happened here?' Mason knelt close to Butch for a better look at his wounds. 'God, look at you—you've been blasted right across the guts.'

With a half grin the sprawling figure looked up at Mason. 'You don't look so good yourself, Ickle,' Butch said as he saw the bloody wound in Mason's head where a shrapnel fragment had embedded itself. Mason had earned the nickname 'Ickle' because of his small, wiry build. He stood no more than 54 kilograms wringing wet.

Butch continued: 'I think I'm pretty well gone. There's not a lot you can do for me.' He was in a great degree of pain and had little doubt that his injuries were terminal. 'Don't stick around. I've run out of ammo, but I'd like a chance to get some more of them if they come this way. Can you leave me your service revolver? I'll take six more of the bastards with me before I go.'

Realising the situation, Mason gave Butch his loaded revolver. He hesitated. 'Nothing more I can do?'

'Nah, mate, thanks—see ya!'

Mason wished Butch the best, feeling a little foolish as he spoke, then disappeared into the jungle.

Butch, meanwhile, was being missed by his men. Cuth Dunlop came round to George Woodward's section with the information that Mason's platoon had been pushed off the rise. He told George: 'See if you can find Butch and tell him we've been cut off. Our position is pretty tenuous.'

Woodward started crawling around the path that he knew Butch would have taken, but after some minutes he was met by Dave Garland, another platoon member. Garland gasped out: 'Butch has been shot. He's in a bad way, machine-gunned through the stomach. Jack Ferguson's also been hit, probably by the same gunner. They're both lying off the track a little, and they need help. Grab Lindsay Elphinstone over there and we'll go back.'

Elphinstone was a stretcher-bearer. The three men quickly slithered back through the bush to where Butch was lying. They found him where Lieutenant Mason had left him not long before. At this stage he was semi-comatose and lapsing in and out of consciousness.

In the fading light, Elphinstone ripped open Butch's shirt and was shocked by what he saw. 'Christ!' he said, noting the congealed blood hiding extensive wounds where the bullets had entered Butch's abdomen.

Through his daze Butch murmured: 'For Pete's sake, Lindsay, you can't do a thing for me—leave me.'

'No way, boss, we'll get you out of here.' Making Butch as comfortable as possible, Elphinstone placed a field dressing over the gaping wounds which were now starting to suppurate.

Not too far away, they also found Private Jack Ferguson, who was badly wounded too and in a great deal of pain. Elphinstone tried to comfort him as well and dressed his wounds.

Other platoon members had now turned up. Jimmy Coy, the section leader, decided that somehow they had to get Butch and Ferguson out and back to the RAP. Murray Bolitho and Col Blume had found their way to the site and offered their help. Butch had placed them earlier in the day in a thickly wooded position just off the Cane Field and they, like everyone else, were exhausted. That morning their good mate Stan Ellery had been killed during a charge. This traumatised them for some time but they recovered their cool and had continued to repulse attack after attack all day.

So, at 9.00 pm, the group improvised stretchers out of saplings, vines and groundsheets and placed the injured men on these, making them as comfortable as possible.

With a guard of six Tommy-gunners, the entourage left the position and in the pitch black night and pouring rain began a nightmare journey along the muddy, slippery track towards the RAP. They sent a runner ahead to warn Dr Duffy that they were coming.

Mokka Treacy's 11 Platoon, fighting next to Butch's 10 Platoon had been encountering the same type of ferocious attacks. With the tenacity and persistence shown by the whole battalion that day, he organised his men to repel the charges, and in the end not an inch of ground was lost. At the same time, his men had inflicted a great number of casualties on the enemy.

As the long day reached its climax, many men from other areas of the battalion came forward and led the way. Every company, platoon and section had encountered various degrees of attack, and it appeared there was always someone of courage and initiative who would step forward and be prepared to risk paying the supreme sacrifice if the need arose. Many times brave deeds went unrecorded as devoted men fought to the last in a lonely jungle corner. Where there were witnesses, they themselves were frequently gunned down—so the courageous actions were never documented. Men like Private Neilson of 13 Platoon, Lieutenant Pearce of 17 platoon and Corporal Winks Wakefield of Stan's old 18 Platoon all set an example of leadership and courage as they unflinchingly led from the front, generally assisted by a spurting Bren gun. The inspiration they provided, together with that of many others who will never be known, enabled the 2/14th Battalion, along with the exhausted 39th, to make a monumental stand that evokes a Homeric image.

The Trojans, like ravening lions, rushed on the Greek ships,
For the heart of Zeus was with them
And their spirits filled like sails in the morning
And the weariness of their legs departed
And their mighty shields grew light in their arms,
And they knew that victory would be theirs.

Towards evening, nevertheless, the battalion's position had become jeopardised, as by sheer force of numbers the enemy slowly filtered through the flanks and to the rear. When 12 Platoon had been pushed off the high ground for the fourth time, Colonel Key realised the position had seriously worsened and phoned Brigadier Potts at brigade headquarters. He requested permission to withdraw to the Isurava Rest House, about a kilometre away, where the battalion might be able to organise a better defence. Potts granted the request at 8.45 pm and set in motion a complete but necessary withdrawal for the battalion.

A little earlier in the evening, Stan had been on his way to Butch's platoon, as at that stage it was still holding the vital ground and it was important for battalion headquarters to know whether the platoon needed reinforcements and how critical their position was. All through that day Stan had been moving

133

from position to position, often under fire, piecing information together and returning it to headquarters to allow informed decisions to be made.

He was almost there when he encountered one of Butch's men, Tommy Wilson, returning from the Cane Field, his hand badly wounded. Using a field dressing, Stan bandaged Wilson's hand and supported the wounded man back to the RAP.

On his arrival he was met by Lieutenant Colonel Key, who said: 'I've been in touch with Potts. We have to withdraw. We're going to reorganise at the Isurava Rest House area. I'd like you and Ralph Honner to reconnoitre the area for a potential defensive position.' Lieutenant Colonel Honner was in charge of the embattled 39th Battalion. Even though they had been ordered back to Port Moresby for a well-earned rest, he had, on behalf of his men, requested permission to stay and support the 2/14th, as he realised the scale of the task given to the 2/14th. The request was gratefully accepted.

Stan was just about to leave with Honner when a runner appeared out of the jungle, searching for him. After regaining his breath, the man blurted out the news. 'Sorry to tell you, sir, the boss's been hit.'

The words hung in the air as Stan tried to comprehend their meaning. The information seemed strangely distant. He suddenly remembered Butch laughing beside the campfire at Efogi a few days earlier and his own eerie premonition as their eyes met.

'How bad is he? What happened?' Stan asked.

'He was delivering some hand grenades to one of the back sections and copped a machine-gun blast through his stomach. I don't think it's good, sir. The rest of the platoon have made up stretchers for him and Ferguson, who's also been shot. They're going to try and blast their way through and get them back to the Doc. They should get out in an hour or so.'

Realising there was little he could do until they brought Butch out, Stan pushed his feelings to the back of his mind and continued on to the Isurava Rest House with Colonel Honner.

When they reached the area, which was about halfway to Alola, they found it was occupied by some of the men of the 53rd Militia Battalion who were having a rest from the fighting on the right flank. Stan asked them to move in order to set up defensive positions there, but was shocked by their refusal to budge and indeed their outright belligerence.

He couldn't find their officers and as they remained uncooperative he was forced to pull out his revolver. Suddenly they saw the importance of his order and the desperation of the moment. They quickly moved out of the area, and Stan and Honner set about preparing the position.

His mind went back to Butch, and after doing what he could at the Rest House he set off to locate Don Duffy. He found the doctor working furiously, as the casualties were steadily mounting from the day's hostilities. Men were also trickling in from the withdrawal which was quietly under way.

'Doc,' he said, 'Butch has been shot. I don't know how bad it is, but I believe it's serious.'

The news troubled Duffy as he had been friends with Butch too for a long time. 'Let me know the minute he arrives,' he said.

The stretcher party of 10 Platoon were slowly extricating themselves from the Cane Field and painfully moving uphill. They had made a decision to work towards 12 Platoon's position and then head back to base from there. The six Tommy-gunners were leading the way, with George Woodward taking the position of forward scout. In the dark he had found the platoon's signal lines half buried in the mud, and knew they would lead the party to battalion headquarters.

Unknown to Butch's men, 12 Platoon had earlier left their position completely and the Japanese were now entrenched there. As the procession struggled up the hill, they heard voices ahead and challenged them. In their briefings they had been told the Japanese had trouble pronouncing certain letters—so when challenging anyone they were to prefix the platoon with the word 'Elizabeth'.

Lieutenant Jack Thurgood, second-in-charge of D Company, was among the group. Elements of his company had earlier filtered into the Cane Field just as Butch was hit, and he remained with them. He called out, tentatively: 'Elizabeth 12?' He was answered by a stream of hand grenades rolling down the hill towards them. Sparks flew off the grenades as they rolled, giving everyone time to spin off the track and take cover before they exploded. This was a trigger for the Tommy-gunners and a fierce firefight developed. Men on both sides were hit as bullets whizzed around in the dark, but it was soon over. They all lay silently till they were sure the inferno had passed, and then slowly regrouped further down the hill.

Up till now, Butch had been silent despite his agony. Every step and movement his carriers made aggravated his condition and he whispered hoarsely to Jimmy Coy: 'For Pete's sake, Jim, this is slowing everybody down. I'm not going to make it. Leave me and get out yourselves.' His head sank back on the stretcher.

'No bloody way, boss, it's unthinkable,' Coy said. He called to Woodward: 'Let's go, George!'

The party started off again. The eight stretcher-carriers slowly lifted the two men and painfully, carefully, felt their way through the slush, still working uphill. After some minutes they heard voices to the side of them, and suddenly found themselves under fire again. Woodward stood up straight and emptied his magazine towards the sound of the gunfire. The other machine-guns opened up as well and in chorus they cut a swathe through the darkness.

In the middle of this fracas, Woodward was suddenly spun around and knocked over, his machine-gun flying into the bush. Disoriented for a few moments, he searched in the dark through the slush of the jungle floor, but failed to find his gun. It was then that he realised he couldn't put any weight on his right hand. He was contemplating this when he found his platoon mate, Bill Jeffrey, who was also bowled over during the incident. Woodward croaked: 'I think I've been hit, Bill.'

Jeffrey replied: 'So have I, mate. Christ, look at you!' In between the gun flashes he saw there was blood everywhere. 'I can't find a wound though—it's too dark.'

The two of them scouted around in the dark and eventually found the rest of the party who were regrouping on the track, consulting with Jimmy Coy.

A couple of the men in the group had been wounded in the exchange, and Corporal Mark Kilburn had been killed. Ferguson, in the second stretcher, had died as well. Regretfully, the party reasoned they should leave the bodies there and that there was no point in continuing towards 12 Platoon's position, so they agreed to branch off and move downhill and then work towards the general direction of the Battalion Headquarters from there.

Taking up their positions, the weary party once again hoisted Butch's stretcher and moved off. They slipped and fell as the vines and roots caught their feet, but they doggedly carried their comrade down the muddy track.

Woodward led the way again. Not having his weapon, he carried a grenade instead, ready to pull the pin at the first confrontation.

Eventually, at about 9.30 pm, they stumbled out on to the main track. Gaining new strength, they moved along the track to where they were met by Stan and Dr Duffy, not far from the RAP. There was tremendous relief as they lowered their patient gently to the side of the path. Most of the men then dropped to the ground, exhausted. Stan thanked them for their efforts, then placed Jimmy Coy in charge and directed them to the Isurava Rest House area.

Duffy attended to Woodward first, who was still quite stunned. After a quick assessment, he said: 'You've been shot twice in the right arm. Your war's over right here. Get back to the RAP—they'll treat it and get you out of here.' Woodward stumbled off down the track, followed by other members from the group, all grateful for the temporary respite. Duffy then turned to examine Butch.

Stan was kneeling beside the stretcher, his hand on his brother's shoulder. 'Hal,' he said quietly, 'it's Stan. Can you hear me?'

Butch slowly opened his pain-racked eyes and, recognising Stan, forced a smile. His words were muted, deliberate, betraying the effort it was to communicate. 'Stan . . . I'm glad to see you. I'm in pretty bad shape. Is Don handy?'

'I'm here, Butch. Let me look at you.' The doctor examined the wounds, then applied a clean dressing. 'You've got several bullet holes through your abdomen. I can't see where they've come out. I'll give you some morphine to settle the pain. When it eases, we'll try and carry you out.' He then injected the morphine. 'This should help. I'll come back in half an hour or so and see how you're doing.'

Stan glanced up at the doctor, nodding his understanding

of the prognosis. He realised there was nothing more to do. 'I'll stay with him, Don, and thank you.'

In the darkness of the jungle, with the tragedy of war all around them, the two brothers huddled together beside the track, oblivious to the insanity of the day's proceedings. Stan held Butch's hand as the badly wounded man lapsed in and out of consciousness. At times they would talk sparingly. Stan would remind Butch of football games, parties they'd been to, characters they'd met along the way. Of the Somers Camp and Power House.

As the battalion continued its withdrawal during the night, muddy, bloodied men would tramp or stagger past the two lone figures. Occasionally someone would ask if they wanted a hand. Stan would quietly say 'We're alright, thanks', hoping his voice didn't betray his feelings of helplessness and grief.

He would talk to Butch of their mother and father and others in the family. His brother's vague eyes would show a glimmer of recognition, then fade as he once more lapsed into insensibility.

Dr Duffy came twice more to check on Butch's condition. Both times he gave him morphine, as the dosage quickly became ineffectual because of the extent of the wounds. Butch's battle continued through the early hours of the morning, until finally his battered body could fight no more. At 4.00 am, he died.

Crouching in the persistent, miserable rain, Stan felt Butch's hand go lifeless—causing him to frantically search for a pulse. His voice broke as he cried out: 'Hal, are you awake?' But it was no use. Stan wept silently to himself, his sobs muffled by the sound of the rain on the canopy.

10

A Fighting Withdrawal

WITH DAWN STILL TO APPEAR, BRIGADIER Potts was feeling reasonably confident that he might be able to move on to the offensive. Even though his losses had been heavy and he was probably outnumbered by as many as six to one, the previous day's battle had rendered a great deal more damage to the enemy than to his own forces. His intelligence estimates were that the Japanese had suffered at least 550 fatal casualties and over 1000 wounded. He suspected the enemy were hurting and might not be in a hurry to risk losing the same numbers in continued open confrontation. So he entrusted two companies of the 2/16th and one company of the 53rd to attack on the right flank at dawn. It was 30 August 1942.

The 2/14th had now set up a perimeter around the Isurava Rest Home area. The battalion had lost twelve killed and 48 wounded on the day before. But their morale was still high after engaging and badly mauling the previously 'unbeatable' Japanese.

In the other camp, General Horii was enraged and frustrated at the setback, and was determined to force the issue. When he found that the Australians had vacated their positions at Isurava, he instructed his army to charge them in their new positions in an effort to keep the momentum going. His men were also keen to administer punishment to the upstarts, so they attacked that morning with great enthusiasm.

As they screamed into the Australian lines, they were met once again by strong resistance from bullet, bayonet and man-to-man conflict. While the Australian perimeter held firm, by 11.00 am the Japanese had attempted to bypass the main battalion and were flanking them via the high ground on the western side. As the battle continued, the Japanese eventually threatened brigade headquarters at Alola and began firing among the wounded in the main Regimental Aid Post there.

Lieutenant Colonel Key communicated with Brigadier Potts by phone and relayed the battalion's situation to him. At 3.00 pm, Potts issued orders for the 2/14th to withdraw to Alola at 5.00 pm, and then ordered the RAP staff to evacuate their wounded from Alola to Eora Creek village. He also ordered the 2/16th to fall back to the other side of Alola, on the Abuari track, as support.

Potts realised that Alola would be difficult to defend, so his extended plan was to further retreat to Eora Creek where they could establish a killing field. It was now obvious to him that conditions had deteriorated to the extent that an immediate offensive would be untenable—he realised the advantage Horii possessed in numbers, firepower and, at this stage, choice of battleground. He made the decision that he would have to conduct a strategic withdrawal, which is one part of the art of warfare. His tactics would be to keep withdrawing to a new ambush position, establish a killing ground, concentrate a swift offensive, then withdraw before Horii's larger force could out-flank and overrun him. At this stage of the battle, Potts realised, his commitment must be to create as many enemy casualties as possible, to extend Horii's supply and evacuation lines to the enemy's disadvantage, and also to play for time until the Australians could be reinforced by the 2/27th based at Port Moresby and eventually by the 25th Brigade, which he knew was on its way from Australia.

Back at 2/14th Battalion headquarters the situation had quickly degenerated. Colonel Key became aware that the enemy had virtually flanked the battalion and that the pathway to Alola was almost cut. He saw that he was going to have to fight his way out, so he gave instructions for two of his companies, C and D, to launch an attack on the western side of the track to clear the newly arrived Japanese who were preventing the battalion's withdrawal. A Company and a portion of B Company were to act as rearguard.

Stan was present when the orders were given, and like everyone else he was tired and working under great pressure. He was devastated at losing Butch earlier that morning, but had consciously put his feelings on hold as the urgency of the moment overtook everything else.

At exactly 5.00 pm, as ordered, Colonel Key, Stan and the rest of the staff from battalion headquarters had secured their gear and were lined up along the track ready to effect their withdrawal. Unfortunately, in another of the strange coincidences of war, it was the precise moment that General Horii had programmed for two of his battalions to launch a massive full frontal attack on the 2/14th.

At the same instant that Horii's battalions started firing into the line, the two Australian companies, C and D, which had been sent up to the higher ground to clear the track, also opened fire—as did the Japanese who were holding the track in the rear.

Suddenly, Key's battalion headquarters area was under tremendous fire from three different directions. A nightmare of devastation and confusion reigned as a blistering fusillade swept the length of the track.

There was no answer to the murderous volley, as it chewed into the jungle and threatened to slash the shocked and tired soldiers and everything else in its path. It was the most intense fire the battalion staff had ever experienced, and it quickly became obvious that if they didn't move off the track nobody would survive the onslaught.

Dividing into groups, the men dived for cover on the lower ground on the eastern side of the track. As the bullets slammed into trees only centimetres away from him, Stan leaped out of the inferno, crashing and falling through bushes and jungle to eventually reach a position affording cover, about 50 metres east of the shattered main track.

After regaining his breath and settling himself, he collected a party of men around him who had also been forced off the track. He found they included three wounded men who had all sustained upper body wounds but were capable of walking, plus nine others—among them Les Tipton, the regimental sergeant major, and Bill Lynn, his 'I' sergeant.

After some discussion, Stan decided it would be suicide to attempt to climb back to the main track again, and that they should try to cut a route running parallel to the main track, and eventually work back to the Alola area.

At about 5.30 pm, they began the difficult process of hacking a pathway through the jungle, using their bayonets to slash the vines and underbrush. Night fell but they continued to bush-bash their way, moving approximately parallel to the track, towards Alola. After seven hours, at about 2.00 am, Stan thought they were fairly close to the Alola Junction, so he called a halt and decided he should conduct a reconnaissance. He knew there was a substantial ammunition and supply dump in this area, and he also wanted to see whether the battalion had held the Japanese off, or whether in fact the enemy had pushed through before them.

Leaving the main group to recover and wait, Stan and Les Tipton began the slow, uphill climb to the main track. The mountainside was covered with very heavy undergrowth, forcing them to slash their way through lantana and typical jungle vegetation. The darkness made the journey very difficult as it obscured crevasses and embankments. As Stan slashed through a vine at one point, the roots clinging to the hillside on which he was balanced fell away and he suddenly found himself plummeting headlong through the air. He crashed against logs and branches on the way down, finally coming to rest, badly bruised, some seven metres down a gorge.

He spent several minutes on his back, dazed, and after catching his breath gently moved all his limbs in turn. Finding no serious damage he crawled to his feet, then climbed back to join Tipton.

There had been light drizzle on and off through the evening, but now the rain eased as they stealthily came out on the track and moved to a position about 30 metres from where they knew the dump was. The moon came out, pouring pale gold light into the jungle darkness and dripping silver-gilt down the wet trunks of the trees. The soft light allowed the men to dimly make out a party of 40 or 50 Japanese sitting chattering around the ammunition dump.

'Blast!' Stan said. 'That means we're behind enemy lines.'

There was a strong temptation to go in and blow up the dump, but Stan had responsibility for ten others, including three wounded men, so he reluctantly shelved the idea. They quietly slipped back into the darkness and retraced their footsteps.

When they reached the other members of the group, they tried to catch a few hours' much needed sleep. At first light Stan decided that, in view of the Japanese presence ahead, they should keep further east in order to flank Alola, cross Eora Creek and hug the ridge on the Abuari side of the track.

Towards mid-morning, they came out at Eora Creek. It was a raging torrent, running fast and furiously. It would have been foolhardy to try and wade through, as one slip would rush the unfortunate soldier to an early death. They eventually found an area where a fallen log would allow a safer crossing.

Once over, they continued to slash a trail through the jungle on the Abuari side of the creek, where they picked up two more Australians who had been cut off. They were Captain Wright, a company commander of the 2/16th Battalion, and his batman. The 2/16th were also in the process of withdrawing from the engagement with the enemy at Abuari, and Stan suggested that the two men join him. His plan, he told them, was to skirt along the ridge they were on, to make a half-circle detour and then cut into the track between Eora Creek village and Templeton's Crossing, hopefully before the Japanese got there.

The going was exceedingly tough, as they had to negotiate very steep ridges, more fast-flowing creeks and some thick stretches of jungle. Every moment was wrought with anxiety and concentration, as they could never be sure just how close the enemy were. The leading pair would cut through the undergrowth until their shoulders and backs were aching, then the rest of the file followed numbly.

On the third day out, they came to a patch that afforded a clear view across the valley to Eora Creek village. Transfixed, they witnessed a bitter clash around the village as the Japanese were closing on the withdrawing Australians. Gunshots, yells and screams echoed faintly back to their side of the valley. Frustrated, they were unable to render any assistance and pushed on with their own task.

Food was getting low, as each man had had only one emergency ration issued to him before leaving Isurava. The men's hunger was affecting their concentration and the quality of whatever sleep they could grab.

Eventually, on the fifth day, they came across a track seemingly heading in the direction they wanted to go. There were signs that soldiers had been along there recently, but they weren't sure whose side they were on. They suspected it may have been the 2/16th Battalion, mainly because the boot prints looked as though they were from standard Australian-issue boots—Japanese boots left an impression like a two-toe imprint. However, the mud prevented clear identification.

Realising they could still be behind enemy lines, Stan forced the pace. If they were Australians ahead he couldn't risk missing them, as his men were close to exhaustion. Suddenly, he turned a corner and was confronted by the rearguard of the troops ahead. With tremendous relief, Stan recognised the man as his friend, Alan Haddy of the 2/16th. He'd met him on the *Aquitania* and again in Lebanon, where Haddy had achieved some fame in the brigade by swimming the Litani River while the Vichy French fired down at him from craggy hills over-looking the river.

He recognised Stan at the same instant and broke into a smile, the scars on his face showing where a Vichy bullet had penetrated one cheek and shot out through the other. 'Jesus, Stan! Where did you come from? I almost shot you! We're the last mob out of there—and the Japs aren't too far behind us.'

Stan explained that they had been bush-bashing for five days since Isurava, and said he'd love some rations for his party of thirteen.

After a quick meal, Stan's knocked-about men joined the withdrawing 2/16th group and finally trudged into Templeton's Crossing that same evening.

The timing was fortunate. They could not have realised how close the Japanese were behind them. Half an hour after this last party arrived at Templeton's Crossing, the Japanese attacked in force. Stan and his men were taken to the rear, where they joined up with the 2/14th Battalion again. He reported in to the commander and was surprised to find Phil Rhoden, his old Power House friend, in command.

'Good to see you, Stan. Thought we might have lost you for ever! We took quite a belting when we were overrun at Isurava that afternoon. After we'd hit the deck we couldn't account for 172 of our battalion. We believe most of them have been separated, as they keep turning up in dribs and drabs, but we really don't know. We've lost Colonel Key and about five of his staff including the Adjutant. It's thought they may have been taken prisoner, or killed. That of course is why I'm in charge.'

He peered at Stan. 'Are you able to resume duties? Roy Watson has been filling in for you admirably but he'd welcome you back if you are.'

Stan insisted he was still fit, but they agreed that most of his twelve charges would be evacuated back to Port Moresby.

Rhoden continued: 'There's some good news—we've been able to hold the Japs at Milne Bay. Our men have got them boxed in along the peninsula and are hammering away at them. The Japs have lost heavily, it appears. Our army, backed up by the Australian and American air units, has virtually pushed them back into the sea. That means General Allen in Moresby has let us have the 2/27th who were waiting in reserve there. They've started marching already, and intend to meet us at Myola. We'll certainly need them, as the 39th and 53rd are both on their way back to Moresby, except for a hundred or so of the 53rd who are maintaining Myola.

'The other thing is that there's now a good buildup of supplies at Myola, so we're moving there today—you're just in time.'

THE STILL PROUD 2/14TH BATTALION THAT had left Port Moresby less than a month before with 546 enthusiastic fighting men had been reduced to 150 strong. Close behind them, as they reached Myola, came the 2/16th, holding the track with only 250 men. Their spirit was still willing and they were even keen to mix it with the Japanese, but their sunken eyes and drained, grey skin, their torn and muddy clothes and wasted bodies underlined their true physical state.

For the first time in ten days, they experienced the luxury of a wash in the icy waters of a stream that ran through the middle of the otherwise dry lake bed. The doctors and medical orderlies at the RAP managed minor injuries and assisted the more seriously wounded on their way. New clothes and socks were issued. For some, the unit's podiatrist had to cut away boots as well as socks in order to air the feet and treat the pulpy, rotting tissues. Each man was given a blanket and a groundsheet and most of them looked forward to a warmer night's sleep.

Most pleasing, however, the cooks had created a substantial meal from the most basic ingredients. Hot urns of bully beef, rice and tinned vegetables met the weary men as they arrived to be fed.

Brigadier Potts had reconsidered his plan to make a stand at Myola, realising it would be a difficult base to defend. He sent a message to General Allen in Port Moresby informing him that they would be moving back to Efogi, where they would prepare defences for a stand at Mission Ridge.

They carried what supplies they could and left a rearguard detail to destroy anything that might be valuable to the advancing Japanese. Alan Avery was selected in this detail and took delight in bayoneting tins of food, allowing bacteria to enter and grow in the punctured containers. He imagined hungry Japanese soldiers ravaging the contents and becoming violently ill after the microscopic fungi had attacked their already overtaxed alimentary system.

Alan's detail began their demolition work in the early hours. Besides the tinned food, they enthusiastically destroyed about 40 000 rounds of ammunition. Bren guns were dismantled and twisted beyond repair. Signal wire was burnt. Sacks of rice and meat were slashed and the contents scattered over the muddy ground.

When the last soldier had left, the rearguard party set fire to the buildings and began their trek to Efogi. As he climbed out of the crater lake, Alan looked back with satisfaction at the smoking, gutted huts and battered supplies that remained for the enemy.

At Efogi, Potts was heartened by the arrival of the fresh 2/27th Battalion which, for the first time in the campaign, allowed him to have his brigade nominally complete.

For the troops, the other welcome surprise at Efogi was the

arrival of the first mail for five weeks. It was timely, as messages from home helped to reinforce the men's determination to see their trials through. They scouted up whatever paper they could find—biscuit wrappers, toilet paper, old envelopes—and then wrote home for the return dispatch. They'd lost their writing paper weeks ago as it became pulp in the wet conditions. The return letters were posted without envelopes and trustingly sent on their way.

Stan Bisset and Phil Rhoden collected their mail together and eagerly opened the letters to hear the news from home. Stan's letter was from his parents, who sadly wrote that the Army had informed them that Butch had been killed and that he, Stan, was missing. But another telegram the next day had told them that Stan had been reunited with his battalion.

Stan saw Rhoden beaming at him. 'Better congratulate me, Stan. I've just become engaged.' He'd proposed to his girlfriend Pat by letter when leaving Brisbane, and she had accepted. The news provided a highlight for the friends after the torrid weeks of mayhem and sadness.

The troops were heartened further that morning as they cheered a flight of American bombers while they unloaded their cargo on Myola and other planes strafed the huts that hadn't burnt down. This action was a great morale booster for the troops, as they had the US Air Force visibly on side. And, unknown to them, the Japanese at Myola were suffering early signs of dysentery as the first hungry troops at the village had wolfed down the tainted rations left behind by Alan's party.

In the meantime, Potts had selected a site dominating the ground overlooking Efogi village as a satisfactory position to make a stand against the enemy. This would give him every chance to create as much damage as possible while he played for time. So, later that day, the three battalions moved into defensive positions behind Efogi, around Mission Ridge—named for the small Seventh Day Adventist Mission hut perched on a spur of the ridge.

The fresh 2/27th Battalion moved into the forward position on the track, eager to take a swipe at the Japanese. They were well received by their sister battalions who paid out much goodnatured chiacking to the fit-looking men.

Earlier, as the returning 39th Battalion had marched into

Mission Ridge, Sergeant Bill Guest was still with them. He was weak, sick with malaria and quite happy to be leaving his Tommy gun and blanket for the 2/27th troops coming through. The 39th now totalled only 185 men and they lined up at Mission Ridge 'Q' Store and passed over their automatic weapons, rations, blankets, signal stores and medical supplies. They then continued on their way to Port Moresby where they would be rested and reinforced, proud of the sterling role they had played in being the first Australians to confront, then hold, the experienced Japanese.

The 2/27th were allocated a position on a grassy spur directly overlooking the old Mission building, while brigade headquarters was situated a little further back towards Menari, the next village on the track. They sat at the highest point of a narrow saddle, commanding a sound tactical position. The 2/16th were deployed on other positions on the ridge, and the 2/14th moved on to the right of the track, covering an alternative route to Menari which had been found earlier by Roy Watson, from Stan's Intelligence Section.

All battalions set up fire lanes and weapon pits, which they dug with their bayonets and helmets, and prepared to wait for the advancing enemy.

THAT AFTERNOON THE JAPANESE WERE OBSERVED moving into Efogi village in their hundreds. At nightfall, high on Mission Ridge, overlooking the scene, Stan and Rhoden watched them move out from the village. Knowing they were out of reach of the Australian weapons, the Japanese audaciously lit lanterns and moved in a long unbroken line from the village across the mountainside and set up opposite to where they knew the Australians were in defence. 'The cheeky bastards,' someone commented. The lanterns were carried about 30 metres apart, and the watching men took delight when the occasional one suddenly went flying through the air as the owner fell prey to a hidden trap on the track.

By morning, Stan and the Intelligence Section men had counted upwards of 1500 enemy moving towards them, causing Potts to call for another air strike immediately.

Nine Boston Havoc A-20s attacked Efogi and Myola, causing considerable damage. They were escorted by four Kitty-hawks which flew low over the village and strafed the immediate area. This, once again, brought great cheers from the Australians, as they gave the thumbs-up sign to the low-flying Kittyhawk pilots. The planes whined in over the treetops, banking expertly to miss the ridge, then, levelling out, locked their sights on the enemy huts at Efogi and the tracks leading out of it. As they screamed into the attack, blue flames burst from their six .5in machine-guns, causing panic-eyed Japanese to desperately propel themselves out of the line of fire. A great many were seen to be flung skywards or to reel backwards as the powerful shells tore into them.

The bombs from the A-20s rained over the village, shattering and collapsing the huts and sending up large clouds of dust and smoke as the impact rocked the area. The thundering explosions continued unabated for several minutes, sending shock waves over to the Australians' lines. As the planes wheeled off through the low-lying cumulus clouds, they left columns of smoke billowing over Efogi and at least 100 troops lying dead.

As the morning progressed, the enemy quickly reorganised themselves and started aggressive probing patrols into the Australian positions. The 2/27th met the brunt of these attacks, as the Japanese continued their now familiar flanking and encircling tactics.

The battle escalated over the next two days and the Japanese were forced to bring up two fresh battalions to help in their attempt to overrun the Australians. Once again, Potts found himself heavily outnumbered and eventually, on 8 September, he realised brigade headquarters had been flanked and was almost completely cut off.

The Japanese had cut all Potts's communication lines and from early morning, while holding off attacks from the 2/16th, they made increasingly violent attacks on his headquarters. Brigade headquarters was usually manned by a platoon of older men, average age 40 years, who led the defence of the corps. They were not normally expected to fight, but this day 'the old and the bold', as they were unceremoniously titled, willingly and ferociously threw everything at the hated invaders. They were supported by every available man—clerks, cooks, signalmen, staff officers and even the commander. They held the enemy to fifteen metres, repelling them with rifles, machine-guns and hand grenades.

The signalman from the 2/14th had managed to contact Potts on a vintage wireless set. Stan was in conference with Phil Rhoden and Lieutenant Colonel Caro, commander of the 2/16th Battalion, when Potts relayed a desperate message for them to try and clear a path through to his embattled position. Quickly they arranged a three company attack to relieve the situation. The 2/16th supplied two companies and the 2/14th supplied B Company under Captain Nye. By now company strength was down to about 40 men, instead of the normal 140. Nye had no doubts about the danger of the mission as his company was to cut through a large section of the well-entrenched Japanese force—and without the benefit of proper reconnaissance. Furthermore, the three platoons of B Company, 10, 11 and 12, all had new leaders, as Butch had been killed and Mokka Treacy and Lieutenant Mason were both missing. And the platoons themselves were all well below strength, having lost greatly at Isurava.

At 2.45 pm they began their uneven battle to save brigade headquarters. Their private war waged for two hours in the jungle as they came under incessant and continuous fire. Slowly but steadily they pushed through, losing men at an increasing rate, until finally eight of them made it through to headquarters. The rest had run out of ammunition and a decision was made to withdraw and evacuate the wounded. The cost was high, as sixteen of the company were killed in the exercise, including Captain Nye and Charlie McCallum, the hero of 12 Platoon's withdrawal at Isurava.

The three battalions were then ordered to withdraw back to Menari, following the alternative route found earlier.

As the light faded on this bloodiest of days, the Australians moved out of Mission Ridge, which was now being dubbed Brigade Hill, and began the difficult slog up the blackened, muddy track. The 2/27th left behind 41 killed and a great number of their 45 wounded members had to be carried out on stretchers. As the heavens opened up yet again, the three battalions were forced to a standstill.

When darkness came, Phil Rhoden halted his 2/14th Battalion —which was at this stage leading the withdrawal—as the terrain made further travel at night impossible. He then proceeded to give the men the finest fighting address Stan had ever heard.

After speaking for several minutes, Rhoden concluded:

'We *must* stop them getting to Moresby. There has been tremendous personal sacrifice, unbelievable bravery and courage, and we all feel the losses greatly. We *must not* fail our friends who are not coming back. We must finish the job they started and for which they died—we owe it to them. Quite simply, the bottom line is this—Australia and our loved ones will not be safe unless the enemy is stopped here and now and thrown back into the sea. We owe it also to them.

'Have no doubts you are going to be tested further over the coming days. I urge you to recommit yourself to this mission, to dig deeper into your reserves—no matter what the consequences.'

Stan's eyes moved over the men as he gauged the effect of Rhoden's speech. He noticed that the faces were a little calmer, the jaws a little more set, and the eyes burnt a little brighter.

The next morning, at dawn, the 2/14th were the first to move out. Components of the three battalions were designated to assist with bringing the stretcher cases along, on what was now a difficult downhill climb to Menari. Each stretcher often needed six or more bearers on the tortuous mountain track. At some stages it was so steep that the stretcher had to be passed from man to man in a painfully slow method of travel.

Brigadier Potts, together with brigade headquarters, had stealthily extricated himself from under the eyes of the Japanese moving along the main track and arrived at Menari before his battalions got there. Finding the place deserted, he sent his men scavenging for dropped cargo from the biscuit bombers, and then set up a supply point for his withdrawing brigade.

At about 11.00 am, the first elements of the 2/14th struggled up from a creek crossing and slowly stumbled on to the level ground of the village. Stan was the first up and was delighted to see his friend Albert Moore, who was waiting beneath his Salvation Army banner. Stan gave him a hand to distribute chocolate, bully beef, biscuits and tobacco, then passed out grenades and ammunition from a dump situated to one side.

It was a privilege to work with Albert Moore. To offer one of the exhausted men a warm mug of tea and to receive an expression of profound relief taught Stan much about compassion. He knew what had driven Moore since his first stint in the Western Desert. To Stan, Moore and the Salvation Army represented everything good in humanity.

As the men savoured their treats, they were joined by Major Bill Russell with fresh troops from Headquarters Company, which had remained in Port Moresby. The battalion now prepared defensive positions around Menari.

General Horii, of course, wasn't about to give up his perceived advantage easily, as he now had five infantry battalions at the front and was keen to keep up the momentum. Before long, just as the 2/16th Battalion started to enter Menari, Japanese mountain guns and machine-gun fire raked the village, confirming Potts's realisation that Menari wasn't going to be easy to defend. He felt he couldn't wait for the 2/27th to come in, and his reconnaissance had reported that there really was no suitable place to set up for another stand until Ioribaiwa. Ioribaiwa was one village further back past Nauro, the next village on the track.

In the meantime, the 2/27th, while carrying the stretcher cases, were experiencing great difficulties effecting their withdrawal. Eventually they were forced off the track into the jungle. Thus began an epic bush-bashing trek that would last several weeks for the hapless battalion, testing every man to his limit.

This loss effectively whittled Potts's immediate command to about 300 men, which meant he was now outnumbered by as much as ten to one. He therefore had little choice but to order a further withdrawal.

ALAN WAS RELAXING WITH A FEW of his remaining Seven Section mates when a lieutenant from battalion headquarters came searching through the lines. 'Is Corporal Avery here?' he called.

Alan called back: 'You mean Private Avery, sir.'

'No, you *were* Private Avery, you're a corporal now! Here's a couple of stripes—put them on and take over as section leader.' The lieutenant smiled, then moved on to the next group of men, pleased to be the bearer of glad tidings.

Alan was surprised. Neither he nor Bruce had ever sought

promotion. They didn't need it—life was fun. Besides, there was always someone around who was happy to assume a position of authority. However, things had changed. Bruce was gone, Jarmbe and the Professor were missing, Teddy was wounded. Considering the circumstances, he decided, yes, it was time to accept some responsibility. And Bruce would approve. There was some goodnatured chiacking when Alan finally had the stripes sewn on, as the promotion was a popular one.

At this stage, in another area of the battalion, a lone, dazed figure emerged out of the surrounding jungle. It was Lieutenant Mason, the 12 Platoon commander, his clothes in tatters, his body emaciated and weighing less than 45 kilograms. He had been wandering, mostly lost, for ten days since leaving Butch at Isurava. He was quickly assisted to the RAP.

Following the withdrawal, to a position some hours forward of Ioribaiwa, Brigadier Potts was recalled to Port Moresby to report first hand to High Command. His recall was worrying as he had become a symbol to the men, epitomising leadership, courage and a never-say-die attitude when faced with great adversity. But their fears were allayed somewhat as his replacement was Brigadier Porter, who had led them bravely at Jezzine in Lebanon.

A second important change was that the 2/14th and 2/16th Battalions were united to form a composite battalion under the leadership of Lieutenant Colonel Albert Caro, the 2/16th commander. Major Challen took over as commander of the 2/14th, with Phil Rhoden becoming second-in-command.

As well, the 3rd Militia Battalion arrived, adding strength to the Australian numbers.

For the next two or three days there was little action on the track as the Japanese were starting to really feel the effects of their long and drawn-out battle. At the end of this time, Alan's section, settled in a group of foxholes, were once again visited by the lieutenant from battalion headquarters. 'Is Sergeant Avery here?' he called.

'You've got it wrong again, Lieutenant! I'm *Corporal* Avery, remember?'

'Not any more, Sergeant,' the lieutenant smiled. 'Here's another stripe to add to the two I gave you a few days ago.'

A deep voice called out from a gun pit a few metres away. It was Hi-Ho Silver. 'Gawd, Lieutenant, we're trying to *win* this bloody war! Soon this little bugger'll be running the place if you keep this up.'

Alan laughed, gave him a two-up sign, and went back to his foxhole, eyes peering again into the jungle, while someone searched for the needle and thread.

During the day the enemy attacked the Australians at several points, and Porter realised that Horii was building up for one last thrust. He decided on a further withdrawal, where he knew he would have to make a final stand. He knew also that the 25th Brigade had now arrived at Imita Ridge and that they would soon be able to assist him.

That night, 11 September, as Porter passed the word to his battalions to prepare for a move first thing in the morning, the forces of nature threw a rude welcome at the newcomers. Black clouds had been building up all afternoon and, by nightfall, freezing northern and easterly gales whipped the canopy and treetops as the intensifying tropical storm reached its top fury. Lightning and thunder raced over the heavens and split the night sky, heralding drenching rain. The men of both armies huddled in their inadequate capes and coats as nature unleashed one of the most violent storms experienced during the campaign.

The storm raged all night. The deluge filled their gun pits and water raced down mountain slopes, bucketing them once again with filthy, slimy mud.

Added to these physical discomforts was the worry that this could be the moment Horii chose to launch a desperate offensive. During the daytime hours the Japanese could hear the droning of aircraft at Port Moresby and at night, when it wasn't raining, they could see the searchlights penetrate the sky. The enemy knew their goal was only a few days' march away, so the Australians had to be prepared for a sudden, large-scale push.

As if the violent storm wasn't enough, at about 3.00 am the area between Imita Ridge and Ioribaiwa suddenly reverberated in answer to a distant earth tremor, further testing the men's raw emotions.

The storm slowly cleared as dawn approached and nature, in all its capriciousness, presented a beautiful, sparkling day.

However, its beauty was lost on the belligerents. At 8.30 that morning Porter's men extricated themselves from their muddy entrenchments and began to move back to positions on the forward slopes of Ioribaiwa, a hard two-hour slog through a quagmire. In these new positions they set up lines of fire and dug foxholes across the track, determined not to give one more inch of ground.

The 25th Brigade now arrived and moved in behind the composite battalion. The arrival of the three fresh battalions— the 2/25th, 2/31st and 2/33rd—was a tonic for the exhausted men of Maroubra Force, and they were delighted to see the fit and tanned men in their green uniforms as they moved into position efficiently and professionally, setting up their camp site.

The composite battalion, though, still held the main position astride the ridge. When the enemy renewed their artillery attack, the Australians didn't have any answer to the larger weapons— mountain guns, mortars and jukis.

Stan had been made Intelligence Officer for the composite battalion and over the next few days he worked tirelessly, helping to coordinate the movements of the five battalions in the field. Inwardly he was still grieving the loss of Butch, but he put the pain aside.

On the third day of the bombardment, Stan asked Alan to come with him to the front lines from his position at the top of the ridge. They set off down the hillside as the Japanese mountain guns set off a tremendous salvo. A number of rounds started landing close to the pair. Immediately they jumped into one of the weapon pits together and to their horror, about ten metres in front of them, they saw an enemy mortar round land in another pit and rip apart the two men in it.

That evening, at twilight, as the unfortunate soldiers were being buried, one of the burial party men fainted. It was obvious to Stan just how much mental and physical trauma his battalion had suffered. There were definite signs of breakdown now, as the composite battalion's doctor, Blue Steward, had to send to the rear several cases of severe battle fatigue.

And it became clear to the commanders that Ioribaiwa was not going to be defended successfully.

So, finally, the Australian force was given permission to make one final withdrawal to Imita Ridge. This great bastion was to be the Australians' last stand. High Command warned them: 'There will be no more withdrawals—you will die there if you have to.'

Imita Ridge presented a vast natural rampart, as its cliffs soared up the steepest section of the entire track, forming a barrier to all but the fittest individuals. The commanders realised it was ideally suited for defence, particularly with an entrenched, organised Australian force waiting at the top.

But it was obvious that the composite battalion was slowly being whittled down as, for the last few days, it had been mercilessly hammered and even the bravest men were now showing signs of emotional and physical breakdown.

Finally, on 16 September, the composite battalion was withdrawn from the field of battle. As the troops prepared to move to a reserve position at Uberi, Stan noted sadly that, of the original 546 men of the 2/14th who had marched over this point four weeks earlier prior on their way to Isurava, there were now only three officers and about 85 other ranks left. The rest were either killed, wounded, sick or missing.

As he slowly shouldered his pack and got ready to move out with the remnants of his unit, the 2/25th Battalion started moving into the composite battalion's positions to relieve them. Stan noticed a young sergeant leading his incoming platoon down to the front lines. He directed his charges with confidence and familiar authority and, seeing Stan, stopped to ask about the local conditions.

Stan noticed the clear, cornflower blue eyes set in a bronzed face and the man's strong corded forearms. The 2/25th had been raised on the fertile Darling Downs in Queensland and, from the sergeant's easy manner, Stan imagined him perhaps to be a farmer.

Even though Stan wasn't wearing any signs of rank, the sergeant recognised him as an officer and commented, with typical country understatement: 'Looks like you and your men have had a rough time, sir. We're to cover you while you go into reserve for a while. You all look as if you could use a break.'

'Yes, thanks, sergeant.' Stan smiled wryly. 'I reckon we're pretty glad you're here—we're just about on our last legs.' The smile opened up. 'What kept you? We could've used you three weeks ago!' Stan paused. 'I got to know a few of your officers in Tripoli.' He mentioned a few names. 'Are they here?'

'Yes, sir, coming down behind me. They're farmers—like myself. Sorry we're a bit late. We had to hop home first, after the Middle East, to make sure next summer's crop was in.' He grinned. 'Besides, I couldn't leave my new wife! I reckon half the battalion got engaged or married during the time on leave—they had to hold the ship back for us.' He laughed enthusiastically. Then, more seriously, he said: 'I guess we all want to get this job done and get back home as fast as we can. And I should have a new kid waiting for me. Anyhow, I heard you chaps got knocked around a bit but accounted pretty well for yourselves. Any advice for us on what's ahead?'

Stan gave the sergeant a brief rundown, and they parted.

By 21 September the Australians who had moved to the front line had managed, through sheer determination and muscle power, to haul two large guns to the top of Imita Ridge. For the first time they had an answer to the enemy's artillery and there was great pleasure in hearing the shells whistle over to the Japanese positions and know they were causing serious damage. In the sky, the Allied airforce had now gained virtual supremacy over the Kokoda Track. And the fresh troops of the Seventh Division were keen and ready for an offensive which they believed would turn General Horii round.

Unexpectedly, five days later Horii received orders from his superiors in Rabaul to cease fighting and to withdraw to Gona and Buna. The Japanese Imperial Army had their hands full fighting the Americans at Guadalcanal in the Solomons. So, reluctantly at first but later in a disorderly retreat, the Japanese withdrew. The Australians followed closely and made their first real contact with the enemy at Templeton's Crossing and Eora Creek. Bitter fighting took place and many casualties were incurred before they were able to push the Japanese back towards Kokoda and finally to Gona.

THE 2/14TH BATTALION—NOW A SEPARATE entity again—relocated to Koitaki, a rubber plantation in the hills about 40 kilometres from Port Moresby. Here they set up tents and a canteen and assumed some degree of permanency as they continued their recuperation. In view of the depleted officer ranks of the battalion, Phil Rhoden recommended that Stan be considered for promotion to captain. The papers came back eventually from Corps Headquarters with a note saying: 'This officer is 30 years of age'—implying that he might be a little too old for promotion. Rhoden showed the note to the brigadier and they both laughed, then sent it back to Corps Headquarters with the comment: 'This officer is the fittest AIF officer in New Guinea.' The promotion was quickly approved and Stan was pleased to become the new Adjutant of the battalion.

Alan had also been recommended for promotion. He was advised that he had been selected for officer training at Bonegilla in Victoria, and that he was to leave in November. Once again he was surprised, but was happy to accept.

When Bruce was killed, Alan knew his family would receive a telegram from the Army as soon as possible, but official war policy meant that he himself had to wait a month before he could mention Bruce's death in any of his letters. On 4 October, he wrote to Mrs Kingsbury and her family. He apologised for not writing earlier, explaining the Army policy. He offered his condolences to the family and said: 'Personally, I am entirely lost without him here as we had been together for such a long time.'

Writing the letter probably aided his own recovery, as he was still grieving. However, it took him another three weeks to find the words to write to Leila. When he did, he explained for the first time the actual details of Bruce's death and tried to use phrases that would help Leila to cope with the loss.

He also wrote to Ann and his own parents and generally kept himself busy, as time was going slowly while he was waiting for his transfer. There was no leave available here, so time had to be filled by playing cards, writing letters, talking or just sleeping.

He missed his card-playing partners—Jarmbe, the Professor and another mate, Jack Gwillim. He had no idea where they were and could only think that they might be dead. He did have some hope, though, as over the last few weeks a number of stragglers from all battalions, including the lost 2/27th, had been turning up at intervals, starving and sick. They had presented heroic stories of hacking through the jungle and making it against all the odds, and Alan privately hoped that his friends might eventually turn up too.

After all, he'd found out that Teddy Bear had made it back, also against tremendous odds, and carrying terrible wounds. Teddy's account of his two week struggle back to Owers' Corner, and of the extraordinarily dedicated help given the sick and wounded along the way by the Fuzzy Wuzzies, encouraged Alan to believe there was a chance the others would make it.

11

Buckler's Party

WHEN ALAN BECAME SEPARATED FROM JARMBE and the Professor at Isurava, on the evening of 30 August, the two were detained assisting and guarding the wounded in the wake of the vicious firefight a little earlier that day. Working into the dark, Lieutenant Mokka Treacy, the 11 Platoon commander, supervised the construction of the remaining stretchers, often under sniper fire, while Captain Ben Buckler and his men, including Jarmbe and the Professor, gave support and protected Treacy's group.

When they were ready to leave, the party set out and carefully moved along the track from Isurava back towards Alola. Unfortunately, the Japanese by now had completely flanked them and were occupying the track ahead.

After consultation with Treacy, Buckler decided to send out a reconnaissance party in an effort to determine the extent of the enemy infiltration. Sergeant Jack Gwillim, who was now sergeant platoon commander of 9 Platoon, and Leo Deeley, who had won his Military Medal beside Alan on Hill 1284 in Lebanon, were sent forward. They had only gone a few metres when they became caught in a fierce ambush. Gwillim got a bullet in his right shoulder, fracturing his scapula, but Deeley was not so lucky and was killed in the melee. Gwillim staggered back to warn the group that the trail was alive with Japanese.

Enemy gunfire then filled the jungle again as the battle escalated in the dark.

Even though the Australians were holding their own, at 8.00 pm Buckler ordered his troops to break off the conflict and prepare to hack through the bush, as he realised they would have to leave the track and find another way out.

Buckler was fairly short in stature, wore a regulation-type moustache and was extremely fit and wiry. He had high standards of discipline, which meant he was not always very popular in the early days of the battalion. But his toughness and training were soon to be put to the test.

As Jarmbe was preparing his bayonet for hacking at the scrub, a burst of gunfire sprayed out of the darkness, knocking him to the ground. He was dazed but not hurt, but realised his pack had been shot off his back. After a vain search he had to forget the pack, surrendering his letters from home and his photographs of Dot and Reg to the jungle. Poor Jarmbe felt a little more lonely now.

Jack Gwillim was being tended by the medical orderly, Tom Fletcher, who supported Jack's hand and arm with a sling. He joined the group of three walking wounded as the party commenced their withdrawal. There were two stretcher cases and one man was crawling. This was Corporal Johnny Metson, who had sustained two shattered ankles as a result of juki machine-gun fire, but refused to be carried in a stretcher. He covered his hands and knees with bandages for protection and, displaying a heroic spirit of selflessness, began an odyssey of courage rarely surpassed in military history. He cheerfully crawled alongside his comrades, plunging through mud and climbing up and down gruelling mountainsides, inspiring every one of the 50 men in the group.

They cut their way through the jungle all that night, and at 4.00 am rested at a creek forward of Alola. Here they were joined by some more withdrawing Australians, including two more stretcher cases, for which Treacy assumed responsibility.

Painfully and steadily, over the next few days, the party worked their way back to a position outside Alola.

There were four men from Seven Section among the party and they stayed together most of the time—Jarmbe, the Professor, Fred Parsons and Ted Jobe. They took their turn on the stretchers and then took it in turns to carry Jack Gwillim's rifle and pack.

By now, a week after the battle of Isurava commenced, Buckler had realised that the Japanese had taken Alola. As his men were beginning to suffer from exhaustion, exposure to rain and cold, and hunger, he found a secluded native garden high on the range, shrouded in cloud, and called his tired column to a halt. The men dug up some sweet potatoes and cut sugar cane for its sweetness. Under cover of the eerie fog they cooked up a sumptuous meal.

Buckler had made a decision to send Mokka Treacy and two others to try to reach the main unit supply dump at Myola. 'I want you to try and obtain medical supplies, food and native carriers and return here with them,' he told the three men. 'If the unit is not at Myola, push on till you find it. We'll remain here for four days. If you're not back by then, I'll leave two men here for a further two days and the rest of us will head north for the Kokoda Valley and then east—to make for the coast.'

On Saturday morning, 5 September, he wished Mokka good luck and prepared to settle in. On the fifth day, following an alert given by Jarmbe, an excellent bushman, Buckler found Japanese footprints not far from their camp area and realised it was time to move on. There was no word from Treacy, so Buckler decided to aim for Tufi, next to Buna on the coast.

The party moved out on the morning of the sixth day, now reduced in number to 47. There were two officers, with Lieutenant Charlie Butler now second-in-command. Of the eight wounded, four were still stretcher cases, three were walking wounded, among them Jack Gwillim, and one was the crawling wounded man, Johnny Metson.

They struggled for the next three days over almost impossible mountain ranges, manipulating the stretchers around tight bends, passing them from man to man down steep descents, and often needing up to eight men to raise each one over sharp inclines.

Food became scarce again; hunger and exhaustion forced a three-day rest at the first native garden they came to. It had a view overlooking Kokoda Valley in one direction and they could see the ocean sparkling beyond Buna in the other. There were potatoes here and delicious bananas, which helped to revive them. To their delight a wild pig was shot by one of their members, Wally Scott, as it nosed around the garden. It was the first fresh meat they had eaten since leaving Port Moresby.

Back on the track, if anybody felt sorry for himself, or needed inspiration, they would cast a glance at Johnny Metson, still crawling on his battered hands and knees, pushing through mud and slime, climbing the slopes relentlessly, never complaining of the pain of his shattered ankles.

On 20 September, they moved out of the dreaded mountain ranges and were elated to reach the warm coastal plain. Towards evening they arrived at Sangai village, which was deserted. When the local people realised these new soldiers were not Japanese, they slowly reappeared from the bush and helped to prepare taros, yams and bananas for the exhausted troops.

Some of the men were now too sick to move on. The village chief convinced Buckler that it would be extremely difficult to transport his charges over the flooding Kumusi River up ahead, and he offered assurances that he would care for the men until Buckler could airdrop food and medicine and send stretcher-bearers in. When Buckler told the party of the plan, Tom Fletcher immediately volunteered to stay behind and assist with the care of the sick men.

Early in the morning, the dishevelled group lined up in their ranks and the order 'Party, *present arms!*' was given. In this way they acknowledged the courage of Tom Fletcher and the seven wounded and sick soldiers who were remaining behind.

With two native chiefs as guides, the party continued along the track until Gorari Creek which, Buckler realised, would have been almost impassable with the stretchers. The fast-flowing creek raced through the bottom of a thirteen-metre-deep gorge which was crossed by a flimsy, swaying bridge. Jarmbe and the Professor encouraged and supported the unsteady Jack Gwillim as he slowly forced his way over the structure.

The next day the men were greeted by the sound of bombers flying low over them. They could hear the distant *Karump! Karump!* and watched with satisfaction as black smoke curled up from the coast in the direction of Buna.

Realising there was no point in continuing towards Buna, Buckler took his party in an easterly direction along the twisting course of the Kumusi River. His idea was to make for Tufi on the east coast and hope the Australians had a foothold there now; failing that, he would try to cut back over the Owen Stanley Ranges again and rejoin the Allied units on the other side.

The party moved a little more adventurously now, as they felt the further east they went the less chance they would have of encountering an enemy patrol. Over the next few days they crossed more dizzying gorges and passed through many unmarked villages. Fruit, sugar cane and taro were a little more plentiful in this area, which helped.

Following a refreshing swim in the river alongside one of the villages, Jarmbe was lying on his back by the stream. It was the first time he'd taken his boots off for the four weeks of the ordeal, and his bruised feet were enjoying the air and the freedom from his soggy socks and tattered boots.

A butterfly with long black wings striped in brilliant yellow flapped easily in the cool morning air. For Jarmbe it evoked memories of lazier, less desperate days back at the Mission, when time and food were not priorities. He could picture the rugged old ironbarks, the twisted box and the tall, scented grey-gums. He could hear the shrieking parrots fight over the honey grevillea and fragrant wattle. And it reminded him of Reg—and his cousin Dickie, the same age as Reg. Back then the three of them were inseparable. Whenever they could, they would go up into the Grampian Mountains, which was part of tribal land. Here they would catch eels and fish from the small rock corrals in the mountain streams—traps which had been constructed and maintained by Jarmbe's ancestors for 20 000 years or more—since Dreamtime perhaps.

This was the kind of spirituality that Jarmbe could relate to. This was his secret and where he knew his God to be. Lake Condah Mission sat on the summit of a gentle slope overlooking land which everybody called 'Murderous Flats'. Two generations previously, most of the full-blood elders of the Gunditjmara tribe had been rounded up and coldly murdered there. It was difficult for Jarmbe to reconcile this atrocity with Christian philosophy, though he had been christened in the Church of England and respected its traditions and principles.

SOME OF THE MEN WERE NOW suffering from malaria and dysentery, so on 24 September Captain Buckler decided he would push forward by himself in an effort to hurry assistance back to them. To reach help he would have to travel west again and go back over the Owen Stanleys by himself. By now Buckler's once neat moustache had blossomed into a thick and bushy beard, and he looked a wild and battered figure as he said goodbye to his men. Everybody had grown a beard but his was voted to be the fullest, closely followed by Jack Gwillim's.

He left Lieutenant Charles Butler in charge. Butler was a larger man, with a strong frame and a mop of fair hair. For the next week they slowly pushed on down the coast following the Kumusi River. Finally, at Jaurei, they headed inland and prepared to tackle the Owen Stanleys again.

The first day's attack on the mountains was an eleven-hour slog up the foothills, where the sun disappeared and the mists and rain closed down on them once more. The exhausted men imagined they were now at the end of their stamina as they contemplated the inhuman task of climbing the 3000-metre mountain range. In their depressed state, they were startled when someone called out: 'White men!'

Coming down from the mountain was an Australian officer —a commando. He had five other commandos with him, all carrying extra supplies for the struggling men.

Captain Buckler had got through!

The officer smiled and introduced himself. 'I'm Lieutenant Nichols from the 2/6th Independent Company. We're based at Dorobisolo, the other side of the Owen Stanleys, and we've been providing flank protection for your units fighting on the main track. Your Captain Buckler came through a few days ago and requested we bring some supplies back for you. He's continued on to Moresby to try and arrange relief for the rest of your party, who he said were waiting at Sangai.'

Soon a meal of bully beef and biscuits was being prepared, and for the first time in five weeks the group felt reasonably confident they were now going to make it—it was a mere five days' walk to safety. The prospect lifted their spirits and somehow they found new energy.

As well, Nichols reported that Mokka Treacy had been

found by the same commandos only a few days before Buckler arrived there. After a heated pistol battle in which he had killed three Japanese, Mokka had left the track to avoid an ambush and become virtually lost. He and his men had remained alive by killing Japanese and taking their rations, until they were found by the commando patrol.

Nichols continued: 'We have to go back over Ghost Mountain. It's hard work—it's about 10 000 feet high and it's a rotten track through cloud and bloody cold.' The men looked at each other, but said nothing.

There was another surprise for the group that night. An advance party of American infantrymen, unheralded, came down the mountain trail from Dorobisolo. The leader introduced himself and said, matter-of-factly: 'We are going to take Buna.' To the Australian men, this meant a new dimension to the war in New Guinea—a helping hand.

The trek over Ghost Mountain was extremely arduous, climbing quickly from 1800 metres to 3000 metres. The party had been struggling for only a few hours when Gwillim suddenly fell on the rotten track floor, severely twisting his knee. It was locked in position and was beginning to swell. 'I've got an old football injury, Charlie. I think the cartilage has gone properly this time. If I don't hurry, I should be able to hobble along after you.'

Butler assessed the knee and agreed. 'I'd like a volunteer to stay with the sarge. I'll arrange to send a stretcher party back for you from Dorobisolo.'

Unhesitatingly, Jarmbe acknowledged the request. They'd been friends from the beginning. 'Jack's my mate. I'll stick with him.'

Jarmbe assisted Gwillim to his feet and, following the main party, they developed a pattern whereby they would walk a few hundred metres, then rest and recover.

By the first night they had made it high into the mountains and, utterly exhausted, were chilled through as an icy wind bit into their frail clothing. They camped in an eerie moss forest, understanding why the local people had called the mountain 'Diriva Gabuna'—a place of ghosts. About this time Jarmbe began feeling symptoms of fever himself. By early morning he realised he was suffering from malaria and cursed his luck. The men tackled the mountain again next day, sleeping where they fell that night.

As the sun rose, they were about to set out for the day's walk when, like a vision, six locals and a commando appeared on the track before them, carrying a stretcher.

At last the effort for Jack Gwillim was over. For the next few days the stretcher party carried Gwillim, and assisted Jarmbe, out of the mountains. At Dorobisolo the pair rejoined the main party who had camped there for three days. They were examined by the RMO of the commando unit and were cleaned up, given medication, and then food. Later in the day they all continued on a gentler track to Trinumu, a further two days' walk to a village on the banks of the Kempwelsh River.

Here Captain Buckler had arranged for the locals to build twenty rafts to transport the men downriver. As the group watched the lush tropical landscape glide past, Jarmbe relished the thought of a comfortable hospital bed at the end of the journey.

BACK AT PORT MORESBY, THE MEN were shocked to hear the fate of the sick and wounded group they'd left at Sangai. Captain Buckler had found that the Japanese had murdered the heroic Fletcher and Metson and the six other defenceless men. It was a sad ending to a remarkable journey and blunted the survivors' sense of achievement.

In hospital to continue his course of treatment for malaria, Jarmbe wrote to his father and, mentioning the action at Isurava, said: 'Bruce Kingsbury was one of the finest mates a man could have. The night it happened, I wept. I still can't believe he's gone.' He also described his own ordeal with Buckler's party, and commented: 'John Metson was our inspiration. If he could do it on his hands and knees, the rest of us just had to be able to do it.' Jarmbe added that there was talk of the 2/14th being returned to Australia for Christmas.

That rumour had changed a couple of days later, as by then, 25 October, the Japanese had dug in at Eora Creek and the Australians' attack had been slowed as bitter and dogged confrontations were taking a heavy toll on both armies.

Jarmbe then wrote to Dorothy, making light of his recent

ordeal: 'I apologise for not writing, but I've been missing in action for seven weeks. I'm in an Aussie hospital with malaria fever . . . I hoped to be able to spend Christmas or New Year with you, but there's not much chance of it now. I think the Army has different ideas from mine . . . I lost my pack in action with all my photos of you in it—how I cursed the little yellow Japs—please could you send me some more.'

In mid-November Jarmbe was discharged, fit to rejoin his battalion which was still resting at Koitaki. After the dust and heat of Port Moresby, Koitaki was beautiful and green. A river ran past the camp site, a native village nestled along its banks and cattle wandered among coconut palms and rubber trees. Jarmbe was resplendent in clean, new clothes and, as was his Aboriginal habit, had massaged oil over his skin and into his healthy head of hair. He fairly glistened as he alighted from the jeep. He was walking along the river bank towards camp headquarters when, among other soldiers, he recognised a familiar figure. He realised with delight that it was Alan Avery.

The two friends held nothing back in their joy at seeing each other again, shaking hands vigorously.

'Geez, Jarmbe, you bastard! I didn't think I'd ever see you again. You look great! How are you after your trip in the bush?'

'I'm pretty fine now, mate. But what's this with the stripes?' Jarmbe pointed to Alan's right arm.

'Yeah, and the silly bastards are going to make me into an officer, f'Chrissake.'

They both laughed, as neither could imagine Alan as an officer.

'I was a private at Isurava, a corporal several days later, and a sergeant a few days after that. Then I was told I was to be an officer—and mate, I have to leave tomorrow. I've got to go to OCTU [Officers' Cadet Training Unit] at Bonegilla. You've caught me just in time.

'I figure Rhoden thought I'd suffered a bit of trauma losing Bruce and wanted to keep me busy. He'll probably be sorry for ever!'

Alan paused, then went on: 'I suppose you heard the battalion won a swag of gongs after Isurava—about eight, you know. Someone said it's the most any Australian or British battalion won in a single day ever. And to top it off—Bruce being awarded the VC! Hell, he deserved it. What a bloody terrible day—talk about desperate! Bruce was magnificent, wasn't he. He virtually threw his life away but he turned things around. God, I miss him.'

He looked down, but recovered quickly. 'They reckon it's the first VC won on Australian soil. I reckon after those four bloody days at Isurava the Japs would've realised they had a game on their hands—and Bruce's VC might've been the turning point. And what about Teddy? They only gave him an MM—should have got more. Hell, he started the charge, after all.

'Mind you, everybody should have got gongs that day. You know, when our chaps got back to the area in front of Butch Bisset's platoon they counted over 200 dead Japs there. They reckon Butch should have got a VC as well. The Japs certainly paid dearly—the whole way across the board. At least they gave Mokka an MC.'

'Fair enough too,' said Jarmbe. 'A few others from our mob got medals as well—Fletcher got an MM and Metson got the BEM. Boy, the battalion was blown apart that day. Must have been hell when you got caught at Mission Ridge.'

'Yeah! They got Charlie McCallum there. He picked up a DCM from Isurava, but I heard they recommended him for a VC instead. You often wonder how they work these things out. Y'know, they call Mission Ridge 'Brigade Hill' or 'Butchers Hill' now. When the 25th Brigade went back there in early October, they found 22 of our boys and about 70 of the other battalions exactly where they'd been killed—with their fingers still clutched around the triggers. The Japs didn't even bury them, though the bastards buried their own.'

Alan stopped and then smiled. 'Still, I suppose there's been some justice. Did you know that yesterday General Horii and four of his officers bought it as he and his bloody rabble were going back over the Kumusi? Their dinghy overturned. I hear they drowned. Serves the bastard right. Y'know, Stan Bisset—who's now a captain, by the way—told me that some of the Intelligence parties had seen the cheeky blighter riding a white charger up in the mountains just like the Lone Ranger. The natives apparently caught and killed his horse when he drowned.

'Mind you, some of the blokes reckon the Japs might be settling in for a last stand at Gona and Buna.'

For a moment the two silently reflected on what had been, unwilling to say goodbye. 'Well, I guess it'll be good to get back home again,' Alan said finally, 'and y'know, I'll probably get married pretty soon. I reckon I'll propose to Ann when I get back.' Jarmbe laughed and wished Alan all the best.

'Well, I'm going one way, you're going another,' Alan said.

Jarmbe smiled wryly. 'I dunno where I'm going . . .' The men shook hands firmly, said goodbye, and Alan left for Port Moresby, on his way home to Australia.

12

Gona

JARMBE HAD BEEN IN HIS NEW quarters for only a few days when the battalion received an order to prepare to move, in battle mode, to the other side of the Owen Stanley Ranges. The Japanese had retreated, being pushed back, and were now entrenched in well-prepared defensive positions at the Gona–Sanananda–Buna beachhead. Over some months, they had diligently transformed the area around Gona Mission House into a lethal trap for any over-enthusiastic enemy, and had been holding off a determined attack by a weary, indisposed Australian force.

The 25th Brigade, with other units, had managed to contain the enemy within a limited area but were now falling casualty to chronic exhaustion from a nonstop ten-week campaign and from malaria, scrub typhus and dysentery. The attack had bogged down and the 21st Brigade was requested to relieve them.

The 2/14th was the first of the three brigade battalions to leave Port Moresby; the men emplaned on 25 November at the Seven Mile drome to fly to Popondetta, some 32 kilometres march from Gona.

The battalion had not been completely reinforced at this stage and many of the wounded and sick from the Owen Stanleys campaign had not returned. The unit was very much understrength, consisting of 341 men all up, including nineteen officers and 322 other ranks. It had been organised into three rifle companies with Mokka Treacy, now promoted to captain, commanding A Company, which of course included Jarmbe's 9 Platoon. Jock Lochhead, the 9 Platoon sergeant who had passed the order that Teddy Bear take over the platoon at Isurava, had amazingly recovered from his critical head wound and was now the commander of 9 Platoon, replacing the injured Jack Gwillim.

Lochhead lead his platoon into the belly of the biscuit bomber and they settled into the aluminium seats lining the fuselage. Within a few minutes they were powering over the craggy Owen Stanleys. Below them, Jarmbe could make out quite clearly parts of the track which now meant such a lot to him. As Kokoda appeared on the horizon ahead, lying at the base of the mountains, he recognised Alola and Isurava perched on the edge of the hillside, pointing down to Kokoda. His mind went back to those terrible few days.

Suddenly he was snapped back to the present by a hefty whack from Hi-Ho Silver, who had been calling him. 'Hey, Jarmbe, wake up, there's Popondetta ahead. Get your gear.' The flight had taken less than fifteen minutes.

Stan was already at Popondetta and, as the Adjutant, was managing the logistics for the battalion to reach Soputa by nightfall. Soputa was on the Sanananda Track and was a hard thirteen-kilometre march.

The battalion slept that night at Soputa, and next morning they began the nineteen-kilometre trek to Gona. The going was as tough as any they had encountered in the ranges, as the track consisted of thick, gluey mud and skirted hot kunai grass patches, humid swamps and fetid jungle areas.

Towards nightfall, and about two kilometres before Gona, Stan was passed on the track by some sick and wounded members of the 25th Brigade. They were slumping, their hollow faces bent over exhausted bodies. By their colour badges he recognised them as being from the 2/25th Battalion, and he remembered the strong, healthy men who had relieved the composite battalion at Ioribaiwa, ten weeks previously.

As the group staggered passed him, he was suddenly shocked to recognise one of them. 'Sergeant,' Stan called. The soldier slowly turned towards the voice, but did not register who owned it.

Stan focused on the eyes. They were no longer cornflower blue, but dark recesses which had seen too much horror. His weight had been stripped from about 80 kilograms to 45, his once strong forearms were now gaunt tendons and his flushed appearance indicated a raging temperature.

'You replaced us at Ioribaiwa, do you remember?' Stan said.

The sergeant's eyes flickered in recognition. 'Yes, sir,' he answered slowly, 'you were in the composite battalion. Glad you're here—we're all bushed, as you can see.' With an effort, he offered the hint of a cheeky smile. 'What kept you?'

His eyes narrowed and were pained again. 'We couldn't quite finish the bastards off. We've been hammering away at 'em and getting nowhere. We think they're being reinforced by sea—but they're so well dug in. They've got machine-gun posts set up for 150 yards around the Mission. The gun pits are reinforced with logs and covered with dirt—even mortars can't hurt 'em. The Japs fire through slits and have set up a bloody enfilading fire pattern so they all cover each other.

'Then there's a coconut palm belt along the whole area. Their snipers strap themselves to the top of a tree and shoot at anyone fool enough to crawl within 50 yards of them.

'We tried to go in several times. It was the closest thing to hell that I can imagine. In one day we lost 64 men. We're down to about 15 per cent strength now—I'm one of the last out.'

'It doesn't sound good,' Stan said, in something of an understatement.

'Whatever you do, watch the bloody snipers. They're deadly, and they go for any bugger silly enough to be carrying a Bren.' The sergeant's voice cracked with emotion. 'I lost too many good mates . . .'

'You'd better get back to the the RAP, Sergeant. You don't look too good.'

The sergeant raised a wry smile. 'That's one of the worst things. The sun just belts down in that dry kunai grass. Most of us have got a fever well over the 100-degree mark as we've all got malaria—but we don't report sick unless we're over 105 degrees. It just adds to the hell!'

Stan wished him good luck and smiled as he called after him: 'That farm's going to look good!' He watched the sergeant move on, stumble, catch himself, then continue towards the RAP back at Soputa.

THE 2/14TH BATTALION WAS NOW COMMANDED by Lieutenant Colonel Hugh Challen. He had been staff captain of the 21st Brigade in Syria and had been awarded an MBE for his work during that campaign. He had also served as brigade major during the Owen Stanleys Campaign and replaced Phil Rhoden—by now Major Rhoden—who had been temporarily leading the battalion. Although Challen had proved to be a competent staff officer, Stan held little confidence in his ability to command a battalion. Stan was also concerned that Challen's judgement might be impaired by fatigue, as since early October he had led a composite battalion known as 'Chaforce' in a gruelling campaign back over the ranges, until he returned to take command of the 2/14th.

As the battalion rested half a kilometre southeast of the entrenched enemy at Gona Mission, Challen received orders that they should move to an area called Small Creek. This was about halfway between Gona Mission and East Gona. From there they were ordered to lead an attack on the Mission on 29 November.

In peacetime, Gona was reputedly one of the most beautiful locations on the northeastern coast of New Guinea. The deep blue Solomon Sea broke onto a long sweep of clean black sand lined with coconut palms and banyan trees. Red hibiscus flowers and yellow crotons highlighted a sturdy church constructed of thatched sago leaf. Behind this sat an ordered Mission House with a red roof, and behind that an attractive school house rested at the edge of a grass cricket field.

Gona Creek entered the sea about 90 metres to the west of the Mission. A belt of trees stretched about a kilometre from Gona Creek through to Small Creek in the east, effectively cordoning off the area.

The Japanese had capitalised on these natural defensive barriers by skilfully interspersing well-entrenched machine-gun pits with deadly snipers hidden among the palm trees, and placing them in a semi-circle on the southern and eastern sides of the Mission. It was an almost impenetrable situation, as the 25th Brigade had found out.

The battalion started to move out on the afternoon of 28 November and Challen called a halt in the bush at 3.00 pm. Even though they had received word from the withdrawing 25th Brigade headquarters that the area ahead was clear, Challen sent out Lieutenant Bob Dougherty with his 11 Platoon to reconnoitre the area forward to the beach and to secure Small Creek to the north, then send a guide back for the main party.

Dougherty, a tough, nuggety soldier with a ready smile and a tousle of blond hair, had been a friend of Stan's back to Power House days, being a handy Rugby player. Stan became concerned when Dougherty had not returned or sent a guide by 5.30 pm, imagining that he may have run into a Japanese patrol. However, the decision had been made at a higher level to attack Gona over Small Creek, and Challen was determined that this should proceed, even without Dougherty's information.

Stan said to Challen: 'Sir, it's madness to try a frontal attack on this position. It's just about dark and it's not been properly reconnoitred. Even though the 25th Brigade reported that the area was clear, it may not be now. Besides, we haven't heard from Bob Dougherty. The fact is, we don't really know who's there or what their strength is.'

Challen accepted the advice, then contacted brigade headquarters. After a heated exchange, he put the phone down. 'I'm sorry, Stan, they want it to go ahead.'

Just on dusk the Australians moved forward, firstly trudging along a gluey, winding jungle track. The last 300 metres entailed wading through chest-deep sago swamps. Moving through the foul-smelling slime, Stan held his rifle above his head and hoped they weren't caught there by the enemy. As he emerged from the filthy ooze, he sought cover behind some scrub and kunai grass. In the dim light he could make out a beach area ahead, made sinister by contorted mangroves bursting out of another swampy area.

Stan's worst fears materialised when, at the instant the first soldiers entered the beach area, they were met with heavy and deadly fire. They had walked straight into strongly prepared positions.

Machine-guns, positioned to cover each other, set up a murderous fire pattern and viciously cut the leading Australians to pieces. Crack snipers then started a deadly, methodical process of selecting and shooting anyone not adequately covered. The Australians could not see where the firing was coming from, as the greenness had melted from the jungle and the near darkness had now settled over the well-camouflaged Japanese positions. As the situation rapidly deteriorated, Stan suppressed his anger and quickly moved to the front.

The signallers had brought a phone and its cable through the swamps and set up a communication point just behind the forward units who were in the immediate line of fire. Stan relayed the situation to headquarters, then searched for Challen for instructions.

He was told the colonel was further back and was not available to make a decision. This can't wait, Stan thought, I have to act myself.

He decided there was only one thing to do—pull the men out and extricate the wounded. He enlisted the help of Sergeant Jimmy Coy. Coy had been in Butch's 10 Platoon and had helped to bring Butch out of Isurava after he'd been hit. Now a sergeant in 11 Platoon, Coy was in the forward party when it was cut to ribbons in the beach area. The company commander, Captain McGavin, was one of those killed by a sniper. Taking control, Coy coolly shot the sniper out of his tree. With rifle and machine-gun fire cutting and lighting the air above him, he crawled forward and rested in a blind spot against the wall of one of the machine-gun pits. Quickly he fed a hand grenade through the slit opening, the screams of the gunners inside being drowned by the exploding grenade and ammunition pile. He then crawled over to a second pit and repeated the act, covering his head as the explosion catapulted logs and sandbags into the air.

Finally he crawled back to the communication point, where Stan had now taken charge.

'Jimmy, I want you to go back to your platoon, if you can find them in the dark,' Stan said. 'Tell them to call off the attack and just keep low. I want to get the wounded out and I'm setting up a holding line to try and evacuate them. Take the message to Lieutenant Evans at the front. Tell him I'll send up some stretcher-bearers.'

Coy scampered out into the darkness again and passed Stan's message on. He then began assisting the walking wounded back to the communication point, where Private Boys of the signals platoon helped them find the telephone cable, which they followed in the dark through the swamp to the RAP.

As he was bending over to help an injured soldier, a bullet from a sniper went into Coy's right scapula. It traced along his spinal muscles and lodged in his hip. He dropped to the ground immediately, but would not allow the wound to be dressed. He continued to direct proceedings until Stan reached him a little later.

Stan had gone forward to all the front positions to supervise the extrication of the wounded. He moved carefully through the dark, organising men to care for and carry out the injured as he found them. It was a difficult and dangerous job, as the cries of agony and the manipulation of stretchers through the kunai grass invited gunfire directly onto their positions.

By the time Stan made it round to 11 Platoon, Coy was in great pain but uncowed, still directing the extrication in his area. He was propped against a tree and insisted on informing Stan of the results of the task. He then slipped into unconsciousness. Stan arranged for Coy's wounds to be dressed and for bearers to carry him out. He was among the last to be evacuated at the end of this devastating day of carnage, at about 11.30 pm, although the firing continued intermittently until well after midnight.

Although Jarmbe and 9 Platoon were not in the melee that evening, they had been helping with the evacuation of the wounded through the swamp. Jarmbe was surprised and upset to see that one of the severely wounded men was Charlie Butler, the second-in-charge during their epic six-week walk out of Isurava in September. Butler, now a captain, had received a devastating machine-gun blast through the eye, jaw and shoulder.

The battalion lost six of their best officers and 40 other men at Small Creek. Gona was proving a costly exercise so far.

Lieutenant Dougherty's fighting reconnaissance patrol had returned in the late evening. Unfortunately, they had pushed

177

too far to the east and had struck a Japanese patrol on the beach, where a willing firefight finished up with twenty dead Japanese lying sprawled on the beach and in the kunai grass. The lieutenant had no chance to report in by the required time, but he did send runners who got in at 7.15 pm. It was too late—the attack was well under way.

BY THE EARLY HOURS OF 29 NOVEMBER, most of the battalion had moved back to the starting position again.

Challen had now taken charge once more, and was ready to accept the new orders for the day as they were phoned through from brigade headquarters. It was a new plan, as the preceding day's encounter had failed to secure the intended positions. He called Stan in and relayed the orders to him.

'Stan, from 9.30 to 11.10 the airforce are going to bomb Gona Mission and the beach area in preparation for an assault by the 2/27th. North of Gona, the 25th Brigade's 2/33rd Battalion and the 3rd Battalion will try and take that area. While the bombing is on, we have to destroy the enemy east of Small Creek as part of the preparation.'

Once again Stan didn't like it. The battalion had carried out no proper reconnaissance. As well, they were still reeling from last night's mauling and there had been no staff planning, let alone adequate time to work out a reasonably coordinated plan of attack. Furthermore, they now knew how well concealed and protected the enemy were.

However, despite his protests, the attack went ahead.

At precisely 9.30 that morning, twelve fighter planes peeled in from behind the Owen Stanleys and each dropped a 300-pound bomb on the Gona installations. At the same time three A-20s screamed down the beach, strafing the Japanese positions with machine-guns. Within a few moments the beach was littered with splintered palm and coconut trees as the bullets shattered and razed the foliage. Smoke and dust rose from the area as the bombs exploded on impact, echoing the sound back to the 2/14th Battalion's location.

Jarmbe and Hi-Ho could clearly hear the crash and crump and feel the slight tremors as the bombs exploded less than a kilometre away from them. They could see the A-20s dive into the attack and skim along the beach, often just below the height of the coconut palms, then accelerate back into the sky in preparation for another run.

While they were being entertained by the aerobatics, A Company, consisting of 7, 8 and 9 Platoons and led by Mokka Treacy, moved off through the kunai and began making their way towards the beach east of Small Creek. With one eye on the sky, Hi-Ho said: 'Boy, the airforce are sure giving them a plastering today. They've been belting away there for close on two hours. There can't be too many Japs left.'

In reality, though, the air attack had not caused a great deal of damage to the Japanese. Most of the bunkers had been built from coconut palm logs and steel drums filled with earth and sand. They were covered with more logs and, in some cases, steel sheeting. They were interconnected by a network of trenches, and as soon as these came under fire the occupants simply retreated into the bunkers and re-emerged when the bombardment ceased. The bunkers also proved to be resistant to 25-pound shells and three-inch mortar bombs. Mostly they were so well camouflaged that they were almost impossible to see from the air. In fact, they were often invisible to anyone crawling a metre or two away from them.

The three platoons steadily moved through the kunai and scrub and at about 11.00 carefully left the protection of the bush and emerged onto the beach. Jarmbe found himself walking beside a mate of his from 7 Platoon, Corporal Norm Stringer. As the platoons started off down the beach towards Small Creek they could hear firing ahead of them, and realised that the 2/27th had engaged the enemy around Gona Mission. They could hear that the conflict was intense and suspected that the air bombardment hadn't greatly dampened the enemy's enthusiasm for a fight.

Jarmbe felt a bit conspicuous, as he was carrying the Bren gun. 'Crikey,' he murmured, 'I hope those planes did a better job down our end.' The adrenaline was starting to flow now, his mouth was dry, and his fingers gripped the trigger and butt of the Bren so tightly that his knuckles blanched.

'Yeah, let's hope so,' said Stringer. The platoons warily advanced down the beach and adjoining scrubland, each man vigilant for snipers and cautious of sites that might conceal a bunker. At the same time they were consciously noting features that would give them cover in case of sudden attack.

They had just manoeuvred through a small orchard growing beside the beach when machine-gun fire suddenly ripped through the air. They had walked into a well-prepared ambush. Several men dropped around Jarmbe. Out of the corner of his eye he saw Ted Jobe fall, wounded. Jarmbe went to ground and spreadeagled himself behind his Bren gun. He aimed at where he thought the fire was coming from. There were screams as his own bullets seared through a camouflaged figure at the top of a coconut palm. The sniper fell out of the foliage and dangled upside down from where he had been strapped in.

Hi-Ho crawled up beside Jarmbe. 'Jesus, I think Bluey Whitechurch copped one too. Just keep firing in that general area. I'm buggered if I can see the bastards.'

Over to the right, Stringer had been caught in the open and a sniper had put a bullet through his pack. A second round quickly followed and blew his tins of bully beef apart in the pack. He crawled over behind a lemon tree as the sniper whizzed shots all around him. He yelled out to Jarmbe: 'This bastard's on to me.' Stringer played dead for an instant as Jarmbe and Hi-Ho fired blindly into the area where the concealed enemy was. The sniping fire stopped, and Stringer quickly moved over to them as they continued to try to locate the enemy.

On the right flank, Jarmbe could see Mokka Treacy leading by example, encouraging his men, occasionally standing up, almost deliberately exposing his athletic figure, firing, then lying down again.

As they lay there, pinned down, they could see their own casualties mounting. Eventually, when it became obvious that the attack had failed, the order came through to withdraw. Carefully, the men started going back along the beach to their starting point. They carried the wounded with them, as Jarmbe gave covering fire.

By 12.30 pm they had all regrouped behind the firing line, Jarmbe being one of the last to withdraw. The company had been decimated, but the remaining men were formed into a composite platoon and were told they were to attack again after having something to eat.

Stringer, Jarmbe, Hi-Ho and several others lay exhausted in

a circle discussing the morning's debacle. 'Shit, look at your pack, Norm,' Jarmbe said. 'They must have used dum-dum bullets.' The pack had been shattered and the bully beef cans blown apart, spraying the contents everywhere.

Stringer laughed. 'Yeah, mate. I thought that was me for a second when I saw the meat. I reckon that bastard thought he'd got me. Thank God he pulled off when he did.'

'Boy, they got a few of us that time,' Jarmbe said. 'I saw them cart off Teddy and Bluey. The bearer said they'll be OK. Y'know, that leaves only you and me from Seven Section, Hi-Ho.'

'Yeah, you're right.' Hi-Ho grimaced, lay back and looked up at the annoyingly beautiful blue sky.

The adrenaline had almost worn off after the morning's conflict and the two men were starting to become anxious about moving into battle again. They missed their Seven Section friends—the section had been pretty special. Now they were down to two.

Jarmbe shared his bully beef with Stringer and the men ate quietly as they contemplated the afternoon assault. All too soon it was time. Jarmbe's hands perspired as he shouldered his weapon and moved to the forming-up area.

COLONEL CHALLEN HAD ARRANGED FOR FULL mortar and artillery fire to precede their onslaught after the break. Stan had moved up with the artillery officer and was lying beside him as he directed fire from a short 25-pound artillery gun. The bunkers were difficult to see, and although he was aware that the rounds were splintering and shredding some of the coconut trees around them, he wasn't confident they were doing much damage to the bunkers.

In fact the bunkers in this section had been constructed under some native huts which were filled with 'Mae West' life preservers—effectively a two-metre padding of kapok. There was a ten-centimetre gap from the bottom of the hut to the parapet of the gunpit. Each pit contained about seven men, including at least one machine-gunner. They were in shadow and the advancing Australians had no idea where they were exactly. But the Japanese had a perfect panoramic view of them.

Once again the Australians had not undertaken proper reconnaissance or planning for the attack. Stan watched with concern as the composite platoon went forward.

They were moving at a fairly quick pace, a few metres apart—about twenty men in line. They had left the cover of the kunai grass and were now crossing open ground. The line extended from the scrub bordering the beach across to the beach itself, where a ledge had been formed by the action of the waves. The only other cover was a few isolated palm trees, silent sentinels to the unfolding drama.

Mokka Treacy was leading from the centre. On the right flank—the beach side—Jarmbe was moving steadily beside Stringer with Hi-Ho a couple of metres behind. Jarmbe had surrendered his Bren gun to George Thompson during the break and was holding his .303. Maurie Valli, Stan's rover in the football team that had won the premiership at Puckapunyal, was next to him. He was a couple of paces in front, carrying his Bren gun at the ready. The other Bren-gunner, Thompson, was similarly alert, as they were both well aware of the intention of the enemy to wipe out machine-gunners first. He was next to the platoon commander, Jock Lochhead, and Maurie Taafe completed the line on the extreme right flank as they boldly moved forward.

Suddenly the tension was broken as a single sniper shot whipped through the air. It slammed into Mokka Treacy, hitting him in the head. He dropped to the ground instantly. There was a moment of disbelief among the men in the line as one of the most admired and heroic figures of the unit was lost to them. Reality quickly followed, then anger, as the scene erupted in a cascade of fire. Guns from both sides blazed, filling the air with whizzing bullets, thunderous sound and smoke.

The two Bren-gunners quickly located the sniper responsible for the attack on Treacy and shot him out of his palm tree, riddling the tree and the man's body. They fought their way forward another 25 metres towards the blockaded positions, replaced their magazines, then streamed gunfire through the small apertures. The slits were too small for a grenade to be pushed through, so accurate and close fire was the only way to clear these pits. After obliterating two enemy posts, they concentrated on the other snipers who were opening up and taking a toll. Jarmbe, Stringer and Hi-Ho moved forward in support, firing as they went, but having difficulty identifying the well-hidden marksmen.

Sergeant Lochhead could see that the Bren-gunners were low on ammunition. Quickly he secured a carton of magazines and moved out of his palm tree cover and up to Valli and Thompson. He didn't make it. A bullet ripped through his throat and he dropped to the ground without moving. An instant later both Bren-gunners surrendered their lives too, as a sniper's bullet hit Thompson through the throat and another got Valli through the head. This was murderous, accurate shooting.

Stan had moved further forward and had witnessed these killings with increasing horror. This can't go on, he thought. Other men dropped near him, killed or wounded.

Then, a few metres in front of him, Jarmbe suddenly fell. During the same salvo Stringer was wounded in the shoulder as a bullet smashed off the palm tree he was sheltering behind. Jarmbe and Stringer dropped to the ground almost simultaneously, and fell under the protection of the wave-formed ledge on the beach. Stringer crawled over to Jarmbe who was lying on his back, not moving, his eyes looking blankly into oblivion. Fearing the worst, he removed Jarmbe's helmet and was shocked to see that the bullet had gone in behind the right ear and had blown the top of Jarmbe's head off. At least it was a quick death, he thought. He placed the helmet over the dead man's face, then pulled open Jarmbe's shirt and searched for his dogtags.

As he was breaking off the bottom half of the tags, he found a locket entwined in them. By now Hi-Ho Silver had crawled up to be beside his mate. Stringer showed the locket to the distraught Silver. 'Look at this, Hi-Ho! It says "Dot, Adelaide".'

'Hell, I didn't know he had a girlfriend—if it *is* his girlfriend. We used to kid him, but he never let on. Jesus!' Hi-Ho looked at the locket for a moment. 'Christ, Jarmbe, I'm gonna miss you.' He pocketed the tags and the medallion and cursed the war; hardly hearing Stan yelling to them from behind to move back.

The company were now ordered to extricate themselves— there'd been too much killing for too little gain. Hi-Ho sadly sought out the RAP and presented the tags and medallion to the orderlies. He pointed at the medallion. 'See it gets back to his family and to Dot, whoever she is.' In a state of shock, he staggered to a quiet, safe area of the beach, his shaking hands fumbling with a cigarette, and looked blankly out to sea.

A further attempt to dislodge the Japanese from their positions was made later in the afternoon. It also failed, and resulted in more casualties. By the end of that bloody day, the day Jarmbe died, 29 November, the battalion had lost thirteen killed and 23 wounded.

Stan could contain himself no longer. He was incensed at the tragic, senseless loss. That evening, at battalion headquarters, he got through to the brigade and asked to speak to Brigadier Dougherty. 'Sir,' he started, 'Captain Bisset, Adjutant, 2/14th. Sir, please forgive me for talking forthrightly. The truth is, open confrontation is not working. The way we're doing it is senseless killing. We are not being given time to pinpoint the enemy's positions. They are too well camouflaged and dug in. We just can't be effective.'

The words came out with pent-up emotion and he was too agitated to judge what effect they might have on the brigadier. But the senior officer thanked him for his advice and said he would consider Stan's assessment of the situation.

The next day the brigadier was still concerned that the enemy might make a strong move in the 2/14th Battalion area. He discussed with Challen the prospects of a sharp bayonet attack on the fortified position, to be preceded by a concentrated 25-pounder artillery attack.

Challen agreed with the idea. But this time the battalion was allowed to instigate and carry out its own battle plan. Challen allocated tasks to various sections in accordance with a well-coordinated overall scheme. Aggressive reconnaissance patrols were sent in to locate the Japanese positions, and after a five-minute artillery softening-up period, one section concentrated on the enemy snipers with accurate, careful, pinpoint firing. A focused blasting of the gun posts with rifle grenades, two-inch mortars and hand grenades, plus harassing tactics employed by a patrol on the beach, overwhelmed the entrenched enemy. As a result of the sustained onslaught, the enemy began to break and run. A bayonet charge completed the victory over the occupied site. Stan noted with pleasure that the final charge resulted in only two minor casualties for his battalion, although they had lost three killed earlier that morning.

It was a significant victory, as it was the first time the Allies had won through to the sea on the northern coast of New Guinea. They now had possession of over a kilometre and a half of beach within the Buna–Gona area. But the task of taking the central Japanese fortifications remained.

In the evening the battalion created a small temporary cemetery on that northern shore. Nineteen of their best men were buried during a solemn ceremony. Jarmbe was placed beside the friends who had died with him and with whom he had gained mutual respect and love.

Hi-Ho and Stringer stood there in a sombre mood as the last of the tropical sun highlighted the hibiscus flowers that had been placed over Jarmbe's grave.

'You know,' Stringer said, 'it's a funny thing . . . there's no difference, is there. Just before we buried Jarmbe and the others, I couldn't tell that he was black or that they were white. They'd all turned grey.'

'Nah, mate,' Hi-Ho said sadly, 'when the chips are down, there's no differences. I never thought of him as black—just my mate.'

FOR THE NEXT FEW DAYS THE remaining battalions in the field concentrated on taking Gona Mission and the Sanananda beachhead. By 3 December the 25th Brigade, with the 3rd Battalion, were completely exhausted and had to be relieved from the field of battle. The 30th Brigade, consisting of the 39th, 49th and 55th/53rd Battalions, replaced them; the last two units having been quickly sent up the Sanananda Track. The 39th, who had fought so bravely at Isurava beside the 2/14th, were allocated positions to assist in attacks on Gona Mission.

From that time on, the battalions in the field were able to fight the enemy in their own way, harassing it with active patrols and gradually eliminating it with all the means at their disposal—aerial bombing, artillery, mortars, grenades and starvation—without taking unnecessary risks. Only after intensive patrols and studied reconnaissance were attacks thrust against the still well-fortified enemy.

The final battles were not without their losses or sadness for Stan. His friend from the 2/16th, Alan Haddy, had been holding a village two kilometres west of Gona with a patrol of about fifteen men. On the night of 6 December, under cover of a severe thunderstorm, a large Japanese force was landed on the beach and overran the small patrol. Haddy and half of his men were killed in a raging battle.

The brigadier, who was in the midst of planning an all out attack against Gona Mission for 8 December, was alarmed at this action. He ordered the 2/14th to investigate the strength of the Japanese force at what came to be called Haddy's Village. Stan's friend, the determined Lieutenant Bob Dougherty, led a patrol of 50 men and surprised the enemy. He immediately launched a fierce attack, and although outrageously out-numbered in hand-to-hand fighting, his troops inflicted 90 casualties on the Japanese for the loss of six wounded, success-fully halting the Japanese advance.

Bob Dougherty personally accounted for fourteen Japanese and was recommended for the Victoria Cross. And the Austra-lians could now attack Gona with some confidence while the 2/14th contained the new arrivals at Haddy's Village.

And attack they did. A large combined Australian force moved on the fortified positions around the Mission after fifteen minutes' mortar and artillery bombardment. Although the attack-ers suffered heavy casualties, nothing was going to stop them this time.

By the night of 9 December, after some of the most bitter hand-to-hand battles of the war, the garrison was wiped out.

Cleaning up Gona was a filthy job. The Japanese had lived in indescribable conditions, and the scene that greeted the Australians' eyes was one of carnage and mayhem. No endeav-our had been made by the enemy to bury the dead—theirs or the Australians'—and bodies were piled everywhere. The stench was terrible, as the Japanese had even used their own rotting and decayed dead in the construction of some of their earth-works. Over the next two days, 650 dead Japanese were found and buried in the area.

But the killing was not over yet. Stan was saddened to hear that Bob Dougherty had been killed during an aggressive patrol in the Haddy's Village area. Even though Gona had gone, there was still a nasty sting in the tail of the scorpion.

Two days after his friend's death, on 13 December, Stan was making a reconnaissance along the beachfront, just forward of the battalion's furthest weapon pit. His senses went on to full alert as he sighted a movement further along the beach, his now experienced eyes identifying a sniper. Shielding behind a palm tree, Stan spreadeagled himself on the ground, took careful aim, and was rewarded to see the man fall. Another sniper then opened up on Stan, only to be dropped also. However, this drew out a third sniper. Stan gritted his teeth as a bullet scythed through the camouflage net of his helmet. Another one ripped through his gaiter and then one more cut through the skin alongside his right eye.

As the blood trickled into his eye, impairing his vision, Stan quickly edged backwards and took cover in the handy weapon pit.

This was the pattern of things until the Australians' final attack on Haddy's Village on 18 December. On that morning, after throwing a constant hail of sniper fire and grenades at the enemy, the combined 2/14th and 39th Battalions moved in, to find only one survivor. Wounded Japanese had been evacuated by barge, but the Australians counted 170 bodies left behind.

A sad but telling discovery was the remains of Haddy's patrol members who had so ferociously defended the village against the seaborne invaders. Haddy himself was found underneath the platform of the command hut, faithful to his post, his body ringed by dead Japanese.

For the 2/14th Battalion, the successful assault on the village signified the end of a relentless, bloody and costly campaign.

A day or two later the battalion returned to the brigade headquarters area. There were only 21 able-bodied combat troops left in the unit: three officers, including Stan Bisset, and eighteen other ranks—barely enough to create two sections. A proud 341 men had marched in from Popondetta some four weeks previously. Including the walking wounded and headquarters camp personnel, just 47 men marched out on the evening of 7 January 1943.

EPILOGUE

13

The Years After

SEVEN SECTION OF 9 PLATOON, IN the 2/14th Battalion, has been described as the most highly decorated section in Australian and British military history. Between them the eleven original members won a Victoria Cross, a Distinguished Conduct Medal and four Military Medals. The eleven members were Private Bruce Kingsbury VC, Lieutenant Lindsay 'Teddy' Bear DCM, MM, Lieutenant Alan Avery MM, Sergeant Ted 'Hi-Ho' Silver MM, Sergeant J. Whitechurch MM, and Privates Harry Saunders (Jarmbe), B. G. Wilson, D. O'Connor, F. J. Parsons, Neil Gordon and E. R. Jobe.

The lives of those who survived followed very different paths in the long years after World War II. Let's take a brief look at some of them.

Alan Avery When Alan returned to Australia from New Guinea, he attended officer training in Adelaide and served in all the rest of the campaigns as a lieutenant with the 2/14th. He married Ann in March 1944. When peace came he went back to working as a nurseryman. Before the war Alan rarely drank, but now he became a heavy drinker. His marriage broke down in 1965. He left Melbourne and began an itinerant lifestyle: various jobs around Queensland, opal mining at Lightning Ridge, woodworking in Townsville. Eventually he worked as a groundsman for

191

the United Service Club in Brisbane. He retired to the beachside district of Clontarf in the early 1970s, finally overcame his addiction to alcohol, and developed into an expert woodworker.

It would be easy to dismiss Alan's life as a classic case of post-traumatic stress disorder—he had seen his best friend killed next to him, he had experienced many bloody battles where life had been cheapened utterly, yet he had survived. But Alan was also a strong personality and lived life by his own lights. He did not suffer fools gladly and his crusty pragmatism enabled him to call a spade a spade. He was highly principled—often to the point of being dogmatic—and was overgenerous to friends he trusted.

In his last days, Alan deteriorated rapidly as his body systems shut down one after the other. He could see the signs clearly. He was determined, among other things, not to compromise his independence, so, following the practical 'soldier's prerogative', he ended his own life on his own terms. He died in May 1995.

Lindsay 'Teddy' Bear After recovering from his wounds on the Kokoda Track, Teddy married Martha late in 1942. In October 1943 he led a charge at Shaggy Ridge in New Guinea, winning the DCM. He was severely wounded three times during this encounter and it took him many months to recuperate in Port Moresby and Brisbane. He attended officer training at Seymour in November 1944, topping the course and receiving the baton of honour.

After the war Teddy gained a diploma in Bible Studies. He and Martha both became counsellors at various secondary schools in the Essendon area in Melbourne.

In their home, over a period of more than twenty years, Teddy and Martha assisted numerous children, and through the 1970s they extended their work to look after alcoholics and 'street people'. In 1991 they helped to found an organisation called 'Shalom Israel', which works in aid of the Jewish cause. Teddy and Martha still live in Eltham, on the outskirts of Melbourne.

Ted 'Hi-Ho' Silver Hi-Ho returned to his father's farm at Launching Place in Victoria, but went to work with the Post

Master General's Department for some years. He never married. One day he intervened, in a typically brave fashion, when at the local pub a man started menacing his wife with a gun. Hi-Ho was killed when the gun discharged.

John 'Bluey' Whitechurch Bluey also returned to work on his father's farm, at Seymour. He spent some time working for Ansett's Woolcord after that, then married Joan Clydesdale in 1954. They lived in the Clydesdale family home while he ran a sheep property not far from Puckapunyal. In the early 1960s the Defence Department bought his farm and he retired. He died suddenly in August 1993.

Ted Jobe 'Tombstone' Ted worked in Melbourne after the war, doing itinerant jobs. He died some years ago.

The Professor A fortnight after the war finished, the Professor found himself sitting in the bush, living in a tent and looking for peace and anonymity. He never married. Rather than going back to teaching, he joined the Forestry Commission. He greatly enjoyed the solitude, and continued working as a forest overseer at Mt Cole in Victoria until he retired.

Neil Gordon Neil rejoined Seven Section after being wounded at Jezzine, but later transferred to the 2/3rd Machine-Gun Battalion. After the war he returned to Rimington's Nursery (with Alan Avery), then in 1953 started his own nursery business. With his wife Muriel, he is now retired at Surrey Hills, Melbourne.

What happened to other people in the story? Let's look at a few.

The unnamed Sergeant from the 2/25th Battalion who met Stan Bisset at Ioribaiwa and, later, near Gona was my father, Hugh.

After the Gona action my father was nominated in the field to attend officer training at Bonegilla in Victoria. However, on the journey south, still weak from the effects of malaria, hepatitis and dysentery, he was sent to recuperate in Queensland. With his frail, shrunken body, he was hardly recognisable as he was greeted by his bride of seven months, now pregnant. On his eventual discharge from the Army he returned to the land and became a peanut farmer at Durong, in the Kingaroy district, until 1960. He died in Brisbane in 1975.

Stan Bisset Stan was awarded the Military Cross for his general leadership and courage at Gona, as well as during the Ramu and Markham River actions. He was also mentioned in dispatches for his work in the Kokoda Campaign. When he returned from Gona, Stan met his first wife, Shirley, and married her in 1944. They had 25 years together.

After the war Stan worked for many years as Director and Secretary of the gas and furnace engineers, N. J. Hurll & Company, in Melbourne. During these years he continued to be actively associated with the Somers Camp and Power House, and was games director for more than two decades.

In 1970 he moved to Gladstone in Queensland, where he met his second wife, Gloria.

On retiring in 1980, at the age of 70, he started to experience vivid memories and dreams of the Kokoda, Gona and Ramu Valley Campaigns, which have troubled him considerably. He is still very active physically, and remains a tireless worker for the battalion association from his home on Queensland's Sunshine Coast.

Phil Rhoden As Lieutenant Colonel Rhoden, Phil commanded the 2/14th from 1943 until it was disbanded in 1946. For his service at Efogi on the Kokoda Track he was mentioned in dispatches; for his general leadership he was awarded the OBE. Phil married his fiancee Pat and, after the war, joined the law firm of John P. Rhoden, eventually becoming senior partner.

In 1954 he took over as Camp Chief at the Somers Camp and directed it until 1959. He also served on many community groups and was Chairman of the National Council of Independent Schools of Australia from 1981 to 1984. He and Pat are now retired and living in Melbourne.

Leila Bradbury and *Gerry O'Day* Alan presented Bruce's signet ring to Leila when he returned from New Guinea. At an appropriate time, Captain Gerry O'Day, Bruce's platoon commander at Jezzine, began a friendship with Leila. They were married in 1944, and Gerry saw the war through. He was mentioned in dispatches for his work at Wampun in New Guinea. After the war he joined the Regular Army, attaining the rank of colonel. He served in many countries, including Laos, and was awarded an OBE for his services. He and Leila are now retired at Buderim in Queensland.

Dorothy Banfield and *Reg Saunders* Dot never received the medallion retrieved from Jarmbe's body at Gona. After his death she moved to Melbourne and joined the Army. Jarmbe's brother Reg visited her when he returned from the Middle East, and the two started up a friendship which led to marriage. Reg continued with his brilliant and extraordinary military career. He became the first Aboriginal to gain a commission, serving with the Sixth Division in New Guinea, and then in Korea as a captain. His battalion won a United States Presidential Citation for the battle of Kapyong.

For many years prior to his death in 1991, Reg worked with the then Department of Aboriginal Affairs. During this time he remarried. Dot retired to Toowoomba where she died on Mothers Day, 1997. She had kept Jarmbe's love letters, which she was happy to share—'It's time,' she said. They are now in the Australian War Memorial.

Bill Guest (39th Battalion) Bill succumbed to a combination of malaria and dengue fever, taking almost all of 1943 to recover. He was posted to the 2/10th and landed in Balikpapan in Borneo in 1945. Seven years later he was back in New Guinea for a lengthy stint with the newly formed Pacific Island Regiment (local troops) and the PNG Volunteer Rifles. He eventually returned to Australia in 1982 and is now retired, living with his wife at Kippa-Ring on Brisbane's north coast.

Andy 'Nicky' Barr Nicky continued to have a distinguished war service, ending up with an OBE, MC and DFC and bar. He served in the RAAF with 3 Squadron in the Western Desert, and was an operational fighter pilot in North Africa, Europe, Italy and the Pacific, being wounded twice. He was a prisoner of war in both Italy and Austria, but escaped each time. He took part in partisan activities in Europe and also flew 108 operational missions from Britain, where he attained the rank of wing commander.

After the war he worked in managerial positions in industry, and is now retired at Carrara on the Queensland Gold Coast.

S. H. 'Ben' Buckler While at Yandina, on exercises in 1942, Ben strayed onto a Maleny farm and met his wife-to-be, Judith. They were married in 1943. Ben stayed in the Regular Army until 1960, when he was discharged with the rank of brigadier, holding the OBE. He then joined the Attorney General's Department, where he worked until his retirement. He died in 1995 after a long illness.

Norm Stringer Norm was evacuated after Gona, with malaria, but returned for the invasion of Borneo. He was discharged in 1945 and worked on his father's property in Victoria. In 1947 he was allocated a Soldier Settlers block at Robinvale in the northwest of the State, where he and his wife Pamela managed the vineyards and dried fruit production until they retired in 1995.

Dr Donald Duffy After the Owen Stanleys Campaign, Don was posted to a military hospital in the Atherton Tablelands, where he met a physiotherapist, Mary Colebatch, who had served in the Middle East. The two soon married. On his discharge in

1945, Don gained his Fellowship and practised as a consultant physician. He became honorary medical officer for the Melbourne Football Club in 1952 and president in 1963. Soon afterwards he joined the committee of the Melbourne Cricket Club, serving for 25 years. Among his peers he was known as 'the quiet achiever'. He died in 1995.

THE DEEDS OF THE MEN OF the 2/14th Battalion will not be forgotten. Nor will those of their mates. At the unveiling of the Cross of Sacrifice at Bomana War Cemetery, Port Moresby, in 1953, Sir William Slim spoke for the men who did not return.

When you go home,
Tell them of us, and say
'For your tomorrow
We gave our today'.

14

The Last Parade

IT IS AUGUST 1998, BOMONA WAR Cemetery, Port Moresby. Stan Bisset kneels beneath Butch's headstone and places a wreath against it. He utters a silent prayer, then stands to attention. With his head still bowed, he clasps his right hand to his breast, then with moistened eyes searching out into space, he offers a last, crisp salute. A few rows away, Bruce Kingsbury's sister Jean Pope is steadied by her son Dennis, a Vietnam Veteran, as they both bid their silent farewells. Across the beautifully maintained cemetery, veterans, sons, daughters, grandchildren and other kinfolk search for the last resting place of their brothers-in-arms or relative and acknowledge the loss.

They are here because Stan picked up the baton from an idea sparked by Brisbane psychologist Graham Scott, who had walked the trail. Along with two MPs, Charlie Lynn and Kerry Chikarovski, he has arranged and coordinated a final cathartic pilgrimage to Port Moresby and the Kokoda Track. Forty-six veterans, aged between 75 and 88, and 40 kinfolk and supporters, including me, fly into Moresby by ministerial jet, compliments of the Australian Government.

We are met by police and Defence Force escorts at Jackson airfield, and given a welcoming party by the Australian High Commissioner, David Irvine. The veterans are overwhelmed by the welcome.

Some apprehension and emotion is experienced as we board

the Air Force Caribou and fly over the Owen Stanleys towards Kokoda. Below, the jungle is compelling, triggering memories and misting eyes as repressed thoughts are confronted, forcing the years to roll back. From Kokoda, we are transported in a thrilling helicopter ride up into the mists of the ranges to land at Isurava. As the clouds part to allow us in, we are met by a colourful sight.

The children and grandchildren of the Fuzzy-Wuzzy Angels have gathered at Isurava over the last two weeks. They have cleared the jungle to make a helipad and prepared a bivouac camp with shelter to accommodate the diggers. In a display of homage, respect and love, they perform a traditional New Guinea Sing-Sing, they sing welcome and farewell songs and perform native plays. The smells of a roast pig fill the air, and women are cooking taro and chicken. The young natives stand by the silver-haired veterans shielding them from the sun with colourful umbrellas and assisting them as their forefathers did a half century ago, maintaining the bond.

The emotional ceremony proceeds as anthems, the Last Post and requiems from a lone piper pervade the jungle. However, a highlight for the men is the acknowledgement that the Australian Government is finally recognising the importance of the Isurava Battle. The Minister for Defence and Support, Bronwyn Bishop, who was flown in especially, formally reaffirmed the significance of the four-day battle. There are no dry eyes as the ceremony continues, the veterans trying to relate this peaceful, idyllic scene to the hell-hole of 1942 and its horrendous events.

After the ceremony, while the veterans search for signs of their old positions, I walk alone into the jungle and look for 9 Platoon's area. I find an area that fits the description I have been given. The dimness and silence call the ghosts out. I see 9 Platoon lined up: Teddy Bear leading the charge, his Bren gun spurting death. I see Bruce Kingsbury take over as Teddy is wounded, the Bren barking as it continues its killings. On his right, I see Alan Avery grit his teeth and move forward firing his Tommy gun, while Jarmbe follows, firing his .303 with deadly aim. I see the Professor, Hi-Ho Silver and the extending line of men blasting their way into history.

No doubt, around the perimeter, the veterans are reliving

their own personal battles and, with the advantages of time, and wisdom of age, hopefully they may finally come to terms with the killing, the sacrifices, the loss, the guilt, the heroism, the courage and the love experienced in this now sacred place. Hopefully they can put the ghosts behind them. They have saluted their mates and dedicated this mission to their memory.

For Stan Bisset, the Last Parade has been a triumph. He has celebrated his 86th birthday during the week, and two of his children, daughter Holly Huon and son Jim, have been able to accompany him. Together they have paid their respects to Butch. Amid tears, Jim and Holly have been able to understand their father better, as have all the kinfolk who accompanied the veterans.

For myself, 'The Silent Men' are silent no more. I understand now the reason for their perceived silence, for their reluctance to talk of the indescribable slaughter they have experienced, and the acts of nihilistic savagery they have witnessed. I understand now their comradeship and strong commitments to each other—an inbuilt support system that renders full credence and authority to the treasured Australian icon of mateship. Through these men, I have also come to know my father. I have come to appreciate the silent burden that war placed on his and their shoulders. In the process, I have also come to know myself more intimately, as I place myself beside him, scrambling and fighting over the stony hills of Lebanon, then stumbling through the mud and jungle of the Owen Stanleys. I lie beside him in the putrid, stinking trenches and beaches of Gona, warding off disease as much as the enemy. Deep wells of grief and love flood me as I put my arms around him, as I would my children, and attempt to shield him from the surrounding horrors, then assist him to stagger out of the holocaust.

As the men bid farewell to the brothers and mates who didn't come home, I feel a stronger bonding with them. After years of pain, examination and conciliation, I pray this Last Parade can release these Silent Men. I will not forget their sacrifice.

Further Reading

V. Austin (ed), *39th Australian Militia Battalion: To Kokoda and Beyond*, Melbourne University Press, 1988.

Australian War Memorial, *Soldiering On*, Canberra, 1942.

Australian War Memorial, *Khaki and Green*, Canberra, 1943.

Australian War Memorial, *Jungle Warfare*, Canberra, 1944.

Australian War Memorial, *Stand Easy*, Canberra, 1945.

P. Bagman, *North Africa, 1940–1942: The Desert War*, Time-Life Books, Australia, 1988.

P. Brune, *Those Ragged Bloody Heroes*, Allen & Unwin, Sydney, 1991.

P. Brune, *Gona's Gone!* Allen & Unwin, Sydney, 1994.

P. Charlton, *War Against Japan, 1941–1942*, Time-Life Books, Australia, 1988.

W. M. Crooks, *2/33rd Australian Infantry Battalion: The Foot-soldiers*, Printcraft Press, Sydney, 1971.

I. Deehm, *Giants in Green and Gold*, Boolarong Press, Brisbane, 1994.

A. Gregory, *A History of Lord Somers Camp and Power House*, St Kilda, Melbourne, 1989.

J. Laffin, *Greece, Crete and Syria*, Time-Life Books, Australia, 1989.

G. Long, *Greece, Crete and Syria*, Australian War Memorial, Canberra, 1953.

J. C. McAllester, *Men of the 2/14th Battalion*, Griffin Press, South Australia, 1990.

J. C. McAllester and S. Tregellis-Smith, *Largely a Gamble: Australians in Syria*, Headquarters Training Command, Australian Army, 1955.

L. McAulay, *Blood and Iron*, Hutchinson, Australia, 1991.

R. Paull, *Retreat from Kokoda*, William Heinemann, Australia, 1958.

W. B. Russell, *History of the 2/14th Battalion*, Angus & Robertson, Sydney, 1948.

Saburo Sakai, *Samurai*, Bantam Books, USA, 1957.

H. D. Steward, *Recollections of a Regimental Medical Officer*, Melbourne University Press, 1983.

S. Tregellis-Smith, *The Purple Devils, History of 2/6 Ind. Co. Squad*, Melbourne, 1992.

Those Ragged Bloody Heroes

From the Kokoda Trail to Gona Beach 1942

Peter Brune

'. . . a triumphant book that is a memorial to men whose sacrifice in the courageous defence of their country must never be forgotten.'

—William Noonan

Those Ragged Bloody Heroes is the story of the Kokoda and Gona campaigns told as never before, through the eyes of the Australian soldiers who fought there.

During July to September 1942 the Japanese set about the capture of Port Moresby by an overland crossing of the Owen Stanley Range, and a landing in Milne Bay. The Kokoda Trail is now a part of Australian military folklore.

To oppose a force of 10 000 crack Japanese troops on the Kokoda Trail, the Allies committed one under-trained and poorly equipped unit—the 39th Battalion, later reinforced by Veterans of the 21st Brigade, 7th Division AIF. These were the men of Maroubra Force. The Australians put up a desperate fight. They withdrew village by village, forcing the Japanese to fight for every inch of ground. Finally at Ioribaiwa, the Japanese turned away, beaten and exhausted. The Australian soldiers' reward for their remarkable achievement was denigration by the High Command—General Blamey called them 'running rabbits'.

Then in December 1942 when the fighting at the beachheads had produced little success, the former members of Maroubra Force captured Gona after heavy fighting—but at tragic cost.

Those Ragged Bloody Heroes is a story that raises serious questions about the planning and command of the Kokoda and Gona campaigns. It is a stirring history of triumph, tragedy and controversy set in the mud and steaming jungle of the Kokoda Trail and the fireswept beaches at Gona.

ISBN 1 86373 264 0

The Spell Broken

Exploding the myth of Japanese invincibility: Milne Bay to Buna–Sanananda 1942–43

Peter Brune

'A well-researched account of the battles that seized the initiative from the Japanese. The analysis is sound but its strength is its vivid description of the fighting from the soldiers' perspective.'
—Dr David Horner, Senior Fellow, Strategic and Defence Studies Centre, Australian National University

In August 1942 the Japanese staged a landing at Milne Bay in Papua New Guinea against an Australian Infantry Force of militia and AIF troops—the prize was the primitive airfield and the eventual capture of Port Moresby. A confused and desperate battle took place against a background of Japanese naval operations by night and Australian fighter support by day—this battle led to Japan's first defeat on land during World War Two.

Then in November 1942, after their defeats on the Kokoda Trail and at Milne Bay, the Japanese occupied the northern beachhead strongholds of Gona–Sanananda–Buna. After repeated American failures at Buna the 18th Brigade's Milne Bay veterans were called in. Despite some of the fiercest and most costly fighting of the Pacific War, the 18th Brigade captured Buna and Sanananda during December 1942 and January 1943.

The Spell Broken is a stirring history of the Milne Bay and Buna–Sanananda battles told through the records of those campaigns and balanced against the recollections of their survivors.

ISBN 1 86448 693 7

200 Shots

*Damien Parer, George Silk and the Australians at war
in New Guinea*

Neil McDonald and Peter Brune

'This is an important book because it tells and brilliantly illustrates a vital part of our history which has been neglected for far too long. And it raises yet again a problem that Australia still has to grapple with—when will we learn to foster and celebrate Australian excellence?'

—Phillip Knightley, author *The First Casualty: The War Correspondent as Hero, Propagandist and Myth Maker* and *A Hack's Progress*

The fierce fighting in the jungles of New Guinea during World War Two provided a primeval environment for some of the most dramatic war photography in Australia's history. *200 Shots* provides a comprehensive photographic coverage of Australia's involvement at that time and highlights the work of two great war photographers—Damien Parer and George Silk.

The photographers' notes and diaries are used to describe the circumstances in which the shots were taken. This is linked with official records, interviews with the participants and a close analysis of the images themselves to explain what the photographs reveal about the human experience of war.

Damien Parer was killed in action shortly after taking the last shots in this book, but for the first time his notes and film of the 2/3rd Independent Company are compared with the sketches of his companion, the famous war artist Ivor Hele, providing a unique insight into the photographer's and the artist's responses to jungle fighting. Neil McDonald interviewed George Silk in the United States in 1996 over a seven-day period. This, together with Peter Brune's research, enables *200 Shots* to put a new perspective on these famous battles.

ISBN 1 86448 912 X